BREAKING
the Patterns of
DEPRESSION

Other Books by Michael D. Yapko, Ph.D.

ESSENTIALS OF HYPNOSIS

SUGGESTIONS OF ABUSE:
TRUE AND FALSE MEMORIES OF CHILDHOOD SEXUAL TRAUMA

HYPNOSIS AND THE TREATMENT OF DEPRESSIONS

TRANCEWORK: AN INTRODUCTION TO THE
PRACTICE OF CLINICAL HYPNOSIS

WHEN LIVING HURTS: DIRECTIVES
FOR TREATING DEPRESSION

BRIEF THERAPY APPROACHES TO TREATING
ANXIETY AND DEPRESSION (ED.)

BREAKING
the Patterns of
DEPRESSION

Michael D. Yapko, Ph.D.

Broadway Books
New York

BROADWAY

A hardcover edition of this book was originally published in 1997 by Doubleday, a division of Random House, Inc. It is here reprinted by arrangement with Doubleday.

Broadway Books titles may be purchased for business or promotional use or for special sales. For information, please write to: Special Markets Department, Random House, Inc., 1540 Broadway, New York, NY 10036.

BROADWAY BOOKS and its logo, a letter B bisected on the diagonal, are trademarks of Broadway Books, a division of Random House, Inc.

Visit our website at www.broadwaybooks.com

First Broadway Books trade paperback edition published 2001.

The Library of Congress Cataloging-in-Publication Data has cataloged the hardcover edition as:

Yapko, Michael D.
Breaking the patterns of depression / Michael D. Yapko.—1st ed.
p. cm.
Includes bibliographical references and index.
1. Depression, Mental—Popular works. 2. Self-help techniques.
3. Cognitive-behavioral psychotherapy. I. Title.
RC537.Y349 1997 96-1070
616.85'27—dc20 CIP

ISBN 0-385-48370-8

16 15 14 13 12 11 10 9

My wife, Diane,
and I recently celebrated our
twentieth wedding anniversary. Every time I think
I couldn't possibly love her more, I find I can—and do.
So, who else could I possibly dedicate this to?

ACKNOWLEDGMENTS

Writing this book has been an interesting, illuminating, demanding, and satisfying project. It brought new people into my life, and reaffirmed the value of those already there. It has been a privilege.

My wife, Diane, makes it all possible in many direct and indirect ways. I am extremely lucky to have someone so wonderful in my life. She is a natural and powerful antidepressant.

Linda Griebel has been my work partner for a long, long time. She is an invaluable and fabulous ally in helping make my professional life so gratifying.

A number of extremely wise and perceptive people shared their time and views unselfishly in agreeing to review and critique earlier drafts of my work. I want to thank the following people from the bottom of my heart for their support and direct involvement in helping this work reach a higher level of quality: Norma Barretta, Ph.D.; Marjorie Coburn, Ph.D.; Gary Elkins, Ph.D.; Madeline Harris; Lynn Johnson, Ph.D.; Jodi Kass; Ellen Kaye, Ph.D.; Michele Weiner-Davis, M.S.W.; and Diane Yapko, M.A.

My literary agent, Audrey Wolf, is a wonderfully skilled advocate for getting my ideas into print. I am indebted to her for her support.

My editor at Doubleday is Frances Jones, and my copy editor, Frances Apt. Both had the abilities to structure, restructure, embellish, and whittle down my work to the essentials. I admire their literary talents very much and feel fortunate that they used them in my behalf.

Finally, I want to thank my clients. In over twenty years of clinical practice, I have been in the position to learn what does and doesn't work in life, and how seemingly average people can learn to do extraordinary things. It has been deeply inspiring being with them. I have great respect and appreciation for my clients, whom I view as my greatest teachers. Thank you one and all.

Now, on the personal side. I have many wonderful people in my life, my family and friends. The Yapko and Harris families have always provided the best possible contexts for learning to be a good human being, a fact I never fail to appreciate. The Horowitz family—Wendy, Megan ("The Hugbug"), and Richard—is my other family. We've been best friends since our early adolescence. It is an extraordinary thing to have lifelong best friends, another fact I never fail to appreciate.

Thanks, everybody, for everything.

CONTENTS

CONTENTS

A NOTE ABOUT
GENDER USAGE

The case examples throughout the book tell stories about men and women who have battled depression. In the case presentations, the mixed use of "he" or "she" is easy, deliberate, and purposeful. However, when I speak in general terms or in terms of principles, I use only masculine pronouns. Why? It is simply too clumsy and distracting to try to work both the masculine and the feminine into each idea. So, to make the book an easier read, I opted for the less-than-perfect choice of the traditional masculine. I hope you will understand that it's a choice made not of ignorance or preference but of necessity.

FOREWORD

George, a 67-year-old, married man, recently suffered a medical crisis. Since then, he hasn't had any appetite. He feels no energy or enthusiasm for life, and his wife reports he seems withdrawn and unresponsive. When questioned, George says he feels he's "just an old man and will probably never enjoy anything again."

Depression is a disorder that can strike anyone at any age. Young children and grandparents, men and women, teens in the midst of school crises or middle-aged executives with a long history of success and achievement, depression strikes across all barriers, making its victims miserable and robbing them of joy and satisfaction. Depression's strength lies in its ability to make you feel that nothing you do will ever bring back a sense of peace or satisfaction with life.

But here is the great secret about depression—it's a sheep in wolf's clothing. It *can* be treated effectively and the treatment's effects can make a difference that will last a lifetime. In the case of George, he saw improvement after just six sessions with a therapist. Now, he and his wife go for walks, he enjoys gardening and working around the house, and he takes pleasure in visiting his grandchildren. He feels that he has a new lease on life.

Contrary to popular belief, most treatment for depression need not last a long time. Many patients recover in less than twelve sessions, many others do well in under twenty sessions; we are not talking about spending your life on a couch exploring your childhood. Today, much treatment for depression is action-oriented, focused on the here-and-now, and looking toward the future.

The book you are holding has this as its clear purpose. It will help you understand depression, help you begin to cope with its effects, and show you how it can be defeated. While it is true depression causes untold pain and suffering, there is hope. Yes, depression is a cruel, unforgiving, and relentless foe. But depression has its weak points and this book effectively prepares you to attack those points.

Dr. Michael Yapko has spent his professional life helping patients confront and battle depression. He is a powerful and kind ally, and his experience and compassion have made the difference between victory and defeat for his patients. He is a talented teacher who has for years taught useful and sensible skills to other mental health workers. He has sought out and studied with the greatest mental health professionals of the twentieth century. He has written unselfishly and helpfully about what he has learned. And he is a man of great personal integrity, whose personal life reflects his commitment to values and priorities.

Dr. Yapko has brought this book to all of us who battle the enemy of joy and peace: depression. In this wonderful guide he will teach you, as he has taught me, how to understand depression and how to defeat it. He will teach you how to look at yourself, the world, and the future in a new way. He will teach you that *you can have a peaceful and satisfying life* and he will teach you *how* to do that.

I heartily recommend this book, because it is based on the best scientific and clinical information, because it comes from a deep understanding of the subject matter, and because it is full of compassion and understanding for those who read it. Most of all, I recommend this book because, when Michael says, "You can recover from depression," he really means it.

Read this book. Do the work. It will help.

Lynn D. Johnson, Ph.D.
Director, Brief Therapy Center
Salt Lake City, Utah

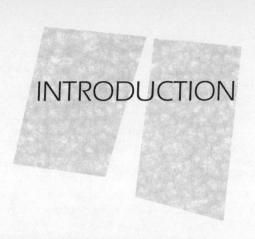

INTRODUCTION

Doubts, Regrets, and Despair

The alarm went off, and Lauren tried to find the snooze button. After several clumsy attempts to hit it, she was too frustrated to drift back to sleep. Already agitated, she found her first thoughts of the day unpleasant ones—waking up feeling tired, dreading the morning routine of getting the kids up and ready for school, wondering where she'd get the strength to get out of bed. Lauren pushed herself to get the wheels turning to face yet another day in a life where it was becoming increasingly difficult to find anything positive.

After being married for eleven years, Lauren and Zack divorced two years ago. The boys spent most of their time with Lauren, an arrangement the couple arrived at quite agreeably. In fact, the whole divorce went pretty smoothly. Neither Lauren nor Zack had been particularly happy with the marriage. It was comfortable, but nothing more. No passion, no shared vision, no true intimacy. The mutual decision to divorce seemed a logical way to be free to find personal happiness, or so both of them thought at the time. Now, though, Lauren often found herself wondering whether divorcing Zack was the right thing to do. Her frequent doubts and regrets felt lousy.

Lauren, only thirty-three, had envisioned a wonderful transformation that would take place after the divorce. She pictured plenty of quality time alone with the boys. She fantasized about romantic and fascinating men she would date and with whom she would rediscover passion. She looked forward to nights out with girlfriends, seeing movies, or just going shopping at her leisure. And she savored the notion of having more time to read, think, and "just be."

But none of these things happened. Lauren's time with the boys was curtailed by their hardly ever being home. They had their own friends and interests, and even when they were home it was tough to pull them away from their computer and video games. Dating had gone badly, too; her work demanded so much of her time and energy. And what few guys she did date in the last two years seemed even less interesting than Zack. She had never thought before of the boys as a liability, but she was beginning to think that they definitely hindered her chances of finding the love of her life. She often entertained visions of growing old alone and lonely, and each time she did so, her despair grew.

Her girlfriends were great, as always, but they were too preoccupied with their lives to have much time for her. Lauren understood perfectly the toll of building a career, being a mother, running a household, maintaining some semblance of a social life, staying physically fit, and all the rest she had to do. She could accept that her friends didn't have any more time for her than she had for them. Still, it left her feeling pretty lonely and isolated.

Time to "just be"? Right. When?

Lauren was overwhelmed, tired, hopeless that her life would ever improve appreciably. In a word, she felt "stuck." At times like this, which were becoming a regular feature of her daily life, Lauren's mind threw up endless questions. What's wrong with me? Why is my life always such a struggle? Why don't other single mothers seem so despairing? Was I wrong to divorce Zack? Should I push him to have the boys more often, or is that an admission of failure? Will I ever find love, or will I always be alone and lonely? Am I some kind of emotional cripple who can't cope with life? What's wrong with me? Why am I so tired all the time? Why am I so negative? Have I always been this way? Is my negativity why no one wants to be around me—not even my sons? Why does my life feel so out of control?

Every question, every thought, drove Lauren's despair deeper. It felt physical—an extra weight dragging her down. It was emotional—a turbulent whirlpool of different feelings, all hurtful. It also felt spiritual—like a journey through a space and time that begged to be understood and worshiped at the place where conscious and unconscious awareness meet. None of it made any sense to Lauren, though.

One time, when she was picking the boys up from a visit with their father, she found herself opening up to Zack about her feelings. Fearing he'd not really listen or understand, Lauren was surprised when Zack opened up and shared his feelings as well. He confessed that he, too, was not finding happiness in being single. He wanted to see the boys more, and wondered whether he was a fit father. He expressed doubts about himself, feeling he had failed as a husband and perhaps was failing now as a father. He said he felt bad most of the time, and life seemed awfully harsh lately. Lauren, who had never heard him talk this way, was mildly comforted by Zack's empathy and sensitive self-disclosure. Each made a point of reminding the other (and themselves) that, despite their self-doubts and loneliness, trying to resuscitate a dead marriage would be a misguided effort. But it felt good to talk about their feelings and reaffirm that they still had some positive regard for each other.

Months ago, Lauren had mentioned to her doctor, during a routine physical, that she'd been feeling out of sorts lately. Her doctor didn't probe much and was perhaps a little too quick to let the subject drop; Lauren appeared to be physically healthy. Lauren thought maybe she was making too much of her feelings, so she too let the matter drop. Now she thought that maybe she should have pursued it. Then the thought occurred to her that maybe she should take it up now—with someone who could really understand her feelings and know what to do about them.

That same day, Lauren began asking trusted friends for the name of a psychologist she could consult. She was given my name, and she took the sensible step of calling me. After our brief telephone discussion about her concerns, she felt comfortable enough to schedule an appointment to see me.

Lauren was wonderful to work with. She learned quickly that she was suffering from a moderate depression. She also learned that her divorce was a crucial turning point in her confronting the sizable gap between her expectations and reality. We had eleven sessions in all. Each involved Lauren's learning specific skills to re-establish control over her life. She learned to address her life questions, make good decisions, and redefine her expectations for herself and her life.

Lauren's depression lifted as she developed these new tools for better living. Soon she began to feel quite different about her life. She even became what she described as "more comfortable and content with who I am and the choices I've made. And, at thirty-three, there's much more to come!" Her newfound optimism led her to make real changes in both her ideas and methods, especially in regard to her relationships with others. She hasn't found Mr. Right yet, but she is content with not having to have Mr. Right Now. She's built up a social life, she dates, and she finds happiness doing other things she feels good about. In short, she's doing well.

Lauren's depression wasn't an "illness"; it was a clear and valuable sign that something was wrong. It was a call to examine more closely what too many people seem unaware of: how expectations, thoughts, feelings, relationships, and all the other aspects of experience that can drift off course can lead you to erroneously believe you'll never have a happy or fulfilling life. It didn't take Lauren long to discover what she needed to do to get better. Good therapy for depression can work reliably and quickly, as you will discover through your success with this book. Here you can learn to act as your own catalyst for personal growth in ways that can break the grip of depression on your life.

Is depression a necessary or inevitable experience? The answer is clearly . . . yes and no. Yes, everyone experiences depressed feelings from time to time; no one escapes the hurtful things in life. No, not everyone sinks into clinical depression. What have we learned about those who do? We've learned they are often missing information or skills that could help prevent depression. When Mark Twain said, "It isn't what you don't know that hurts you; it's what you know that isn't so," he was only half right. What you don't know *can* hurt you.

Depression can be a completely normal response to painful circumstances, or it can be a sign that a person is "going down in flames" because he doesn't know how to handle sensitively something that must be handled with skill. The more complex our world gets, the more things we face that need to be handled with great care. That includes both internal experiences, such as sadness over the breakup of a relationship, and external ones, such as being laid off from a job.

I am a clinical psychologist who has treated depressed individuals for the past twenty years. I have written two earlier books and edited a third on the subject of depression exclusively for my professional colleagues. Through my experience, I have come to believe that the chief problem with most depressed people is that they think, feel, and act out of a depressive perspective that is distorted and hurtful, and then make the mistake of actually believing this perspective is a God-given truth. When a relationship ends painfully, they may tell themselves, "I'll never fall in love again." When they get laid off from a job, they may think, "I'll never be able to get another job." When they respond imperfectly to a situation, they may say to themselves, "I'm an idiot." Having internal dialogue is normal. Believing the negativity, though, is unnecessary and hurtful.

The most important point I can make at the outset, the point that succinctly represents all I have written here, is that people become absorbed in ways of being (thinking, feeling, doing) that they mistake for "real" or "true." They lose sight of the fact that much of life experience is not clearly "this" or "that," but is instead a product of personal beliefs. So when people tell themselves, and then actually believe, "I'm a terrible person" or "Life is just no damn good," depression is a predictable consequence. The worthy skill to develop is how to step outside your personal beliefs. Only then can you determine whether they are accurate and serve you well, or whether they are distorted and the cause of unnecessary pain.

Let's consider an everyday example. You call a friend just to say hello, but your friend isn't home. You leave a message on his answering machine, but he doesn't return the call that day. Naturally, you wonder why. No return call is made the next day either, and so you call him again and leave another message on the machine, this one betraying just a hint of irritation. No return call. Now, pause. What do you tell yourself about this situation? Do you tell yourself that whoever you're calling is an irresponsible jerk? Or that you are *always* being ignored or abandoned by others? What *do* you tell yourself? How are you and your mood affected by what you say to yourself? Does telling yourself these things help or hurt you? What is the right way to respond to such a situation? In this book you will learn to respond to such everyday situations skillfully and in ways that minimize your chances of believing something that is detrimental to your self-esteem.

Depression is not a fixed "thing." And despite the oversell of drug companies, treatment centers, talk shows, and books that suggest you think of depression as an illness "just like diabetes," the best evidence to date states that for *most* people depression is *not* a biologically based disease. The "disease model" of depression and the value of antidepressant medications have been exaggerated. Biology is only a part of the depression story, and antidepressant medications are only part of a total solution.

For most people, depression is the product of a hurtful way of interpreting and responding to life experiences. Depression involves an intricate set of projections about yourself, life, the universe, *everything*. By projection, I mean the way you interpret the meaning of something that is ambiguous or unclear.

You may know of the psychological test called the Rorschach Inkblot Test. The Rorschach Test involves showing the client an inkblot that is ambiguous in shape, then asking the client to interpret its meaning. People will "see" all kinds of meanings in the inkblot through their projections about it. The relevant principle here is called the "projective hypothesis," which says that whenever you encounter an ambiguous stimulus, you inevitably interpret it from your own perspective.

What is the most ambiguous stimulus any person ever faces? As best as I can tell, the answer is LIFE! Life is like an inkblot—an "experiential Rorschach," so to speak. *Life doesn't have an objective or assigned meaning. We give it meaning by our individual values, beliefs, relationships, careers, hobbies, and other life experiences.*

Depression is also an inkblot of sorts. It is interpreted from many different perspectives or frames of reference by different mental health professionals. Each interpretation has the potential to help someone suffering the pain of depression, but extensive research has made it clear that none should be applied to the total exclusion of other approaches. For example, just giving someone antidepressant medication, without teaching thinking (cognitive) or social (interpersonal) skills, is not doing a depressed person any favors. Antidepressants alone, valuable as they are, cannot address faulty patterns of thinking as effectively as cognitive therapy can. Doesn't it make sense to address *all* dimensions of the problem of depression in order to arrive at a more complete resolution?

I will emphasize throughout this book that *depression is not a single problem with a single cause and a single treatment.* Depression can have many points of origin, and many paths can lead one out of its grip. Therefore, I will give many perspectives and many tools that you can work with to "custom design" your treatment plan in the most intelligent manner. I am keenly aware that the experience of depression is as different from person to person as are the individuals who suffer it. Most of the common denominators are well known, however. There *is* a legitimate basis for you to be optimistic about overcoming your depression.

The tendency of depressed people to interpret life experiences negatively helps fuel the negative expectation that when life is going badly, it will *always* go badly. It is essential that you take this into account and make a deliberate effort to change your thinking in the area of expectancy. Few experiences, good or bad, are enduring. The majority of experiences are, in fact, transient. When you know that, hopefulness can start to take the place of hopelessness.

When you are depressed, almost everything is overwhelming. Simple tasks seem difficult, difficult tasks seem impossible, and the energy to deal with much of anything—easy or hard—is missing. Now, at a time when depression may make you feel anything but ambitious, I am encouraging you to be actively involved in this book. At a time when you are depressed and hopeless, I am suggesting that you work at building hope. At a time when your future seems entirely negative or, at best, uncertain, I am telling you in a firm and deliberate way that your future can be much better than anything you have ever experienced before. But you need a realistic plan to make it happen!

I can tell you with absolute confidence and sincerity that the perspectives and skills you will learn here hold great potential to help. The path to recovery will be created by your learning about depression, understanding how it affects you and why, and honing the skills to deliberately change your thoughts, feelings, and behavior quickly and efficiently. This book isn't "emotional popcorn." It's a serious manual for building the life skills that can make your depression go away. The path to recovery isn't something done *to* you, however; it's done *with* you. I hope you'll be an active partner, willing to experiment with your beliefs and perceptions and thereby evolve new ones when they seem appropriate or desirable.

LET'S PUT DEPRESSION IN PERSPECTIVE

As you and I both know, the world has changed dramatically in the last several decades. The changes have been primarily sociological and cultural. Certainly, many of them were positive and progressive. Significant steps have been taken in the direction of civil rights. There is greater mobility and broader freedom to choose an individual and personally satisfying lifestyle. Families can actually be planned, and the technology now exists to cut short the amount of time spent on drudgery, like cleaning or balancing the checkbook. Communication is instant, and valuable information of all sorts is so plentiful that it's easy to become overwhelmed by it.

All the gains of so-called higher consciousness, technology, and personal freedom have not been without cost, however. On the contrary, the costs to all of us have been enormous. "Getting high" used to be taken lightly as an adolescent exploration of consciousness. Now, America is being strangled by a nightmare drug problem that includes murder and mayhem in all neighborhoods. AIDS has made "free love" something you may eventually pay for with your life. Relationships that endure "till death do us part" are found most frequently in old late-night movies.

In addition to these obvious costs, one of the liabilities associated with all the social changes is our national mental health. A major research finding that is startling, even to the mental health professionals who uncovered it, is that *the rate of depression has increased by a factor of nearly ten in those born in the years following World War II* (the baby boomers). The 1950s and '60s were times of rapid economic and social change that forever altered American values and lifestyles—and apparently deeply affected people's feelings about themselves and their world. The 1970s, '80s, and '90s have seen life get more complicated than ever.

The fact that depression is more likely to occur in someone born after 1945 than in someone who was born at the turn of the century is highly significant. That it affects people at younger ages is equally significant. It means biology isn't likely to be the chief culprit; after all, human genetics and biochemistry do not change dramatically from one decade to the next. Nor do they change dramatically in some age groups but not in others. Social change, however, *is* swift and dramatic. And it readily affects specific age groups.

The factors that have caused depression to be *the most common psychological problem in America* are far more likely to be environmental than biological. This interpretation of depression as much more than biology gone awry is supported by the recognition that in other cultures around the world, depression increases as the society becomes more Westernized (that is, culturally similar to the United States). Thus, hope for depressed people of all ages can be built on an understanding of the social and psychological factors that have caused such high rates of depression in so short a time.

Depression affects people of all ages. But the high concentration in certain age groups enables us to observe more carefully the factors that underlie the serious problem affecting you and millions of others. Can these factors be identified and successfully treated? Can depression be overcome? The answer to both these questions is a definite and unhesitating *yes!*

Depression is among the psychological problems most responsive to appropriate treatment. When the treatment is aimed in the right direction, and is organized and carried out appropriately, depressive symptoms can usually resolve relatively quickly. Questions about the causes of depression are many and will be talked about throughout the book. I will, however, provide brief answers in the next section.

SELF-HELP FOR DEPRESSION

Depression comes about for complicated reasons that, at first glance, may actually seem simple. If you consider the recent changes in society that have shaken many of our basic ideas about life, and observe the rising rate of depression as an obvious consequence of these changes, it becomes obvious that our lifestyles and values contribute to our overall sense of well-being. As a clinician who routinely treats depressed clients, and as a teacher and writer in the field, I have identified many key patterns, including ways you think and ways you relate to others, that can either contribute to or prevent depression.

Throughout the book, I will describe specific patterns that are the basis of your perceptions and moods. You can learn to recognize these patterns in the ways you do things that may end up hurting you. Once you can recognize the patterns that lead to disappointment or despair, you will be in a good position to learn to do things differently. At that point, you can teach yourself, with the help of this book, how to approach life situations in ways more to your satisfaction. A primary goal I have in writing this book is for you to *feel good* about who you are and what you do.

Central to the self-help methods described throughout the book is the idea that *your experience can limit you* enough to depress you. Sometimes, depression evolves from noncritically absorbing a cultural belief that is erroneous (such as "You should *always* put other people's needs ahead of your own"), or from reaching an incorrect conclusion about an experience. ("You should never trust the opposite sex"). For example, if you have never had a good, close relationship with someone, then my saying to you, "What you need to do is go out and have a good close relationship with someone" isn't likely to help. Why doesn't my advice provide relief? Because you may know *what* you want (a good, close relationship), but your lack of experience in ever having had one prevents you from attaining it. *Knowing what to do does not provide you with the skills for doing it.* Therefore, I will often focus on *how* to do the important things you want to do.

I consistently discover that the depressed people I treat are missing some very specific and vital skills, such as thinking clearly, relating positively to others, or gathering and weighing important information. This lack of skills is usually not recognized by my clients, naturally, because they don't know what they don't know, nor do they recognize what they know that just isn't so. A lack of relevant knowledge leads them to mismanage important situations. The experiences go badly, they get hurt, and then become depressed in the aftermath. Even years later, they can still feel that way. Learning how to step outside yourself at times to recognize and avoid your vulnerabilities can help change such hurtful scenarios.

YOU CAN LEARN FROM OTHERS, TOO

Throughout this book, you will be exposed to many examples of good, intelligent, healthy people sinking into depression when their lives don't work in the way they'd like. Sometimes they know why they are depressed but don't know what to do about it. At other times, they have no idea why life is so painful. Developing life skills and building a reserve of many resources on which to draw in facing life's demands is what depression-free living is about. That's also what this book is about. If you are depressed, I hope you will learn to see how the patterns leading to depression, described throughout this book, may apply to you. Perhaps more important, I hope you will feel good about developing the skills to manage your life better and thereby get more of what you want out of life.

As a general principle, if you see other people do the things you want to do, then you already have some evidence that such things are possible. While it may be a total mystery to you that someone else succeeds in an arena in which you'd like to be successful, it's motivating to realize that other people's skills are usually learnable. The goal is to learn *how* it's done so that you can do it, too. My job is to explain many of those skills in ways that make sense to you, and motivate you to find others who can also teach you what now seems so mysterious. I'll do my best—if you do yours. Plan to be an active force in your own recovery from depression by participating in the exercises and answering the thought-provoking questions scattered throughout the book. As your thinking and responses begin to change, you can expect relief from depression to follow soon after. Once you learn how to respond with a variety of abilities and clear thinking, to situations that trigger depressive reactions, you will be in a stronger position to prevent future episodes of depression.

HOW TO USE THIS BOOK
TO YOUR BEST ADVANTAGE

The practical methods of this book do not emphasize rehashing the past. Examining your history may *explain* aspects of your depression but will not *change* it. Rather, recognize that you are reading this book with the hope that things will be different in the future—next week, next month, next year, and all the rest of your life. The focus is on change in the present with an eye on the future. With that in mind, I intend to provide *new ways of looking at depression* and will also provide opportunities for *experiential learning*, because there is no better teacher than our own direct experience. I must emphasize to you that the best way to benefit from this book is to *participate* in the activities that are suggested in each of the chapters. Action is the emphasis here, because mere passive reflection on important but abstract ideas is not likely to produce the results you want. The ideas presented in each chapter are valuable, of course, but the real help comes as you expand your range of personal experiences (and therefore your range of resources) through the structured activities presented in the book.

There are two types of participatory experiences here. One is the "Pause and Reflect" exercise, which asks you to carefully consider some important concepts related to the topic at hand. (In order to encourage you to pause and reflect on your answer to these thought-provoking questions, and thereby derive more personal value from them, I have made my responses to them a little more difficult to jump into by printing them upside down.) The other is the "Learn by Doing" exercise, which structures a learning experience for you to actively carry out. These typically encourage the development of specific new perspectives or life skills.

I must clearly state that this book is *not* meant to be a substitute for personal therapy. There is a great deal a good therapist can do to expand and personalize the points I make, so I encourage you to consider seeking a good therapist to consult. I offer some specific guidelines for how to do so in Chapter 12.

There is much to look forward to as you participate in these practical methods of self-help. I sincerely hope that you will benefit from what you learn here. After all, some of the best experiences you will have in your life haven't happened yet!

AUTHOR'S NOTE: GETTING STARTED

You may want to get right to the "tell me what to do to feel better" parts of the book. You are welcome to do that, of course, perhaps starting with Chapter 4. However, you should know that the first three chapters provide a strong framework for understanding what depression is about and why the methods contained herein are being offered to you.

I think you can do a much better job of building a successful self-help program if you know more about what you're dealing with. If, though, you want to skim, or even to skip over, the first three chapters, then I suggest you read at least the chapter summaries. Once you're feeling better, you can go back and read in greater detail the things about depression that I think are important to know.

Chapter 1

DEPRESSION: A GROWING PROBLEM IN MORE WAYS THAN ONE

From the time I first let others know I was researching the latest information on depression for a self-help book, many openly expressed their reservations about the project. They'd ask, "Why do you want to write about something so, well, depressing?" Or "Self-help? Hasn't Prozac made that unnecessary?" Some even suggested that "depression is just self-indulgent feeling sorry for yourself. Why try to get people to help themselves who don't really want to?"

I can't honestly say that any of these comments or questions surprised me. Having worked with depressed individuals, couples, and families for the last two decades, I've heard such reactions and misstatements all too often. To me, these responses simply highlight the necessity for this book. Someone suffering through depression, or someone who cares about a person suffering through depression, needs realistic answers to these and many other such questions. There is a great deal of current and objective information that I intend to share with you in this book, all of it designed to help. And, beyond the facts, I intend to present a way of thinking about the facts that can continue to help long after you've finished reading the book.

Let's start with people's reactions to my letting them know what I was working on. Is researching and writing about depression depressing? The internal experience of depression is painful on many different levels, as you undoubtedly know. It can drain the pleasure out of life and make life seem a difficult burden. But this book isn't about experiencing depression. It's about *changing* it, *stopping* it, *recovering* from it, even *preventing* it. That isn't depressing, on the contrary, it's exhilarating! So much has been learned about depression in recent years that it is not overstating the case to say, truthfully and with conviction, that almost anyone suffering the pain of depression can be helped *if* he truly wants to be and is willing to take the necessary steps. Even those who judge themselves to be "hopeless" can be helped. After all, hopelessness about life isn't a fact. It's merely a viewpoint.

The second common response was to question the need for self-help because of the advent of so-called miracle drugs, like Prozac. While it is certainly appealing to think that "a capsule a day will forever keep the depression away," it simply isn't true, nor is it ever likely to be. Prozac and other antidepressants will be discussed in the next chapter, but suffice it to say that antidepressant medications, although they can be effective allies in treatment, are not a total solution in most cases. They can provide symptom relief, help ease distress, and even lessen other symptoms that may co-exist with depression and further complicate an already complex clinical picture. What they can't do is magically transform most personalities (despite the optimistic excesses of some drug advocates), teach vital coping and problem-solving skills, resolve associated personal and interpersonal issues, or erect strong protection against the recurrence of episodes. The clinical research evidence is perfectly clear on this point: psychotherapy that emphasizes skill-building and problem resolution is not only desirable but *necessary*.

While this book is no substitute for participating in psychotherapy with a qualified professional, it does provide many of the benefits by emphasizing many of the same things. I have made every effort to offer you important ideas and practical methods for acquiring the kinds of skills known to the mental health profession as the most vital ones for overcoming depression now and preventing later episodes. I have crystallized here the essence of many effective interventions over twenty years of my clinical experience of treating depression sufferers. These have addressed and resolved the core components of depression, and are both sound and therapeutic. They work! The body of treatment literature supporting these views is considerable.

The third common response from others about this project was the damning suggestion that depression is a product of self-indulgent self-pity by weak people who may complain but don't really want to change. This tendency to blame the victim permeates our culture in a variety of ways, whether for rape victims "who asked for it," or for cancer patients who "caused" their cancer by not expressing anger appropriately. In the case of depression, far too many people hold the outdated and incorrect view of depression as a problem stemming from a person's character defects or moral weaknesses. This viewpoint was common in the 1940s, '50s, and '60s. Those individuals who were "weak" enough to openly confess their depression may well have been given such "helpful" advice as "Pull yourself together" or "Be tough and quit complaining."

The person who went for therapy decades ago—a less common course of action than is now the case—was likely to be given trite sayings to repeat: "It's always darkest before the dawn"; "Behind every cloud there's a silver lining." Worse, he may even have been blamed for his depression: "You have a decent job, a nice home, nice kids, a loving spouse, and you have your health. What can you possibly be depressed about?" The depression continued, of course, but now he felt guilty, too!

As you can appreciate, depression is a complex disorder. There is no single cause; there are many. There is no single solution; there are many. Suggesting that depression is mere self-pity is both hurtful and *wrong*. No one likes the idea of being depressed and letting his life waste away, one painfully slow day at a time. No one wants to lead a crummy life. My experience leads me to believe that people want to feel good and want their lives to be worthwhile, but through their life experiences they have evolved perspectives that make a good life seem impossible. People become absorbed in their own views of relationships and careers, and these views take on the aspect of inescapable reality. What they discover in therapy—and what you can discover in this book—is that you *can* escape, you *can* recover, and you can go well beyond what has been painful to you in the past. *Experience is negotiable, not fixed.*

Just what is depression? Who gets depressed? What causes depression? And how do you overcome it? These fundamental questions will be briefly addressed in the following sections of this chapter.

LEARN BY DOING #1

Before You Begin, What Do You Think?

Purpose: To define and discuss your ideas about depression before beginning your self-help program.

In this first structured exercise, the goal is to find out something about <u>your</u> ideas on depression <u>before</u> you learn all that you will learn later. By answering the questions below <u>in writing</u> and <u>in detail</u>, you have the chance to express your current ideas clearly. Later, after you learn more and more, you will probably discover that what you believed at this point was incomplete or even wrong. It will help you in the future to remember this key concept: <u>It isn't you that's the problem</u>. Instead, there are two problems: what you believe that is incorrect or incomplete, and how you go about doing things based on those beliefs.

So, in writing and in detail, please set out your responses to these four questions:

1. What is depression?
2. What sort of person gets depressed?
3. What causes depression?
4. What should someone do to get over depression?

I suggest that, for easy reference, you keep a folder or journal of the work you do on this and the written exercises to come. Not all the exercises involve writing, but it will be helpful to have the written replies in one easy-to-find place.

DIAGNOSING, DEFINING, AND DESCRIBING DEPRESSION

TOUGH LIFE

There is a popular bumper sticker that says LIFE IS A BITCH, AND THEN YOU DIE. To people who are not depressed, the bumper sticker is amusing. Those who are depressed tend to nod in solemn agreement.

Life has definitely grown more complicated. For many people today, the hassles of life overwhelm their ability to cope realistically. For others, the complications of life do not necessarily exceed their abilities to cope, but may exhaust them as they try to stay on top of everything. Stress is a basic component of depression. Each person experiences and manages stress in his own way, which is the main reason that depression takes so many different forms and can often be difficult to diagnose. For this reason, and some others, many of the people who are depressed do not even know they are.

The Case of Alex

Alex, in his late thirties, came to therapy hoping he would find a way to overcome what he called his "aimlessness." He had been unemployed for about a month. His most recent job, as an educational program planner and administrator, came to an abrupt end when funding for his program was cut off. Alex had been married for sixteen years, and described his wife as "ambitious for me." Her attempts to motivate him to go out and get a new job led to nearly constant friction between them, and caused Alex to feel "emotionally abandoned." He was well aware he would need to work again soon, since his financial responsibilities were too great to meet solely with his wife's income. But he couldn't seem to get himself to go out and look for a job. He couldn't say exactly why, even though he asked himself that question constantly.

Alex attributed his anxiety to career and financial worries. He could not make a decision about whether to work for someone else or begin his own business. He doubted his ability to run a business, but feared that if he worked for someone else, he'd get laid off again. He acknowledged a tendency to be a perfectionist about things, and did not want to make any decisions unless he was absolutely sure they were the correct ones. He could not bring himself to fill out applications and pursue interviews for jobs until he had established a clear goal, nor could he make plans to start his own business unless he knew he could "pull it off and make it work." He thought the "right" business idea would eventually "just come" to him.

Beyond his career and financial worries, Alex complained that his attention span was so short that he could not follow through on business ideas or even mundane domestic tasks. His wife was frustrated by his lack of follow-through, his friends annoyed him by asking him his job plans, and his parents were considered no potential help since "they are a part of my original self-esteem problem." He couldn't seem to find a sympathetic ear anywhere, and felt alone and misunderstood. He was sleeping poorly, waking early much of the time, and had little ability to find anything good in his life. So Alex turned to therapy to try to find out what to do.

Although Alex's original complaint was simply "aimlessness," he was experiencing helplessness, hopelessness, anxiety, indecisiveness, paralyzing perfectionism, diminished concentration, social isolation, marital discord, poor self-esteem, sleep disturbance, fatigue, and a loss of any sense of pleasure. Aren't these enough warning signs for even an amateur to have said, "Gee, I think you're depressed"? And yet Alex didn't realize it! However, once Alex was diagnosed and treated, using some of the methods in this book, he got his life back on track. He opened his own educational-consulting business and is gradually building it up. He is challenged, excited, and doing well.

HOW THE "PROS" SEE DEPRESSION

This book is about the category of disorders known to the mental health profession as "major depression." The profession has a well-established and widely used diagnostic system that is embodied in a thick book called the *Diagnostic and Statistical Manual of Mental Disorders*, or *DSM*. Now in its fourth edition—hence called *DSM-IV*—this American Psychiatric Association publication is considered the essential guide in making a formal diagnosis of *any* disorder. *DSM-IV* categorizes depression as a mood disorder. Because it may interest you to know how major depression is characterized, the diagnostic criteria are presented on page 7, with the publisher's permission.

DSM-IV further suggests distinguishing single-episode depressive disorders from recurring ones. A single-episode disorder is exactly that—an apparent one-time phenomenon. A recurrent disorder is said to exist when another episode of depression occurs after an interval of at least two consecutive months in which there was no depression.

The diagnosis of depression can be a very tricky thing. A phenomenon called "co-morbidity," which complicates the clinical picture, refers to other psychological or physical problems that may exist along with depression. Someone with a diagnosable clinical depression may also be abusing drugs. He may have a serious physical disease associated with depression or perhaps a more serious psychological problem alongside the depression. Statistically, the majority of depression sufferers also suffer a co-morbid condition.

The important point about co-morbidity is that your depression may be more complicated than you think, and you may be helped by a qualified professional. I suggest such an evaluation if you are in doubt about yourself, because I do not want you to miss or underestimate any problem that may slow down recovery.

Major depression is not the only type of depression. In manic-

<u>DSM-IV</u> Criteria for Major Depression Episode

A. Five (or more) of the following symptoms have been present during the same two-week period and represent a change from previous functioning; at least one of the symptoms is either (1) depressed mood or (2) loss of interest or pleasure.

    <u>Note</u>: Do not include symptoms that are clearly due to a general medical condition, or mood-incongruent delusions or hallucinations.

    1. Depressed mood most of the day, nearly every day, as indicated by either subjective report (e.g., feels sad or empty) or observation made by others (e.g., appears tearful).

        <u>Note:</u> In children and adolescents, can be irritable mood.

    2. Markedly diminished interest or pleasure in all, or almost all, activities most of the day, nearly every day (as indicated by either subjective account or observation made by others).

    3. Significant weight loss when not dieting or weight gain (e.g., a change of more than 5% of body weight in a month), or decrease or increase in appetite nearly every day.

        <u>Note</u>: In children, consider failure to make expected weight gains.

    4. Insomnia or hypersomnia nearly every day.

    5. Psychomotor agitation or retardation nearly every day (observable by others, not merely subjective feelings of restlessness or being slowed down).

    6. Fatigue or loss of energy nearly every day.

    7. Feelings of worthlessness or excessive or inappropriate guilt (which may be delusional) nearly every day (not merely self-reproach or guilt about being sick).

    8. Diminished ability to think or concentrate, or indecisiveness, nearly every day (either by subjective account or as observed by others).

    9. Recurrent thoughts of death (not just fear of dying), recurrent suicidal ideation without a specific plan, or a suicide attempt or a specific plan for committing suicide.

B. The symptoms do not meet criteria for a mixed episode.

C. The symptoms cause clinically significant distress or impairment in social, occupational, or other important areas of functioning.

D. The symptoms are not due to the direct physiological effects of a substance (e.g., a drug of abuse, a medication) or a general medical condition (e.g., hypothyroidism).

E. The symptoms are not better accounted for by bereavement, i.e., after the loss of a loved one, the symptoms persist for longer than two months or are characterized by marked functional impairment, morbid preoccupation with worthlessness, suicidal ideation, psychotic symptoms, or psychomotor retardation.

depressive illness, the individual's mood can go from euphoric highs to depressing lows. Often, there are many lows for every high. It is important to consider whether you have ever had a manic episode (characterized by high energy and no sleep for days, euphoria, and a greatly inflated sense of self). Called "bipolar disorder," because it features the two polar extremes of mood (major depression is a unipolar disorder in that it features one), this disorder has a primarily biological basis and can be effectively treated with appropriate medication and psychotherapy.

Some episodes of depression may be caused by physical diseases, and the side effects of certain medications may also cause some depressions.

One of the peculiarities of depression, in comparison to most other disorders, is that there is no single defining attribute. If you look again at the *DSM-IV* criteria for a major depression episode, you will see that they represent a general checklist; not all the symptoms may apply to a given individual. Can someone be depressed and have only one or two of the listed symptoms? Yes. Can someone have none of the symptoms and still be depressed? Yes. Can the experience of depression differ markedly from individual to individual? Yes.

Talking about depression as if it were manifested by a single symptom helps maintain the misconception that it is basically the same kind of problem for all sufferers. There are indeed enough similarities to warrant a *DSM-IV* category—and shared language about the disorder—but there are many important differences. These are most evident in the different ways depression is experienced by individuals in particular and even by cultures in general.

The face of depression is as unique as that of the individual sufferer. Often in my presentations to my professional colleagues, I speak of *depressions,* the plural, rather than of depression as a single phenomenon. The implication is that whether or not you fit the *DSM-IV* criteria for depression, you can benefit from the life-enhancing perspectives and skills offered in this book. After all, *your* depression is unique to you and your circumstances. Not all the tools in this book will be equally useful to everyone. In later chapters, I will help you to identify those which are especially pertinent to you so that you can concentrate on them.

PROJECTION AND THE AMBIGUITIES OF LIFE

In the Introduction, I briefly mentioned the key concept of "projection," a psychological term that describes the interpretation of the meaning of an ambiguous stimulus. A stimulus is simply anything you react to; an ambiguous stimulus is one that has no clear or precise meaning. For example, it may be something someone says that you can interpret in different ways. Or it may be an event that you can interpret in different ways. It may be anything that causes you to wonder about its meaning.

Through the process of projection, you give meaning to whatever happens. This occurs because of a basic psychological need to make sense out of life. All the elaborate beliefs we develop about life, death, and everything in between are motivated by our desire to make sense out of confusion, order out of chaos. Life constantly presents us with ambiguities to interpret and respond to: What is the right job for me? Should I buy or rent a place to live? Which school should we send the kids to? What should we do with the Christmas bonus? Where should we go for dinner? Should your mother come to live with us, or should we place her in a nursing home?

The ambiguous stimulus of "life" can lead one person to project that it "is a wondrous adventure." Another person, clearly depressed, projects that life "is just no damn good." Can you see how each projection carries emotional and behavioral consequences?

The idea of projection will come up at different points in this book, but I mention it here for a very specific reason: depression is itself an ambiguous stimulus. No one can identify *the* cause, because there are many. No one can say, "This is the right way to treat depression," because there are many right ways, ultimately defined by successful treatment in individual cases.

In response to the inkblot of depression, mental health professionals project a variety of interpretations onto depression and then suggest treatments according to their interpretations. For example, the psychiatrist is trained to view life through the lens of physiology. Naturally, then, he "sees" depression as a "disease" and attributes it to genetics or presumed biochemical imbalances in the brain. The traditional psychoanalyst is trained to view depression as a result of childhood formative experiences, such as the loss of a parent or a deeply shaming incident. A cognitive therapist looks for errors in thinking; a behavior therapist looks at the consequences (reward or punishment) of specific behaviors.

There are hundreds of therapies, each involving projections about a problem and its causes. Some projections about depression are clearly more sound than others, and are well supported by objective evidence. These are the ones presented in this book.

Any projection, even by educated professionals, can be arbitrary and *wrong*. Knowing this can help you better understand why I wrote this book, for each person who suffers depression—and there are millions of them at any given moment—asks, "Why me?" Each asks, "Will it ever go away?" Each wonders, "What, if anything, can I do about it?" These and many other such questions invite you to speculate, leaving you vulnerable to the implications of your own thought processes or else the presumably expert advice of well-meaning professionals. You can see how your responses to such questions can either help you or hurt you. I want to facilitate your thought processes in order to have them working *for* you rather than against you.

How would I describe or define depression? I would say that it involves an intricate and hurtful set of projections about life, the universe, other people, and yourself. Simply put, people think about their life experiences, they project hurtful or distorted meanings, and then make the mistake of believing themselves.

Your projections are patterned; that is, they are your repetitive, characteristic ways of thinking, feeling, responding, relating, predicting, and engaging in perceptual processes. Identifying and *actively* breaking these hurtful patterns, and *actively* establishing new and positive ones, is what I encourage throughout this book.

WHO GETS DEPRESSED?

Depression is the most common mental health problem in the United States today. It affects all age groups, but the rates are currently highest for those aged twenty-five to forty-four. Unfortunately, adolescents are the most rapidly growing group. The average age of onset is currently in the mid-twenties, although the trend over time is for an even earlier age. Major depression is three times more likely to affect those living in urban rather than rural settings. At any given moment, nearly twenty million Americans are suffering a depressive episode.

THE COSTS OF DEPRESSION

Depression can be called a disorder of superlatives. It is the *most common* disorder affecting Americans and is potentially the *most lethal*, since suicide is all too often chosen as the permanent solution to a temporary problem. It is, arguably, the *most debilitating*, since it impairs a person on so many levels, ranging from emotional and physical to social and financial ones.

The emotional costs are, perhaps, the most obvious. The grief, pain, despair, and the unattained potential for a higher quality of life are all heavy prices to pay.

The physical costs associated are also significant. Numerous illnesses, physical discomfort, frequent trips to the doctor's office, an unwillingness to maintain one's health, an inability to follow prescribed treatments, and even earlier death are all among the physical consequences.

The social costs are of grave consequence, too. Family conflict, divorce, poor parenting, lost loves and friendships, and even antisocial behavior (such as drunk driving) are just some of the costly interpersonal consequences.

The financial costs may be the least personal of the consequences of depression, but they are the ones that affect everyone the most directly. A 1995 study concluded that the annual cost of depression in the United States at that time was $53 *billion.* You can safely assume the cost has gone up since then. It represents hundreds of millions of days lost from productive work by people too depressed to show up. And it represents poor performance on the job—tasks needing to be redone, careless accidents, and so forth. The financial costs of psychotherapy, medications, and even the loss of lifetime earnings when someone takes his own life are additional costs at the individual level.

Depression is clearly a costly disorder in many ways. Your individual suffering is naturally of the greatest concern to you, but it is not the only concern. I think a primary goal of living well for *anybody*, not just for a depressed individual, should be to make sure that, since you inevitably affect others, you must strive to affect them positively.

GENDER AND DEPRESSION

One of the most controversial aspects of the prevalence of depression is the differing rates for men and women. The data indicate that women are two to three times more likely to be diagnosed as depressed than men. Between 2.3 percent and 3.2 percent of men meet the *DSM-IV* diagnostic criteria for major depression at any given moment, in comparison to 4.5 percent to 9.3 percent of women. In statistical predictions, as many as one in four women will develop depression in their lifetime, compared with one in ten men.

Some researchers have suggested that the gender differences are more the product of data-gathering methods than true differences in rates of depression. Certainly the hypothesis deserves further examination, but most mental health professionals seem to affirm the higher rate in women. It is theorized that the higher rate of depression stems from both biological and sociological causes.

Biologically, women have more physiological triggers for depression, such as reproductively based events (menstrual cycles, postpartum episodes, menopausal episodes). Sociological research suggests that social inequities account for the greater likelihood of women evolving the perception of helplessness so often associated with depression. The inequities are such things as: (1) a higher rate of emotional and sexual abuse in childhood; (2) a higher level of economic deprivation associated with poverty or divorce; and (3) a greater socialized dependency on others. It is a fact that nearly three quarters of antidepressants in this country are given to women, further affirming the disparity according to gender.

Regardless of the gender differences in the prevalence of depression, the most important thing to appreciate is that at the level of the individual—that is, as far as you're concerned—the numbers are less relevant than what they imply for the effective treatment of the problem. They suggest that biology, psychology, and sociology all play important roles in the development of depression. Let's consider this point next in addressing the matter of causative factors.

WHAT CAUSES DEPRESSION?

Depression is an ambiguous stimulus that can have many causes. In plain language, it is difficult, if not impossible, to establish a simple cause-and-effect relationship. Even when it seems clear, as with the onset of depression following a painful event like the death of a loved one or the loss of a job, it isn't so simple to be sure of the cause. Not everyone who suffers such an event becomes clinically depressed. Why, then, do some people? If it isn't necessarily what happens that triggers depression, what is it?

There is an enormous body of scientific literature indicating that depression has its roots in three general areas: biology, psychology, and sociology. Within an area are many variables, each of which may play an important role and so must be considered in every case. I want to consider briefly each of these areas and offer some of what we know about its influence on depression. Let's consider the role of biology first.

THE BIOLOGICAL COMPONENT OF DEPRESSION

One of the oldest questions in the field of human behavior is: How much of human experience is governed by biology (nature) and how much is governed by experience (nurture)? The nature-nurture controversy, as it is known, is important because it addresses a deeper question. How much can we hope to change our lives if the quality of our lives is biologically predetermined? Ultimately, of course, we *are* biological creatures. Our genetics and biochemistry play a considerable role in all experiences; even when we consider how much our families or culture influence us, we can say that we are biologically predisposed to be sensitive to our environment! In addressing depression, though, one has to determine the nature and degree of influence of the specific biological variables.

IS DEPRESSION A DISEASE?

Depression has often been called a disease by mental health professionals. Some compare it to diabetes or hypertension. Is it a disease? In most cases, the answer is no. Is it purely a consequence of genetics or some physiological aberration that strikes the brain? In most cases, the answer is no.

Depression is 1.5 to 3 times more common among first-degree biological relatives, meaning parents, children, and siblings. This has been known for quite a long time, and it clearly indicates that family history is important. There *is* evidence for what is called a genetic transmission factor, but there is no specific "depression gene." The existence of the transmission factor has merely been deduced from family studies and the study of twins reared apart, and it is known to account for only a very few cases. Genetics is a tempting explanation for a family history of depression, but we have come to realize that your family is largely responsible for shaping your personal view of life experiences. There is a strong relationship between the depression-causing patterns of perception in parents and those of their children.

Many doctors suggest depression is caused by a "chemical imbalance in the brain," but there is no reliable test to identify any such imbalance. It is simply assumed to exist whenever someone is depressed. Then, if the person responds well to antidepressant medication, it is taken as confirming evidence. Such a conclusion is not fully justified, however, because mood-altering drugs can have an effect even when there is no "chemical imbalance." Brain chemistry can indeed be related to mood, since specific brain chemical messengers, called neurotransmitters, are known to be directly related to mood. But which comes first? Do life experiences and associated mood shifts alter the brain's biochemistry, or do biochemical anomalies alter mood? The question is difficult to answer at this time.

The view that suggests biochemical imbalances as the sole cause of depression are too simplistic and one-dimensional to be entirely true. Clearly, a person's experience, like the death of a loved one, can cause a biochemical shift, just as a person's biochemistry can lead him to seek out or avoid certain kinds of experience. The evidence for the value of experience in reducing depression is overwhelming, considering that certain psychotherapies are every bit as effective as drugs in treating the disorder. They are even *more* effective than drugs in certain aspects of treatment, such as minimizing the likelihood of relapses.

And, interestingly, some recent research suggests psychotherapy also changes physiology to some extent, just as medication does. It seems evident that experience can change biochemistry just as biochemistry can change experience. To be sure, there is a biological correlation with depression, but a correlation is not the same as a cause. It is more accurate to speak of depression as a complex disorder than as an illness.

The notion of depression as a disease has clearly been oversold to the general public for three primary reasons. First, as mentioned at the beginning of this chapter, depression was viewed as evidence of a character weakness, and depressed individuals were blamed for their depression. With heightened social awareness came the well-intentioned goal of trying to take the stigma out of acknowledging depression and seeking treatment. Calling depression a disease redefined it as a biological problem, not a personal weakness. Second, as our culture evolved a philosophy of personal blamelessness, many problems, not just depression, became defined as diseases. It is not uncommon to hear some people denote as "sexual addiction" and "shopping disease" the behavior of those who like frequent (and often irresponsible) sex and those who spend considerably more money than they earn. Third, the development of newer, more efficient drugs that can alleviate depressive symptoms with fewer side effects serves as a powerful reminder that biology influences mood, and thus lends strong support to the not entirely correct conclusion that depression is an exclusively biological problem.

There is another line of strong evidence to indicate that depression is best viewed as a disorder rather than a disease. In the section "Who Gets Depressed?" I noted that the incidence of depression is growing in all age groups and that the average age of onset is becoming lower. While a strictly biological viewpoint might suggest that the increase results from reduced exercise or changes in diet, other evidence suggests that these are much less significant factors. The more significant factors are psychological and sociological. Depression is *not* caused by chemical imbalances or genetics in the majority of cases. *As far as most people's depression goes, nurture is more influential than nature.*

This should not be interpreted as my playing down the roles of genetics and biochemistry. I can't ignore the abundance of data showing that antidepressant medications work. Nor can I ignore the link established between the onset of depression and the ingestion of particular medications, such as certain diuretics and heart medications. I also recognize the established link between depression and some disease syndromes, such as congestive heart failure and hypothyroidism. The evidence for a relationship between biology and mood is unequivocal and strong. But it is not the total picture.

WHY DOES IT MATTER WHETHER
DEPRESSION IS A DISEASE OR A DISORDER?

Why do I emphasize so strongly the point that depression is not a disease in most (but not all) cases? Because how you think about depression plays a huge role in how you respond to it and, ultimately, whether you recover from it. If you believe you are destined to be depressed because of a genetic predisposition or a biochemical imbalance, then you are more likely to assume there is nothing you can do except sit around passively and "wait for the pills to work." This is perhaps the most dangerous result of thinking of depression as a disease. Depression's passivity often leads the sufferer to give up without really trying, and then sink into despair. Believing the medication will cure you and that you don't have to do anything but take the drug on time is not only unrealistic, it is potentially detrimental.

Any patient who takes prescribed antidepressants and seeks no other intervention is not doing himself a favor. There is a higher relapse rate when antidepressants are the only recourse than when they are taken in conjunction with effective psychotherapy.

There are a lot of good reasons not to think of medication as the best or only solution. Antidepressant medications can and often do work well, and they can be considered an integral part of a comprehensive treatment plan for many individuals, but I wouldn't want anyone to hold the view that "depression is a disease that must be medicated" as if it were true in all or even most cases. It isn't.

THE SOCIOLOGICAL COMPONENT OF DEPRESSION

Consider your answer to this question: What do you think accounts for the growing number of depressed individuals? When I pose this question to colleagues at my clinical training sessions, they talk of things like the breakdown of the traditional nuclear family, the changing roles of men and women, the ever-present fear of nuclear destruction, greater geographic mobility and the subsequent lack of stable and close relationships, and an increasing emphasis on technology (such as television and computers), resulting in an information overload and a de-emphasis of significant human contact.

I would agree that these are all important cultural influences leading to higher rates of depression. I believe there are many other factors, too. Life *has* become more stressful and more difficult for most people. Do you have more spare time now than you did a decade ago? Or less? Do you engage in more restful leisure activities now? Or fewer? Do you feel more in control of the quality of your life now? Or less? Many have suggested that every era has its share of challenges and stressors. That's true. But the things people deal with now are far more complex than those they handled before.

Consider some of the changes in our society. People used to have job security. A loyal employee might stay with an appreciative company through his whole career, and eventually retire with a nice pension and a gold watch. Now, people change jobs every five years, on average, and many companies make no apologies for firing a long-time employee when he turns fifty-seven in order to avoid paying his costly retirement benefits.

People used to have economic security. They counted on Social Security benefits. Now they are told to count Social Security out of their retirement plans. Banks go under, government-assisted programs get slashed from the budget, and making ends meet is getting more difficult. Jobs are hard to find, and competition for them keeps getting tighter.

People used to have family security. Now, people move all over the world, and family relationships are often conducted on a long-distance basis. Families break up, child custody is a matter to be negotiated, and visitation schedules get sandwiched between work and other pressing obligations.

Even for children, life is getting tougher. When I was eight years old, my biggest concern was whether I'd be the starting pitcher on my Little League baseball team. I didn't have to choose between Mom or Dad for my primary residence. I didn't have to set up a complex visitation schedule following their divorce, because they never divorced. No one instilled in me a fear of people who might want to do "bad touches" to me. No one tried to scare me away from drugs, because drugs weren't a kid's issue. No one lectured me in fourth grade about safe sex and AIDS. No one brought guns to school and opened fire. It *is* a different and tougher world for today's youth, who do face these sorts of things every day. It is no coincidence that depression strikes younger and younger targets.

Our society promotes depression, albeit unwittingly. You may be surprised to learn that there are substantial differences in the rates of depression in various cultures around the world. There are even some cultures in which depression is a minimal problem. Invariably, though, these societies are those we consider primitive, ones that place great emphasis on a tight social structure, meaning a strong sense of community. "Self" is not as heavily emphasized as what the "self" does for the greater good of the society.

One of the chief consequences of recognizing the sociological influence on depression is that you cannot think of it as only your individual problem. Instead, you can think about the influence on you of things you learned while growing up and living in a society that powerfully shapes your views. Your culture helps define what it means to be a woman or man and influences your views about all things, including love, family, time, money, social order, politics, art, religion, fashion, government, education, career, and everything else you can think of.

Society shapes us from the moment we are born, usually in ways that are so deeply ingrained as to be unconscious. This is the "programming" of individuals, which is inevitable in every culture. It is not a thing to be avoided (as if it could be, even if you wanted to). Instead, it is best to understand that what you learn to be and value is, in some ways, an arbitrary aspect of whatever culture you happen to live in. But people absorb the messages, and they live them. Consider, for example, the gender differences in the most common triggers of depression. For men, the most common triggers are job failures and a

Pause and Reflect #2

What About the Emphasis on Self?

How does an increasing emphasis on self increase the likelihood of depression? In years long past, the "common sense" remedy for depression was to "go volunteer at a hospital and see people with <u>real</u> problems." Why <u>wasn't</u> that such a bad idea?

My response: An emphasis on self can lead to a preoccupation with your feelings, a self-awareness that may cause an overreaction to every fluctuation in your mood. It can also mean less awareness of and sensitivity to the needs of others, followed by poor or unsatisfying relationships (because the unrealistic expectation is "my partner should meet *my* needs," which provides little motivation to try to meet the other person's). Finally, a connection to others fosters the learning of other viewpoints, discouraging a preoccupation with your own possibly distorted perspectives.

loss of status. For women, the most common trigger is the cut-off or disruption of an intimate relationship. Do you see male and female cultural stereotypes at work here?

You are exposed every hour of every day to countless messages that shape your perceptions of yourself and your life. So, not-so-thin women see the skinny beauty on the billboard, compare themselves unfavorably, and then despair over being "a fat pig." Not-so-successful men see the other guy's fancy car and nice house, compare themselves unfavorably, and despair over being "a big loser." I've had clients who could sink into deep despair watching *Lifestyles of the Rich and Famous* ("I'll never own my own Greek island . . . I'm such a failure")! Not funny, though.

Unless you are aware of, and can selectively choose among, the messages from our society, you can be too easily drawn into living a life that is depressingly at odds with your real self. Our society encourages all kinds of things as "the right way to be," but they may not fit you at all. If these standards become the basis for self-deprecation—or even self-loathing, when you discover you cannot live up to them without paying too great a personal price—the result is an unnecessary tragedy.

I have been using the term "culture" in the broadest sense. But what is a culture? It is influential people—parents, relatives, lovers, teachers, religious leaders, doctors, and all the other important folk you encountered directly as a child. It is also those you were only indirectly exposed to, like politicians, scientists, and artists. In most cases, the truly powerful agents of socialization were your parents. No one was more significant in shaping your views than those who reared you, trained you, and taught you everything, from how to brush your teeth to how to contain or express your feelings. Your parents taught you what they knew, and, by omission, didn't teach you what they didn't know.

I've been building up to this main point: the kinds of experiences your parents encouraged you to have, and the kinds they discouraged you from having, all helped shape your individual patterns for responding to life. Thus, if you were taught that your feelings were unimportant ("Don't speak unless you are spoken to, because children are to be seen and not heard"), you may have learned not to notice or express them or give them any credence. If you were taught that your worth came only from what you did for others, you may have learned not to follow the obvious (to others, anyway) steps for basic self-care (like taking time off or having vacations) or basic self-management (like getting enough sleep or enough exercise). If you were taught that your worth came only from your achievements ("You'd better bring home only A's from school, or else"), then you will have a hard time enjoying those things which don't lead to achievement, like leisure reading or just lying on a beach, doing nothing at all.

Our perceptions of others and ourselves are crucial to our mental health. In fact, how we relate to others is a powerful influence on all aspects of our health; it has been well known for decades that people who are satisfied in their relationships live longer and get sick less frequently than others. They also get depressed much less often. Good relationships promote good health, yet in this crowded, overpopulated world of ours, too many people are dying of loneliness. Even when a person is in a relationship, the absence of any true intimacy or emotional connection can leave one feeling lonely. It may sound trite, but it happens to be true: the best way to have friends is to be one. Almost every interaction you have with others gives you a chance to show you are approachable, interested, and open to friendship or closeness. How well you relate to others is a product of your level of social skills. If you feel you don't relate well to others, I would encourage you to learn such "people skills" as starting and maintaining conversations, expressing interest in others, and sharing appropriate things about yourself. Are you aware that workshops and seminars on these topics are routinely held all over the country? If you get catalogs from a variety of local learning institutions, you'll find them. More is said about the importance of good relationship skills in later chapters, but it's important to appreciate from the outset how much the quality of our relationships with others affects us.

The fact that others can exert such strong influence on our well-being emphasizes that what we are taught to do also defines what we are not taught to do. And, as you will see from Donna's story, it is often what we don't know how to do that leads us to try, fail, give up, and, ultimately, sink into despair.

The Story of Donna

Donna sat in front of me, trying to catch her breath between her grabs for more Kleenex. Crying softly, she repeatedly pressed a tissue to her face to wipe away her tears and blow her nose. Donna frequently became tearful in our therapy sessions, usually right from the beginning of our time together, no matter what my opening remark or question was. From our very first session, it was obvious that Donna not only was in a lot of turmoil and emotional pain, but always had been.

An intelligent, articulate, and attractive woman, Donna saw herself as a total failure. She had married and divorced three times, struggled to raise her four children alone, and had been battling the abuse of drugs and alcohol most of her life. She had engaged in countless affairs, driven by an intensely desperate wish to be taken care of by a man—almost any man. Donna became very anxious if she was left on her own for long, and her urgent priority was to have a man around to be there for her and support her in every way.

Donna was highly dependent on and therefore reactive to others. In fact, she barely managed in her job, because she was so prone to emotional outbursts if she felt her security threatened in some way, which frequently happened if her colleagues were just too preoccupied to say good morning to her. Donna was so wrapped up in her desire for a man to rescue her from the realities of her life that she became involved with guys she would have been wise to avoid. Naturally, these destructive episodes made her feel even worse about herself, deepening her depression and drug abuse, further impairing her ability to function.

Donna, having described her most recent sufferings to me,

paused and waited for me to say or do something to alleviate her pain and get her life moving in a positive direction. I couldn't expect her to be hopeful, could I? After all, she'd never known anything but a struggle to survive from the time she left her abusive home at the age of fifteen. Clichés about dark clouds and silver linings wouldn't help Donna. What would?

What Donna wanted for herself are reasonable, positive things. She wanted a healthy and committed relationship with a man and better coping skills and problem-solving abilities, so that she could handle life stresses and wouldn't feel so strong a need to "escape" through substance abuse. She wanted more "living" and less "just being alive," and, overall, a more even approach to life. It's the way that Donna went about these things, though, that prevented her from achieving them. I fully supported each of Donna's goals. The fact that she had no realistic idea of how to bring them about was where I came in. My job was to provide a safe environment and the means for Donna to learn the things she never learned, the lack of which had caused her pain.

TURNING POINTS

Most often there are many small turning points in a person's life rather than one huge one. In one session, I made a point of mentioning to Donna that I would be hiking in the mountains with a friend later that week. On previous occasions, I had mentioned my love of the outdoors and how hiking provides a necessary counterbalance to the stresses of my life. I emphasized that balance in life, like balancing play with work, is vital to a sense of well-being. Some balance in her life was a skill I hoped Donna would eventually achieve. Nowhere in her life had she ever developed recreational interests; everything she did was work, and she did not know how to play.

Donna, expressing a polite interest in my hiking, admitted that she had never in her life gone on a hike. I asked, "Why not try one?" but she was immediately gripped by mixed feelings, wanting to go yet being afraid of going. When I encouraged her to try something new, she said she had a friend who would probably go with her. She asked for and received massive amounts of reassurance that I would suggest to her and her friend an easy but beautiful hike that would not exceed their physical abilities. I gave her directions, a map to the trail head, some ideas about what to expect, and my best wishes for a very good time.

Some days later, she drove with her friend to the state park I had suggested. As she approached it, she could see Stonewall Peak, the top of which was to be her destination. Donna said she momentarily panicked, and then felt helpless, as she viewed the impressive peak. She said to her friend, "I don't think I can do it." Donna told me her immediate mental image was one of laboring intensely as she climbed straight up the vertical side of the mountain, her life in constant danger. She had no experience—no frame of reference—for knowing that the climb is made safe and easy by a continuous series of switchbacks, small inclines that go back and forth, eventually leading to the top. The climb did not require courage, just enough physical endurance to handle the slow but steady climb up the graduated inclines. Hesitantly, and proceeding only on her trust for me and the encouragement of her friend, Donna began the hike.

Once on the trail and after a few easy switchbacks, Donna relaxed and began to enjoy the beauty and peacefulness of the environment. She soon laughed at herself for her fearful and mistaken images, and all along the trail she felt more alive and happy than she ever remembered feeling. A few rest stops and several snacks later, she was at the top, looking down on the rest of the world below her. Donna was delighted, animated, and wonderfully pleased with herself. The whole way down she and her friend talked about other hikes they might go on. In one morning, a whole new world had opened up for Donna!

Whether Donna ever hiked again was not the issue; the value was in the lesson she learned from the experience. Donna saw the peak—the goal—but did not know how to get there. She automatically assumed it to be too overwhelming for her. Yet, with the right kind of strategy— a realistic and appropriate one—she reached the goal and experienced the proud satisfaction of having done so.

Completing the hike was a turning point. She discovered *from her own experience* how she could easily overwhelm herself by thinking she couldn't succeed in doing something others do routinely. Instead of striving to learn *how* to do what she wanted, she had focused only on the fear, the emptiness, and the pain of her shortcomings. This hike led her to think of setting goals, and highlighted for her that the real task is learning to develop realistic plans to do what she wants. She learned that most goals have at least one path to accomplishment, and she learned how to tell achievable goals from impossible ones. She started to understand that she is competent when she plans in advance, and she discovered that not knowing how to do something reflects only a lack of experience. It is *not* an indication of her inadequacy or a lack of intelligence, as she had so negatively assumed previously. She also found that she has the power to take care of herself and make herself happy. It is not necessary to depend on a man.

Was that the end of Donna's therapy? No, not at all. It was simply a structured opportunity for Donna to discover that there was a world of difference between how she looked at things and the way things really are. Get the message?

WHERE DOES DEPRESSION COME FROM?

It may be easier for you to understand Donna's depression, and your own, too, if you consider how she approached getting the things she so desperately wanted for herself. She valued relationships highly but didn't have the skills to choose wisely. She wanted to have some fun in her life, but she focused only on problems, not solutions. Trapped in her negative world, she felt powerless to do anything to change it. So, Donna stayed depressed, struggling to cope by deadening her feelings of despair with drugs and alcohol, running to stand still.

When people have developed only ineffective ways to manage the demands of life, they get hurt by what they don't know how to do. Whether you want to attain a loving relationship, a promotion in your job, a healthy physical appearance, self-esteem, *whatever* it is you beat yourself up for emotionally, depression is a predictable result if you feel powerless to experience what matters to you.

I constantly see clients in therapy who are hurting terribly because they do not get the approval they want, the recognition, the love, the support, the intimacy, the self-acceptance, or any number of countless basic requirements necessary for living happily. I find it very easy to support my clients' goals, and I work with them to bring their goals about. As I work with them, I challenge their views, create opportunities for them to experiment with their perceptions, practice new skills, and expand many other ways, too. That's why it is so important that you actively participate in the exercises throughout the book. Challenging your views, experimenting with your perceptions, and practicing new skills will break the grip of depression.

Donna has come a long way since that hike. There was no overnight miracle, just a slow and steady climb over the mountain of her depression. She worked hard to develop specific skills. She has since learned to manage anxiety without substance abuse. She is better at assessing men so that she can avoid those who would abuse her if she let them.

LEARN BY DOING #2

Analyze Donna's Case

Purpose: To learn to make the shift from focusing on symptoms to focusing on learnable skills.

Sometimes it's easier to start learning through someone else's experience, so let's use Donna as the teacher. Go back through "The Story of Donna" and make a list of Donna's goals and a second list of Donna's symptoms. Are any of her goals inappropriate or unrealistic as far as you're concerned? How do her symptoms reflect her inability to accomplish them?

Now, the <u>real</u> task: identify and list specific abilities Donna needs to develop in order to live more happily. If you get stuck, reread the last paragraph of her story to see what I mean by specific abilities. Try to list <u>at least</u> five more than I did in the vignette. Use this model below. I did three for you!

Donna's Goals	Donna's Symptoms	Skills Needed
To have a stable, committed relationship	Casual affairs	Assessing men, greater independence
Greater independence	Urgency, desperation for a relationship	Ability to establish a stable network of supportive friends to reduce the urgency for social contact that leads to destructive affairs
Better manage anxiety	Drug, alcohol abuse	Relaxation training; leisure skills; more detailed identification of goal-oriented behavior

She has learned to contain her feelings and prevent her old emotional outbursts, and she now has greater trust in her own judgment. She still experiences some twinges of depression now and then, but her life is going well, and Donna feels good about herself for the first time ever.

You may have your own mountain to climb. A step at a time, you can learn the switchbacks that will make it possible.

THE PSYCHOLOGICAL COMPONENT
OF DEPRESSION

From Donna's story, you can probably appreciate how biological, sociological, and psychological factors can combine to create intense personal misery. In the discussion thus far, I have described some biological and sociological components as having clear and significant effects on the experience of depression. However, it is at the individual psychological level, in a case-by-case consideration, that the battle against depression is ultimately fought. Knowing abstract statistics about the frequency of genetic transmissions, or the differences in cultural configurations of depression's symptoms, is not as powerful in helping you overcome depression as a deeper understanding of your personal psychology. Thus, most of the rest of this book addresses that specific level, describing in detail models of depression, dimensions of depression, and the specific skills known to be essential to both manage and prevent depressive episodes. Not all points will apply to you, of course, so I encourage you to read critically and focus on what pertains to your individual needs.

Psychological models of depression have been developed by many different theorists over the years, ranging from the abstract to the concrete, from the merely explanatory to the highly practical. Let's briefly consider some of the psychological models of depression developed to this point so that you can get a general idea of what they say. Then you can glean from each whatever may apply to you.

THE PSYCHODYNAMIC MODEL

Freud's view of depression was "anger turned inward," and he associated its origin to unresolved grief over childhood losses, such as parental rejection or a parent's death. A child's dependency on his parents is real, and can lead to a fear of abandonment. His need can make it difficult for him to express anger to them if they seem or really are unavailable. So the child's anger is turned against himself, which accounts for the typical self-loathing of depressives. This model is now widely considered incorrect, however, since research has failed to support even its most basic tenets. Furthermore, treatment-outcome studies based on such approaches ("Let's examine your childhood") consistently show the lowest rate of success. For reasons described in the next chapter, objective evidence makes it clear that this "focus on your childhood feelings" approach is not as useful in treating depression as are some others.

THE COGNITIVE MODEL

A cognition is a thought. Cognitive therapy, as developed by its originator, Aaron T. Beck, M.D., is based on the recognition that depressed people's thinking almost invariably shows errors, or "cognitive distortions," in specific areas (*not* everywhere). When the client is taught to identify and correct his distortions, improvement is generally rapid and lasting. I said earlier in this chapter that the key problem is people's erroneous and hurtful thoughts about themselves and the belief that they are true. That was in part the acknowledgment of the huge role of cognitive distortions in creating and maintaining depression. Cognitive therapy works well in the majority of cases.

Beyond the straightforward cognitive distortions model just mentioned, there are two variations worthy of your awareness, each accepting cognitive distortions and noncritical thinking as the basis for depression. One, the "learned helplessness" model, was developed by Martin Seligman, Ph.D. Observing the passivity often manifested by depressed individuals, Seligman set up laboratory conditions that involved the use of aversive and uncontrollable stimuli, such as an irritating noise that could not be escaped. Many research subjects became passive and depressed when they discovered there was nothing they could do to stop the offensive stimuli. Later, in situations where they would have been able to stop what was offensive merely by trying, many didn't make the attempt; previous experience had taught them that their efforts were destined to fail. They "learned helplessness." Their error was believing that what was true in one circumstance was also true in another. Therapy involves learning to be more accurate in gauging what is and is not controllable. This topic is so important that it is the sole subject of Chapter 9.

A second variation of the cognitive model involves your "attributional style," which refers to the meanings you attribute to other people's behavior and the way you explain life events. As with the earlier example of someone not returning your phone call, you naturally form an explanation for an occurrence. The quality of your explanation, or attribution, holds significant potential to depress you. If you decide that the person didn't call back because he hates you, you feel terrible. If you decide that he didn't call back because he didn't get the message, you feel neutral. Neither attribution is known to be true, but clearly one holds much greater potential for making you feel bad. Learning to suspend attributions and to seek objective evidence for your views is the essence of therapy based on attributional style. This, too, is so critical that I have devoted Chapter 6 to helping you understand and master attributional skills.

It is vital that you never underestimate the role of cognition in your experience of depression. Recovery now and the prevention of relapses depends in large part on "learning to think straight."

THE BEHAVIORAL MODEL

Just as the things you *think* have consequences, so do the things you *do*. Your actions, your observable reactions, what you say, what you don't say, what you do, and what you don't do all fall into the realm of behavior. Your behavior influences which experiences you seek or avoid, the quality of your interactions with others, the courses of action you will take, and whether or not those will lead to success.

The basis of the behavioral model is that consequences shape behavior. We want to do things we will get rewarded for, and avoid things we will get punished for. So we are more likely to repeat actions we have been rewarded for in the past and to avoid things that have caused us hurt.

The behavioral model also takes into account that people are sometimes rewarded for the "wrong" things and punished for the "right" things. For example, a bank robber who gets away with his crime is likely to try it again. A person who richly deserves a promotion for working hard, but who is passed over for the boss's nephew, may then lose interest in working so hard.

Someone who is depressed may get all kinds of extra attention and personal favors from others out of sympathy. This can actually reinforce his depression. Likewise, if a plan to do something new backfires, the person may stop seeking fun things to do, things that would have provided reinforcement for feeling good. (What are *you* doing to feel good?) Behavior therapy strives to develop a plan of action that will probably be successful and involve plenty of rewards along the way. Toward that end, this book heavily emphasizes *action* that is well planned and on target. The reward is that you will feel better.

THE INTERPERSONAL MODEL

Good relationships serve as insulation against physical illnesses and emotional disorders of all kinds, including depression. Other people can provide love, support, companionship, and alternative viewpoints. When relationships go well, it is wonderful. When relationships go badly, it is painful.

Depression can be and often is caused by relationship issues and problems. The reverse is equally true: relationship problems can be and often are caused by depression. The death of a loved one, divorce, breakup, rejection, defiance and hostility, humiliation, abuse, emotional abandonment and isolation all occur in the context of close relationships.

The interpersonal model addresses these kinds of issues and more. The cultural factors I described in the section on sociological components of depression are obviously also interpersonal. Thus, family relationships, social roles, and role transitions (such as retiring or becoming a parent), and the lack of desired and necessary social skills are all targets for interpersonal intervention.

In studies of therapeutic outcomes, interpersonal therapy rates as the most effective psychotherapy for the treatment of major depression. *Good relationships are essential for good mental health.* Chapters 10 and 11 are devoted to helping you develop specific relationship skills so that you'll bring good people into your life and so that your current relationships will improve.

WHAT CURES DEPRESSION?

This fourth and last of the questions on which this chapter is based leads me to describe the rest of the book. I wrote the book to address this question as realistically and completely as I could.

The answer to this all-important question is, paradoxically, both simple and complicated. The simple answer to what helps depression is this: good psychotherapy, of which self-help is an integral part (hence, this book), and sometimes antidepressant medications. The complicated part is this: everyone is different and so is each person's depression.

Does depression get cured? Or does it simply recede into the background, where it lies dormant until another episode is triggered? The

LEARN BY DOING #3

Discovering the Relevance of Models

Purpose: To identify the specific ways that each of the psychology models of depression may apply to you.

You have now been introduced briefly to the most important psychological models of depression. The ideas and methods each model offers will be more fully developed later, but even on a first reading you may have had some affinity to one model more than another. Which model(s) most attracts you or seems most relevant to you at this early stage of exposure?

Write a paragraph or two about what relevance you think each model may have for you. Do you recognize, for example, that your thinking is sometimes distorted, even if you're not yet sure what to do about it? Or do you recognize, perhaps, that it's almost always relationships (interpersonal events) that get you down?

As always, date and keep what you've written so that you can later see where your thinking was at the time you began your self-help program.

Use the models below to get yourself started.

The Cognitive Distortion Model   I sometimes see myself reacting to situations in very emotional ways, only to find I have erred in my thinking. The kinds of errors I seem to make are . . .

The Learned Helplessness Model   I have often felt or been victimized in my life, and I usually think, "Why bother?" I think I'm powerless to change things and make my life any better, so I don't even try . . .

The Attributional Style Model   I interpret situations in ways that usually depress me, and often find later that what I thought was happening really wasn't. My knee-jerk reaction is to see things in the worst way possible . . .

The Behavioral Model   I'm afraid to try new things, meet new people, or try new behaviors, and the things I do now don't work; they make me feel inadequate, incompetent, and depressed. I do things I know don't bring about the results I want, yet I keep doing them . . .

The Interpersonal Model   I am very sensitive to other people's reactions to me, and it is important to me to have good relationships with others. But I seem to turn people off, or I get so attached to them that I can't cope without their support. My relationships often go off in wrong directions that hurt them . . .

Pause and Reflect #3

What's Your First Impression?

How do you feel right now? Hopeful? Intrigued? Uncertain? How do your feelings influence your expectations of receiving benefit from this book? Take the positive approach of being open to new ideas and ways of doing things, and learn what you can do to improve your responses to life. I believe you'll be happily surprised with the results!

My response: I hope you are feeling hopeful. A dose of realistic optimism to motivate your participation is a solid base on which to build the skills you'll learn here. You will learn to do things differently and successfully. Feeling good will be the result of your focused efforts.

conventional wisdom in the mental health profession has been that you can recover from depression but not cure it. It has been called a "cyclical," or recurring, disease. The goal for clinicians has typically been for their patients to have fewer episodes, each of which lasts for a shorter period of time and causes less discomfort.

I see it very differently. I don't think of depression as a "recurring disease." I don't believe it is depression that is recurrent; I believe it is *life* that is recurrent. No one faces loss only once or rejection only once. Hurt and pain are sprinkled liberally into the lives of people. If each time you face a negative event your response is to become depressed, then, yes, depression will be a frequent companion.

As the crude but popular bumper sticker says, SHIT HAPPENS. But be reminded also that *"good* happens." A primary goal of mine is to help you make sure you do not create your own problems. After all, life will hand you plenty without your adding to them with preventable mistakes. *Managing skillfully the problems you can't prevent while striving to avoid or prevent others is the primary way to reduce and even prevent relapses.* Prevention isn't always possible, but it is possible more often than you may currently realize. I place great value on prevention, as you will see.

So, what cures depression? A realistic understanding of the nature of depression, a realistic treatment plan that involves established principles and techniques of effective resolution, and the willingness to expend intelligent and focused effort in the appropriate direction. All of these things are readily available in this book.

In the next chapter, I describe in detail the characteristics of effective psychotherapy, including self-help therapy. Let your recovery begin!

SUMMARY OF KEY POINTS . . . AND WHAT THEY CAN MEAN TO <u>YOU</u>

- Depression is a complex disorder. There is no single cause, single treatment, or single defining characteristic. So don't try too hard to look for either THE cause or THE solution!

- As an ambiguous stimulus, depression invites projections of all kinds from researchers and clinicians. Many are well thought out and validated through good research; some are not. That's why it's important to learn what works for you as an individual.

- Depression affects all age groups, regardless of education, socioeconomic status, or gender. Women are more likely to be diagnosed as depressed than men. Adolescents are the fastest growing age group affected, but those between twenty-five and forty-four are the largest group suffering depression. These facts highlight that *anyone* can become depressed.

- Depression is extremely costly on many levels: emotionally, physically, socially, and financially. How it affects you specifically, though, is the basis for deciding how soon and how actively you need to start your self-help program. In general, why wait?

- Depression is more accurately considered a disorder than a disease. There are biological influences underlying depression, just as there are sociological and psychological ones. You are not a diseased or sick person; you *are* someone who has not been taught to develop the specific ways of thinking, feeling, or behaving that insulate you against life's difficulties. You *can* learn now.

- The most prominent psychological models relevant to the self-help nature of this book are the cognitive (including learned helplessness and attributional style), behavioral, and interpersonal models. These models emphasize specific skills that will help you deal with life effectively and thereby minimize the chances of sinking into depression. Life events are repetitive in nature, so even though "the names and faces may change," you will be dealing with many similar situations throughout your life. Once you develop the ability to manage them effectively, and once you learn to adapt your skills according to changing circumstances, you'll have some valuable tools for managing life without depression.

Chapter 2
LESS ANALYSIS, MORE ACTION

WHEN YOU'RE EXPERIENCING depression, the idea of experimenting with a bunch of different therapy approaches can be pretty unappealing. It often takes a lot of energy to try *anything*, so naturally you want whatever effort you put forth to be effective. Having worked with so many depressed clients over the last couple of decades, I am acutely aware that often, if the person isn't in a particularly patient frame of mind, I have only a short time to figure out what's going on, get him pointed in a useful direction, and start him on the path to recovery.

In this chapter, I will describe the essentials of effective treatment for depression. This information is vital on two counts. First, you will learn how best to help yourself with effective approaches by focusing on important and helpful things, while not getting stuck in analyzing aspects that may be interesting but hold little potential to help you. Second, should you ever decide to seek professional help, you will have some current information about how therapy may best be done so that you attain the greatest benefit.

TREATMENT FOLLOWS DIAGNOSIS

Research indicates that most of the depressed people who would benefit from therapy never seek or get the professional help they need. As valuable as a professional consultation may be, only about one in four depressed individuals are likely to consult a mental health professional.

There are at least two reasons for this. First, many of those who are clinically depressed don't know they are depressed. (Remember Alex from the first chapter? He is typical.) Instead, they may think they have a physical malady that is draining their energy and happiness, so they are likely to consult a physician and present some of the classic *DSM-IV* symptoms described in the previous chapter.

This would be all right if the person is correctly diagnosed as depressed by the physician. Unfortunately, research indicates that only about half of the people with depression seen by general practitioners are correctly diagnosed. The evidence further indicates that the chances of a correct diagnosis appear to be even less in health maintenance organizations (HMOs). Thus, it comes down to a flip of the coin as to whether your physician will recognize and treat your depression or miss it completely. Why is this so? For several reasons. Some physicians may lack knowledge about depressive symptoms. Some clearly have a bias toward identifying only physical or organic disorders, or they may underrate depression's importance in comparison with co-existing medical problems. Others may not ask the relevant questions as part of their medical evaluation.

Another reason that many depressed people go untreated, despite the fact that *good treatment works,* is the very nature of depression. Typically, the depression sufferer feels hopeless—perhaps about ever feeling good again, perhaps about whatever seems to be at the base of the depression. When you feel hopeless, you usually don't want to spend the time and energy to shop for, find, and then build a whole new relationship with a therapist. It may seem far too big a project, especially when your underlying hopelessness has you say, in essence, "Why bother? No one can help me anyway."

Although *recovery from depression is not only possible but highly likely,* you may convince yourself that getting help—even self-help—is a useless endeavor, one that will result only in failure. That's not true, of course, but that's where depressed thinking can lead. Or you may actually seek help from a therapist or a self-help book but stop trying when there are no immediate, dramatic results. In fact, research indicates that nearly a third of depressed people will drop out of treatment before it is completed. Sometimes this is because of unrealistic expectations of "instant cures" (partly generated by the popularity of Prozac), and other times because of the therapist's missing the target when choosing treatment. It is fair to say, though, that with the right focus in treatment (both self-help and professional approaches), and with a realistic client who recognizes the need to participate actively, recovery is a realistic expectation. Stay with the program!

Let's consider what has been learned in recent years from the research and clinical literature about successful treatment. Knowledge about what works in the treatment of depression can help motivate you to apply relevant principles and methods to yourself. As I present these to you, I want you to know that they are not the product of just my experience or my personal viewpoint. Rather, they are derived from the experiences and viewpoints of thousands of experts who have contributed their knowledge and methods to the scientific literature. These were accumulated, analyzed, and integrated into a set of comprehensive treatment principles that are widely considered to be the core elements of good treatment, whether provided by a mental health professional or by a good self-help book. Familiarizing yourself with the information in this chapter sets the stage for you to apply it in your own behalf.

PROFESSIONAL CLINICAL PRACTICE GUIDELINES

In December 1989, a U.S. federal public law was passed mandating the development of clinical practice guidelines for health care providers who treat depression (as well as six other common disorders). Depression was chosen for inclusion for several reasons: its prevalence, the great opportunity for early detection to prevent unnecessary suffering or even suicide, and its high level of responsiveness to good treatment. The formal treatment guidelines were established to reduce the likelihood of inappropriate treatment by individual clinicians, and to encourage them to adopt methods with a proven value. In order to establish the treatment guidelines, the Agency for Health Care Policy and Research (AHCPR) was established within the United States Public Health Service. The AHCPR set up a multidisciplinary (psychology, social work, psychiatry, etc.) panel of experts to oversee the project.

The panel initiated a review of the huge body of recent research data gathered about depression and its treatment. Over 100,000 publications were reviewed, all published between 1975 and 1990. After these were analyzed, only the most well-structured and meaningful studies were chosen for use in formulating the treatment guidelines. These made up a data base of nearly 3500 studies.

Several things should now be apparent to you. First, depression has received a huge amount of attention from researchers and clin. The fact that there were over 100,000 studies published between 1. and 1990 is just one indication of the seriousness with which the subject of depression is treated by the mental health profession. Second, it may be comforting to realize that depression is a subject about which a great deal of information exists. That means you don't have to rely on just one person's word (your doctor's or therapist's) about what may be wrong with you and what you should do about it. Rather, you can be an informed consumer of health services who knows something about appropriate standards of care and methods of treatment. Third, it means that in establishing your own self-help program, as you can with the guidance of this book, you don't have to try just *anything*. Instead, your efforts to help yourself can be focused and sensible. You can aim at specific problem targets instead of blindly trying things you hope will somehow make a positive difference in your life. Fourth, instead of trying to absorb abstract advice or well-meant clichés ("It's always darkest before the dawn"), you can recognize that living life well and feeling good require specific, carefully defined skills. The need to learn and master these life skills has been well defined in the clinical and research literature. Through the vehicle of this book, I will identify and teach you many of them.

In April 1993, the AHCPR guidelines were released to both health care providers and the public following careful peer review by no fewer than seventy-three professional organizations and three consumer groups. Without a doubt, the treatment guidelines were subjected to a great deal of scrutiny by many, many experts. Thus, it is no accident that they have been extremely well received by the majority of experts, who believe they provide a solid perspective about the nature of depression and good, clear recommendations for its treatment. Despite some minor differences of opinion, I include myself among them. You can obtain copies of the *Depression in Primary Care* guidelines by calling the Government Printing Office at (202) 512-1800. There is a cost for purchasing them. There is also a briefer, more conversational patient's guide you can order if you think you'd prefer it to the more clinical documents.

Bear in mind that the panel's guidelines are necessarily general in nature. They can provide some specific recommendations about the types of psychotherapy that are appropriate and a rationale for employing antidepressant medications. But they cannot specify which medication, if any, *you* should be taking, or what *you* should be talking about in *your* fourth therapy session. These choices must, of necessity, be a product of both clinical judgment and personal choice. In this book, I address the common denominators of *all* effective treatment modalities without focusing on any one exclusively. This is not a book about cognitive therapy, though I clearly advocate and include its principles and methods. Nor is it a book about behavioral or interpersonal therapies, though I readily acknowledge them as invaluable and thus include their techniques liberally. The goal is for you to *discover what works and do it!* My job is to help you do exactly that.

SO, WHAT WORKS?

The AHCPR treatment guideline panel concluded that both psychotherapy and pharmacotherapy (treatment with medications) are effective in treating depression. It is not false hope, but *realistic hope*, which has been gained from years of accumulated clinical research and practice. The task now is to translate all of this information into a realistic plan for *you* as an individual. Let's turn our attention to what we know about each of the two main approaches to treatment. We'll start with medications.

ANTIDEPRESSANT MEDICATIONS

In the first chapter, I addressed the misuse of the term "disease" in association with most cases of depression. In fact, research indicates that no more than one in five cases of depression has an underlying physical cause. It is not an accurate reflection of everything we know about depression, from its onset and treatment to its prevention, to call it a disease. It is more accurate to think of depression as a "disorder," with obvious biological consequences and correlations. On that basis alone, the appropriate use of antidepressant medication may be wholly justified. I remind you of that point now so that you can avoid thinking in misleading terms of "disease" and "cure."

The AHCPR suggests medication as the first-choice approach when the following conditions are in effect:

1. The individual's depression is severe.
2. The individual has suffered at least two prior depressive episodes.
3. There is a family history of depression.
4. The individual seeking treatment specifically states that he prefers medication as the sole intervention (refusing psychotherapy).

I can add a fifth condition. If the person has responded well to antidepressant medication in the past, he can try the same one again or perhaps another of the same type.

Antidepressant medication is a broad term for several categories of drugs that are known to reduce some of the most basic symptoms of depression, like sleep disturbance or loss of energy. These categories include tricyclic antidepressants (TCAs), monoamine oxidase inhibitors (MAOIs), selective serotonin reuptake inhibitors (SSRIs), and a group of drugs so different in their chemical makeup that they are simply called "structurally unrelated compounds." All of these antidepressants work by altering the concentration of certain brain messenger chemicals, called neurotransmitters.

The TCAs and MAOIs have been in use for decades. They are effective drugs, but are used less frequently now, with the emergence of the newer SSRIs and structurally unrelated compounds. The reason? The newer antidepressant drugs have considerably fewer side effects, though they are not by any means fully free of such effects. The more pronounced side effects of the older antidepressants often made users so uncomfortable that they would stop taking the drug, thereby rendering them useless. What good is a drug if the patient is unwilling to take it? This is known as a "treatment compliance" issue. Some of the greater success of the newer antidepressants is attributed solely to the higher rate of compliance, meaning that more people are willing to stay on them.

THE PROZAC PHENOMENON

With the release of Prozac, in January 1988, came a new era in the pharmacotherapy of depression. Prozac worked more directly on the relevant neurotransmitter (serotonin), thus generating fewer side effects. (In fact, Prozac is actually old news. Newer SSRIs and structurally unrelated compounds are becoming even more widely used.) Prozac quickly achieved a near star status, especially when its enthusiasts broadly promoted it. One therapist in Seattle, known locally as the Pied Piper of Prozac and featured nationwide in an episode of PBS *Frontline*, prescribes it routinely for all his patients. Questioned about his "one size fits all" practice by the government licensing board, he stated that depression is a basic component of *everyone's* life, and that if it were solely up to him, he'd put Prozac in the community water supply!

Prozac has been the subject of books that glorify it, declaring that it can enhance entire personalities and help people be "better than well." It has been the star of television documentaries and has been featured on the covers of numerous national publications. Prozac, as well as some newer medications, is certainly a valuable treatment tool, but what should we think of this kind of glorification of a drug well beyond its appropriate clinical use?

Despite its popularization in the media, neither Prozac nor any drug is a guaranteed solution. For some, it does seem to work near miracles. For others, though, it gives the "jitters" but no relief from depression.

In fact, Prozac and the newer drugs are no more effective than the older drugs; the success rates are about the same. What *is* true, though, is that the newer antidepressants not only have fewer bothersome side effects, but they are not likely to be lethal if overdosed (unlike the older TCAs, which would be prescribed for depression and the potential for suicide, and then, ironically, would be the very drug suicidal persons most commonly overdosed on). Furthermore, they are not addictive, and they can be used successfully for a co-existing condition, like an eating disorder or obsessive-compulsive disorder. In fact, about a third of the prescriptions for Prozac are for other conditions, not for depression.

ANTIDEPRESSANTS AND YOU

Can antidepressant medications help *you?* Quite possibly, since they do help the majority of those who take them. It is important, however, that you approach them realistically. It is equally important that you recognize their appropriate value and not refuse to take them because of some misguided notion that you're somehow weak and "giving in" to depression merely by taking medication. It's not weakness to use every available tool in breaking the patterns of depression.

If you choose to consult a physician, particularly a psychiatrist, about beginning a course of treatment with antidepressants, here are some points to keep in mind. No one antidepressant is clearly more effective than another. It is unknown how your body in particular will respond to medication in terms of side effects or symptom resolution. You will, though, usually know relatively quickly. If your body reacts negatively, you'll know within a matter of days; be assured that serious complications are rare. You'll also know within two to six weeks whether the drug is helping. In fact, the AHCPR suggests that if no improvement is evident by six weeks, a change of medication should be seriously considered. If the medication facilitates improvement, the depressive episode should largely be over in twelve weeks' time; if not, then a switch to another medication may be indicated. In general, they should not be used if you are pregnant or plan to be pregnant soon.

How long should you be on an antidepressant? If the episode has been resolved and you're feeling a lot better, the panel recommends that you continue the medication at the same dosage for *at least* four months but *no longer* than nine months. Some recent research suggests the patient stay on the antidepressant up to eighteen months. Regardless, you will not and should not be on antidepressant medications forever.

Let's weigh the benefits and risks of pharmacotherapy. In its favor, antidepressants:

1. Are not addictive;
2. Are considered relatively safe to take over long periods of time;

3. Rarely show any serious complications;

4. May show a higher response rate in more severe depressions (there is still considerable debate about this point);

5. Show a faster (but not better) rate of symptom remission than does psychotherapy alone; and,

6. Do not depend for therapeutic effect on the skill of whoever writes the prescription.

The risks of pharmacotherapy include:

1. The higher rate of relapse when drugs alone are used in treatment;

2. The potential for overdoses with the TCAs;

3. The presence of unpleasant side effects, ranging from mild to severe from individual to individual, which may lead to reduced treatment compliance or serious complications in patients with certain medical conditions (such as cardiac disease);

4. The significant (50 to 60 percent) chance that the first drug tried will not work;

5. The lack of any clear advantage of medication's success over psychotherapy for most individuals;

6. The unfortunate and undeserved social stigma often associated with taking mood-altering drugs;

7. The tendency to reinforce the "disease" viewpoint, which suggests depression happens to you (perhaps reinforcing passivity and a "victim" mentality); and

8. The significant risk to pregnant women, or to women about to become pregnant, for fetal damage.

As long as the medication is not the sole intervention and is taken as prescribed, its benefits generally outweigh the risks. I want to make it clear that the use of antidepressant medication as an aid in your recovery from depression can be a good and realistic choice. I also want to make it clear, though, that approaching drugs cautiously and sensibly shows good judgment (unlike the fellow who wants to dump Prozac in the community water supply!). You would be well advised to talk in detail to a knowledgeable physician about the value of medication in *your* particular case. You can and should be an intelligent co-creator of your own treatment plan, and not just ask for a Prozac prescription because it was on the cover of *Newsweek*.

There is far more to say about pharmacotherapy, of course, but psychotherapy, not medication, is the major focus of this book. Let's consider the suggested psychotherapy guidelines of the AHCPR panel.

LEARN BY DOING #4

Why Is Prozac Popular?

Purpose: To help you consider the role of medication in your case by evaluating what is "hype," misconception, and good common sense in the opinion of others.

Many people still hold the naïve and outdated notion that to take a medication for depression is a sign of personal weakness. Yet Prozac (and its relatives) has caught on with people in ways no other drug ever has. Why do you think this is so? After you list your own reasons, ask at least half a dozen people for their perspective on Prozac—why it's so popular, when they think its use is appropriate, and when they think it is inappropriate. What do you find out? You can use the outline below to record your answers.

Those I Asked	Why They Think Prozac's Popular	When Is It Appropriate?	When Is It Inappropriate?

PSYCHOTHERAPIES FOR DEPRESSION

The AHCPR clinical practice guidelines are especially valuable for their consideration of the essential role of psychotherapy in treating depression. Psychotherapy is at least as much art as science. Therefore, the level of skill of the clinician does matter. In the case of self-help, *you* are the practitioner, so it is necessary for you to know what constitutes effective treatment.

The panel evaluated many different therapy approaches for each phase of treatment, including the *acute phase,* when someone first appears for treatment of his symptoms; the *continuation phase,* in which therapy continues to provide support, education, and relief; and the *maintenance phase,* in which results are maintained while greater attention is focused on preventing relapses. The panel concluded that therapy:

1. Should be an *active* process;
2. Should be *time-limited* (and not go on indefinitely);

3. Should focus on *solving current problems* (and not on rehashing old issues); and,

4. Should specifically *aim for symptom reduction* as a goal (rather than assuming the symptoms will disappear if some deeper abstract personality issue gets resolved).

The panel's recommendations are clear and specific about the chief characteristics of good psychotherapy as derived from thousands of key studies. The evidence that not all therapies are equally effective in treating depression is simply too great to support outdated notions suggesting that, essentially, "any therapy will do." (Many therapists are still being taught that all therapies are equally effective, giving them the erroneous belief that they can practice whatever therapy they prefer.)

What psychotherapies, then, are the most effective for treating depression? The panel concluded that cognitive, behavioral, and interpersonal psychotherapies are the most efficient forms of treatment, even more effective than antidepressant medications in some important respects (though not all). It is interesting to note that the panel also specifically made a point of identifying brief dynamic psychotherapy—a category of therapy generally aimed at personality change and focusing primarily on historical issues—as the weakest approach. By the end of this chapter, you will know why this is so.

Psychotherapy is considered by the panel to be the first-choice approach when:

1. The depression is mild to moderate (as it is in the majority of sufferers), although it may reasonably be used in more severe cases as well;

2. The depression does not involve psychosis, or severe impairments of judging objective reality;

3. The depression is not extremely chronic (long-term) or highly recurrent; and,

4. The individual specifically requests psychotherapy as the desired form of intervention.

Can psychotherapy and medication be combined? Yes, absolutely. In fact, many depression experts suggest this sort of "combination therapy" as a matter of course. A combination approach may be especially sensible when:

1. There are recurrent depressive episodes in rapid succession without a full recovery between episodes;

2. Neither medication nor psychotherapy alone seems to be working;

3. There is evidence of a personality problem that goes beyond major depression; and,

4. The individual expresses the desire for a combination approach.

The panel concluded that any of the three major psychotherapy approaches—cognitive, behavioral, interpersonal—may sensibly be used alone or in combination. These approaches are summarized in Table 1, on page 46. Which approach to use is determined by the specifics of an individual's case. Positive results should be evident within six weeks, and it is realistic to expect a remission of the depressive episode within twelve weeks. This gives you an idea of how long you can reasonably expect to be actively working on overcoming your immediate experience of depression.

To be realistic, the remission of your present episode should *not* mark the end of your self-help efforts. I place strong emphasis on prevention. Although it is not possible to prevent all future episodes of depression, many—probably most—such episodes can be prevented when you have mastered the skills taught in this book. I don't want you to think that once your depression lifts, that's all there is to it. That would be a mistake. One of the key ways good psychotherapy outperformed medications was the probable reduction of relapses. I consider this preventive component a vital part of the self-help plan you will develop. Much more will be said about prevention later, when I turn your attention from the general discussion to the identification of your specific needs.

WHAT'S SO THERAPEUTIC ABOUT COGNITIVE, BEHAVIORAL, AND INTERPERSONAL PSYCHOTHERAPIES?

The AHCPR clinical practice guidelines make a point of emphasizing the superior value of active, time-limited approaches that focus on symptom resolution and the resolution of current problems. These are general characteristics that provide some insight into desirable treatment. But what is it about the cognitive, behavioral, and interpersonal models that make them more effective in treating depression than other approaches? And is it that the approaches themselves are effective, or do they have some common denominators that lend them their roughly equal rates of effectiveness?

Table 1. Recommended Treatment Models of Psychotherapy for Depression

Model	Focus of Treatment	Goals	Methods
Interpersonal Therapy	Identifying and correcting social skill deficits	Define and resolve issues in main areas: 1) abnormal grief following significant loss; 2) interpersonal disputes; 3) role transitions; 4) interpersonal deficits	Exploratory techniques, encouragement of affect, clarification and communication analysis, use of therapeutic relationship
Cognitive Therapy	Identifying and correcting errors in thinking (cognitive distortions)	To teach self-identification and self-correction strategies when interpreting events or making choices that may be depressingly inaccurate	Use of behavioral "experiments," homework assignments, Socratic questioning, exploring thought content and style
Behavioral Therapy	Diminishing hurtful or unsuccessful behaviors while learning and increasing the use of rewarding behaviors	To identify and develop the skills necessary to manage interactions and tasks skillfully with maximum reward value	Relaxation training, assertiveness training, role playing, modeling, graduated task assignments, time management

Let me answer the latter question first. Yes, there are common denominators that I identify and describe in the next section of this chapter. These are factors not tied to any one approach, but contained in *any* approach that holds the potential to help. In that respect, it does not matter that you study and learn one method of treatment; what matters is that you learn to identify and manipulate the variables of good treatment in your own behalf.

Let's consider the three models now in order to identify what they do and what they teach.

COGNITIVE THERAPY

As you learned in the first chapter, a cognition is a thought. Cognitive therapy is founded on the simple understanding that both *what* we think and, more important, *how* we think significantly affect our physical, behavioral, and emotional responses. If what you think is hurtful, and if the way you think is distorted, depression is a common result. The cognitive model places great emphasis on first identifying and then correcting errors in your thinking process. These errors are called "cognitive distortions."

Let's consider the following example. Mary is jilted by the new fellow she is seeing when he decides to return to his old girlfriend. Although they dated only a few times, Mary really liked the guy and had visions of a serious, committed, long-term relationship with him. Hurt by his returning to his former girlfriend, Mary concludes that "men just can't be trusted, because they always leave you." She sinks into deep despair as she repeats this to herself, and soon refuses to date anyone.

Can you see how Mary's thinking is in error, much to her detriment? It is a huge and unjustifiable leap to go from *"this* man" to *"all* men." Mary's thinking shows a cognitive distortion called "overgeneralization."

Cognitive therapy is an active form of both education and remediation; it involves the process of learning to distinguish between errors in your thinking (what you tell yourself) and what's actually going on out there in the real world. Thus, it means developing the ability to step outside your thinking (feelings, interpretations, projections, reactions) long enough to gather relevant facts, weigh them, draw sensible conclusions, plan a realistic course of action, and assess your plan's effectiveness. These are all vital problem-solving skills, invaluable in living well and staying out of depression. The history of how you came to develop your cognitive distortions is unimportant in cognitive therapy. Learning to "think straight" now and for the future is the primary goal of treatment, whether in formal therapy or in self-help.

Chapters 6 and 7 will present the cognitive distortions in detail so that you learn to recognize and correct them. Without the ability to monitor and correct your errors in thinking, you would continue to be at risk for more episodes of depression, and it would take you longer to recover from the one you may be in now.

BEHAVIOR THERAPY

Behavior therapy focuses on what you do in specific situations, like meeting someone new or going to a party, and how the the way you behave then affects your later actions. As you are no doubt aware, the behaviors you engage in that lead to success or failure in a given situation can play a significant role in how you feel about yourself and your world.

Let's consider Mark, who works constantly. If he's not actually at work, he's working at home. He has a position of considerable responsibility, and he is convinced that if he doesn't stay focused on his job, he'll miss something that will result in his being fired or kicked off the career ladder. Mark has not taken a vacation in several years. Although he wants to continue to get pay raises and promotions, as he has each year, he is also painfully aware that life is passing him by. He feels stressed, depressed, and hopeless about ever having a "normal" life.

Mark clearly feels rewarded for his one-dimensional life with praise, pay raises, promotions, and the absence of mistakes for which he might get punished. Mark's behavior is governed by his work focus. He engages in no social activities, lives alone, and does not organize his time to include anything but his work. If he wants to improve his quality of life, and his outlook on life, Mark must learn some very specific new behaviors. (Can you name them?) He will need to organize his schedule so that he'll have time for social and recreational opportunities. He will need to actively and deliberately do things that are fun and pleasurable. He will need to practice new ways to meet people and form social relationships (friendships, dating). He will need to practice relaxation skills to reduce his stress. All of these represent new behaviors that will help Mark restore a sense of control over his life and bring him the rewards and good feelings associated with living successfully. Simply put, if you don't do things to feel good, how can you expect to feel good?

The role of action (behavior) is vital to recovery from depression. It is no coincidence that I have included dozens of activities in this book that are meant to stimulate new behaviors and new approaches to experience. The ability to act in a manner that is purposeful and effective in achieving the desired result is a major influence on your quality of life. *If what you've been doing hasn't worked, then it's clearly time to do something else.* The structured learning experiences included in this book are to help you develop the ability to "do something different."

INTERPERSONAL PSYCHOTHERAPY (IPT)

In the first chapter, I mentioned that some societies on our planet seem to have considerably lower rates of depression among their members. These are societies that typically place a greater emphasis on community than on self. I also noted that people who are in good relationships are less likely to be depressed than those who are not.

We live in times that are not particularly kind to relationships. The national divorce rate exceeds 50 percent; the average person moves every seven years; the average person changes jobs every five years; and the local community typically keeps growing and outgrowing easy opportunities for close social ties. More people work at home, interacting only with their computers and fax machines. Consequently, people now commonly date through classified ads and computerized dating services. I must get asked ten times a week by lonely people some variation of this question: "Where can I go to meet members of my species?"

Getting connected to others becomes increasingly difficult as the pace of life gets faster. When the emphasis is on work or other interests, it's not on people. Developing social skills is less a focus and less an opportunity for many. The unfortunate result is that the absence of such skills makes it difficult, if not impossible, for people to create the kind of social network that could effectively insulate them from depression.

Let's consider an example. Sue, in her early twenties, wants a good, long-term relationship and, eventually, marriage. She is now dating a new guy named Bill. Bill is a fun guy to be around. He can "party" at any given moment of any given day, and often does. Sue finds him enjoyable to be around. But he doesn't work or go to college, and he still lives at his dad's house. He doesn't have any money or any apparent ambition. He treats Sue reasonably well, and she likes him. When prodded by her friends about why she goes out with this "loser," Sue angrily attacks their criticisms of Bill as emphasizing career and money over being nice. Meanwhile, Bill shows up at Sue's whenever he wants to, raids her refrigerator, borrows her car, and tells her to "forget your friends—they're obviously not interested in your happiness." Sue is aware of her mixed feelings about Bill, but figures "time will tell."

Meanwhile, she is getting more resentful of Bill's taking but not giving, yet feels that she "shouldn't feel this way." Slowly, she becomes ever more unhappy with her circumstances.

Sue is in a relationship that involves "give" but no "take." It is not a healthy sharing on most or all levels—it is a one-sided deal. Bill may eventually develop a career or an interest in assuming adult responsibilities, but, then, he may not. How can Sue tell whether her time with Bill is growth-oriented and healthy, or just "emotional popcorn," good for the moment but going nowhere?

Can you identify Sue's social skill deficits? Certainly, she is making excuses for Bill to herself and to her friends, despite some evidence that they are correct in their assessment of Bill as a man who does not have the resources to be what Sue ultimately wants. Sue lacks the ability to effectively set limits on Bill's "show up whenever" behavior, his frequent borrowing of her things, and his taking for granted his right to Sue's refrigerator and whatever else she has. Sue needs to assert herself with Bill, and she needs to negotiate clear and realistic guidelines for the relationship to continue satisfactorily (if it can). Sue has to be able to express her feelings openly and honestly, and be heard by Bill (even if he disagrees). Without these and other relationship skills applied by Sue, her relationship with Bill, and with others, too, will suffer and be a source of pain instead of happiness.

Interpersonal psychotherapy emphasizes the development of specific skills in managing relationships with others. They include handling the building of new relationships, adjusting to new transitions in ongoing relationships (like going from being a spouse to being a parent), and dealing with the loss of important relationships (perhaps through death or divorce). IPT teaches skills for resolving disputes, clarifying expectations, setting effective limits, asserting oneself— everything it takes to establish and maintain good relationships with others. And if you go the next step in your thinking, you can appreciate that the same skills are helpful in your relationship with yourself, too.

You live in a world filled with other people. Good relationships are wonderful, but even the best relationships have their hard times. Unless a person has the skills necessary to move through the hard times, good relationships can turn bad and cause much hurt. The development of good skills with people is a fundamental part of avoiding the pain of depression, and it is emphasized in detail in Chapters 10 and 11.

THE ESSENCE OF WHAT HELPS

While each person's path is inevitably different from anyone else's, because of his unique symptoms, patterns, personal history, and so forth, there are common denominators among what may, at first glance, seem like very different approaches. Now you have at least some familiarity with several of the key concepts and methods of each of the major approaches to the treatment of depression. You can start to sift from them the core ingredients available for an intelligent design of your self-help program. In the remainder of this chapter, I briefly discuss each of these core ingredients. They represent the foundation for everything else in this book—all the ideas, methods, exercises, *everything*. Sound important? Right you are!

ISSUES VS. PATTERNS (CONTENT VS. PROCESS)

I begin the final section of the chapter with this topic because I consider it the most important element of all. Here's why. I have spent a significant portion of my career not only treating people with problems, but treating people who, despite their problems, can do some things in life very well. After all, no one is a total failure. You may be depressed but still be a wonderful friend, a creative artist, a loving partner, a productive employee, or any of a million other worthwhile things. So, while I treat some aspect(s) of a person's life, I also have the opportunity to discover the admirable skills he has in other areas.

Consider this example. I once treated a woman named Vicki who had recently learned she had terminal cancer and had only a short time to live. She came to me to learn psychological approaches to manage pain. She wanted to minimize her use of painkilling medications, which she feared would cloud her thinking. Now, if *you* were told you would die soon, would that negatively affect your mood and outlook? Most probably, your answer is yes. Isn't a terminal diagnosis a legitimate reason to be depressed? Of course it is. What fascinated me about Vicki, and people like her, though, is that while she could, and perhaps even "should," have been depressed, she was *not*.

This is one example of the difference between the content and the process of a person's experience. The "issue" in her life, the content of her problem, was pain associated with terminal cancer. The "patterns" with which she responded to the issue represented the process of her experience. Simply put, the content refers to the "what," and the process refers to the "how" of the problem. *What* happens in your life that depresses you is one consideration, but *how you respond to what happens* is the far more important consideration in treatment.

Vicki had terminal cancer and did not get depressed. Another individual has terminal cancer and gets *very* depressed. Clearly, it is not the event (or the content of the problem) of a cancer diagnosis that is the sole determinant of whether depression develops. Rather, it is the patterns with which an individual responds to the event (the process) that have the greatest influence on the development of depression. What are these patterns, and how do they affect the degree, if any, of depression? I will identify these patterns in future chapters, always stressing the point that the primary goal of therapy—and of self-help—is to identify and break the hurtful patterns with which you respond to life experience. Please be clear about this. I am stating in no uncertain terms that *it is less what happens to you and more how you interpret and respond to what happens to you that regulates your experience of depression.*

Let's apply the same content-process principle to each of the therapy models. Cognitive therapy focuses on *how* you think, not *what* you think. When you change *how* you think (from "crooked" to "straight"), *what* you think will also change. So, when you learn not to jump to conclusions without evidence, for example, that process of clear thinking will apply to many other things and will help you for the rest of your life, not just the problem you started with. *Whenever you learn a principle, push yourself to examine whether it applies to other situations as well.* It usually does.

Behavioral therapy focuses on *how* you behave in a given situation, and how it leads to desirable consequences (or not). It teaches you how to approach many situations skillfully, not just the initial problem. Likewise, interpersonal psychotherapy teaches you *how* to relate to others (how to set limits, for example) and how to use social skills with everyone to whom you relate. The current problem relationship can be used as the place to learn, and you can practice your new skills in other relationships.

In each case, the therapy teaches specific skills that transcend the immediate situation, skills that apply in many similar situations. And, to be realistic, life involves lots and lots of similar situations.

Are you clear about the difference between content and process? We are aiming in this self-help project to change not only your current depression, but how you deal with whatever caused it or kept it going;

Pause and Reflect #5

Learn to Distinguish Content from Process

A woman says, "I've been married and divorced three times." She describes each of her husbands as alcoholic and abusive. She wants to know what she does to attract such men to her.

What is the content and what is the process of her problem?

Answer: The content is each husband; the names and faces change, but not the type of person. The process is how she chooses (although she'd probably say she's chosen by) the man she marries.

If you change the process of how she chooses men, what will happen to the content?

Each new person you meet represents a change in content. The process is _how_ you meet someone new, whoever it may be. Each time you go to the store to buy something, you make a content choice. How you decide what to buy is the process. Who your best friend is is the content. How you build close relationships is the process. Whom you date is the content. How you decide whom to date is the process. What you do on a date is the content. How you conduct the joint decision-making for what to do on a date is the process.

that's the way to prevent similar episodes. It's too easy to fool yourself into thinking you are depressed simply because something bad has happened to you. That same bad thing, or something like it, has happened to others who did *not* become depressed. How was their response to the bad event different from yours? And, most important, how can you learn to respond in ways that don't lead to depression?

PROBLEMS VS. SOLUTIONS

One of the things I never liked about my formal academic training as a clinical psychologist was the exclusive focus on pathology, or "mental illness." You may ask, "Isn't that what you signed up for—an intensive study of the emotional disorders, including their diagnosis and treatment?" Well, to a certain extent, yes. However, if you focus your studies on people mired in problems, how do you learn to recog-

LEARN BY DOING #5

Learn from Those Who Succeed

Purpose: To discover that when you ask specific questions about the way others do things successfully, you can often (not always) learn effective strategies.

Pick a problem that isn't very emotionally charged for you. Got one? Good. Find at least half a dozen people to talk to who once had the same problem and arrange to speak to them privately. The goal is to find out how they dealt with the problem. Make sure your questions are very specific. Now ask some people who never had this problem how they managed to avoid it. Again, make sure your questions are specific. If you ask questions that begin with "how," you'll learn to recognize skillful strategies by their process, not content.

This is one way I learn effective therapy strategies. I go up to people, like guys who work out at my gym, and I ask lots of questions. How do you get yourself to come here regularly? What happens when you're too tired to come; how do you get yourself to do a workout anyway? How do you decide how hard to push yourself during a workout? How do you decide when you've had enough for today? When I compare the answers given by guys who are in great shape to those of guys who aren't, I learn things. You will, too, when you get used to focusing on "how" instead of "why."

nize solutions? Is wellness only the absence of sickness? What about studying people's strengths or people's capacities to overcome problems creatively?

If you look at the broad spectrum of human experiences, you'll see that many events in the average person's life are hurtful. People we love die, trusted friends betray us, we lose jobs, and on and on. Why, then, isn't *everyone* depressed about the miseries of life? Is there something to be learned about the positive frame of mind many people have that seems to insulate them from depression?

I believe there is far more to learn about overcoming depression from people who have maintained optimism in times of adversity, and from people who have faced terrible times and "bounced back" quickly and forcefully, than we could ever learn from people who got hurt and then just gave up. Thus, I have spent a great deal of my time studying people who do things *well*. For example, consider the person who is depressed about getting older year by year. Compare him with someone who doesn't view aging as a problem. I want to know what the person who ages comfortably is "doing inside." I want to know what he is thinking about, focusing on, or telling himself that makes him so comfortable with getting older. Then I'll know what I have to teach the depressed person to "do inside" that can help him better deal with getting older.

If you really want to learn how to go through life well, one of the most effective things to do is talk to the people who are doing well. Often, the person you talk to will not have the insight to explain how he does what he does. When that is the case, you may not learn anything new. But it has cost you nothing to ask and find out whether he can share something useful. If you persist and ask many people "how," some will be able to tell you meaningful things that can help you. They may provide valuable perspectives that can give you targets (ways to think, feel, and act) to aim for. As you learned in the introduction, everyone forms projections about life and life experiences, but clearly some feel better and some feel worse.

Do you focus on problems, or do you focus on solutions? Do you constantly spin around the same negative thoughts and feelings about how terrible things are, or do you actively search for and identify new things to do that will help? You may not have realized it before, but now that I draw your attention to it, you can start to define what a renewed focus on solutions might involve for you.

Focusing on solutions means knowing that your circumstances are, at *some* level, changeable. Even if you can't change the external circumstances that seem so hurtful, you *can* change your reactions to them. Focusing on solutions means being observant enough to recognize *you are not your depression*. You are *more* than your depression. You can observe that there are times when you feel better and there are times when you feel worse. What goes on at the times you feel better? What's different at those times? How can you learn to do more, have more, and be more of the things that work in helping you feel better?

In her refreshingly honest and self-helpful book *Change Your Life and Everyone in It,* the therapist and author Michele Weiner-Davis discusses what it means to have an orientation toward solutions instead of toward problems. She points out that it is no coincidence that each of the proven therapies for depression, as well as for many other problems, emphasizes the value of developing problem-solving skills in order to move quickly toward solutions. She further emphasizes that explaining the origin of the problem, as you'll see in the next section, offers little potential for solving it. Her emphasis is on active self-help that recognizes the importance of little changes that can add up to big results. Let's strive for solutions!

PAST VS. FUTURE ORIENTATION

One of the most innovative and influential psychiatrists of this century was Milton Erickson. Erickson was unique in his uncanny ability to find creative solutions to people's problems, and he did so without spending much time rehashing his patient's past to explain why things are the way they are. This was a new viewpoint in the middle of this century, when most of his contemporaries were still focusing heavily on people's childhood experiences. Erickson's view, now validated by research data about what works in helping people change, was well stated when he said, "People don't come to therapy to change their pasts. Rather, they come in to change their futures—they want things to be different tomorrow, next week, next month, next year." I fully agree.

Many people automatically assume you *have to* explore your past, investigate every memory, and express every feeling before you can get better. Untrue! In fact, the evidence is clear that depression doesn't improve or remain improved if the person gets caught up in focusing on things that aren't central to the problem. Focusing on your past is generally not an effective way to gain improvement. I know this may run counter to what you have heard or been led to believe by the conventional wisdom that says if you don't understand your past, you are doomed to repeat it. However, there is a huge difference between explaining a problem and changing it. I wish I had a nickel for every time a client said to me, "I know why I'm doing that; I just can't seem to stop it." Insight does not necessarily, and often will not, lead to change.

If you allow yourself to be absorbed in the pain of rehashing the hurtful past, or in negative predictions for the future ("I'll *never* be able to do it"), you are working against yourself. All the information I share here is meant to make it clear that you are not a hapless victim of circumstances, destined to suffer. Your past may be hurtful, your present circumstances may be excruciating, but your future hasn't happened yet. *Your future has not happened yet!* Yes, you need to shift your focus from the past to the future, and yes, to create a better future you need

Understanding the Past May Not Change the Future

Do you have to know exactly what happened to someone before you can help? Pretend you're a therapist. Someone comes to see you for therapy and is very guarded. He says he has "trust issues," meaning that he finds it difficult to trust anyone.

What can you infer about this man's past without even asking him about it? His belief that no one is trustworthy is clearly untrue and is limiting him. Even if you ask for the details about whom he trusted who hurt him, aren't you still faced with the task of teaching him how to determine who is trustworthy and who is not? Explaining his past is not the same as changing his future.

My Response: Understanding the past is not necessarily a vehicle for change. This fellow with trust issues is a perfect example. If you explore his relationship with those he feels have betrayed his trust, he will better understand his fear of trusting others and being vulnerable to them. But he will not have learned a very specific skill, namely, how to distinguish who is trustworthy from who is not. Because he is missing that skill, he plays it safe by using the "one size fits all" strategy of trusting no one. The price he pays may be paranoia and loneliness.

to *take action now*. Doing things in the same crummy way only assures you of the same crummy results.

The need to "do something different" is obvious when what you're doing isn't working. However, what happens when you need to "do something different" but you don't know *what?* Ah, now you're catching on to why I wrote this book. The ideas and the methods I have included here, chapter by chapter, are meant to help you "do something different." And rather than have you try anything out of desperation, I will encourage you to develop *focus*—to aim your efforts at a meaningful target. I will emphasize the value of setting realistic, attainable goals and defining the steps necessary to reach them. The more time you spend focusing on the unchangeable past, the more time slips by and the less focus you'll have for the future you are trying to build from this moment on. You do not have to ignore your past; you just don't have to be limited by its negative influence.

MOTIVATION VS. ABILITY

One of the most destructive ideas to come out of "pop psychology" seems, on first consideration, to be useful: "Where there's a will, there's a way." This is a truism, a statement that seems so obvious that it discourages any deep consideration. Thus, countless people believe that if they truly want to do or succeed at something, their ambition will ultimately bring it about.

"Deep" psychology has fared no better on this point than has pop psychology. Generations of therapists have been trained to believe the same peculiar notion: if you want it badly enough, you'll find a way to get it. Then, when a client does not do well in treatment, the therapist may question his motivation to get better and offer such "interpretations" as these:

1. The individual suffers an "unconscious fear of success."
2. The person has an "unconscious fear of failure."
3. The client has an "unconscious need to sabotage his progress."
4. The "secondary gains" (the clinical term for indirect rewards) for staying stuck outweigh the person's need to improve.

Each of these explanations for failure focuses solely on the person's motivation. The underlying assumption is that if the client had the proper motivation (at conscious *and* unconscious levels), he would naturally succeed. The client is blamed for the lack of therapeutic progress, and the therapist sits back comfortably and either states or implies that therapeutic progress is solely up to the client. Doesn't it seem peculiar that there are two people in the relationship, yet the efforts of only one are thought to control the outcome?

In my clinical trainings, I do my best to give my colleagues a taste of this "blame the victim" mentality. I ask them all to think of a problem that has been a source of distress for a long time. I ask them to think about the efforts they have made over the years to change the problem—the reading they may have done, the therapy they've had, and the many hours and dollars they've spent trying to solve it. I ask them to think about the emotional distress the problem has caused them over the years—the self-criticism, the self-blame ("What kind of therapist am I that I can't even solve my own problem?"), and all the other distressing psychological consequences. *Everyone* has long-term, unresolved issues, so no one in the room is exempt. Then, when they are aware of their problem and their associated despair, I state smugly, "Well, if you really wanted to get over your problem, you would have." Instantly, I have a room full of *very* irritated therapists! And they quickly get the same point I'm making here: motivation isn't everything. No matter how motivated you are to watch a sunset, if you face *east*, you'll never see it!

Beyond motivation, there must also be ability. Unless you have the ability to do something, *whatever* it may be, it simply will not happen. And as motivation without ability means little, the reverse is true as well; ability without motivation is equally empty. Things really get cookin', though, when a person has motivation *and* ability!

Have you been accused of wanting to stay stuck in depression? If so, you know how hurtful such an accusation can be. The most important message I want to get across in this section is that you could easily get sidetracked into thinking that you must want to be depressed or, worse, that you unconsciously enjoy your depression. Then you'd waste time exploring those ideas instead of developing the skills to overcome your depression.

My experience is that clients come in hurting and want the hurt to go away as soon as possible. Typically, they know exactly what they want—a good relationship, a good job, freedom from depression, and the like. But when I ask them *how* they'll go about getting what they want, I discover they have either no idea or one that won't work. They think that if they just "try" hard enough, they'll succeed. (They've been told, "If at first you don't succeed, try, try again." Okay, I'll accept that, but I'd add "and when you try, try again, do something different!") When I hear them describe *how* they go about trying to do whatever they're trying to do, I almost inevitably discover what I call an "experiential deficit." An experiential deficit is a gap in a person's awareness of a vital skill or a missing step on the path to the goal, an absence that virtually precludes his success. In such instances, it's what you don't know that hurts you and prevents you from succeeding. *Good motivation does not compensate for poor strategies.* Both are important.

I strive to teach my clients specific skills that can make it possible for them to succeed. Often, someone puts forth a great deal of sincere but misguided effort, fails miserably, and then sinks into depression. The sequence is obvious: more desire, more (misguided) effort, more failure, more depression. That's a pattern we need to break!

LEARN BY DOING #6

Identifying What It All Means to You

Purpose: To make general information about depression more personally meaningful and therefore more helpful.

This chapter has covered many of the most important aspects of what works in treatment and why. Now is the time to start personalizing the information.

Go back through this chapter and mark key points with a highlighting pen. Next, make a brief written statement (either in the margins or on separate sheets of paper) about what each point means to you specifically. What do you get from the government treatment guidelines? What do you get from each of the common denominators of good treatment? How does each point I discussed compare with what you thought about that topic <u>before</u> you read what I had to say?

If you use a separate sheet of paper, you could set it up to look like this:

Page Number	Key Concept	How It Applies to Me As an Individual	How It Confirms or Challenges What I Originally Thought

People frequently do not know their blind spots, their experiential deficits, but think they know what they're doing. When people don't recognize their cognitive distortions or lack of certain social skills, for example, they do what they know how to, and then rise or fall with the consequences. *It is no coincidence that every proven therapy for depression emphasizes building skills, not analyzing unconscious motivations.* It is essential to your recovery that you focus your efforts on identifying *your* experiential deficits and developing the necessary skills to build the kind of life you want. Consider your motivation, too, but if you're reading this book carefully to learn all you can, I think it's reasonably safe to say you're well motivated. The real challenge is to use your motivation to develop your ability to live well.

In this chapter I have presented most of the critical concepts you should know in your quest to overcome depression. What follows, then, in all the remaining chapters is how you can use these ideas and methods to devise and carry out your self-help plan. Use your growing knowledge about what works in general to discover what works *for you* in particular.

SUMMARY OF KEY POINTS . . .
AND WHAT THEY CAN MEAN TO <u>YOU</u>

- Depression, unfortunately, often goes untreated because the sufferer doesn't know he's depressed or because the health professional he consults misses the diagnosis. Depression can be tricky to diagnose because it may differ greatly from person to person. *You* have to judge how you're feeling about yourself and your life.

- The Agency for Health Care Policy and Research established formal treatment guidelines for clinicians, based on the best objective research. The guidelines underwent substantial peer review and are widely accepted by experts. It means that a lot is known about what it takes to help depression, so you can afford to be optimistic that things can improve for you.

- Effective treatment may involve the use of antidepressant medications, psychotherapy, or a combination of the two. It's for you to decide what you're comfortable with, balanced by what makes sense in your particular case. Keep all your options open!

- Psychotherapy is at least as effective as medication in producing successful results, and even more effective in reducing the likelihood of relapses. Taking medication only is not necessarily the best choice, though it may seem an easier one. The disease model (genetics or biochemical imbalances) has been oversold, and you should know that there are many reasons to pursue a good program of building antidepressant life skills.

- Cognitive, behavioral, and interpersonal psychotherapies are known to be effective approaches. You can use ideas and methods of each, with the help of this book, to aim your self-help efforts in the direction of learning to think clearly, take appropriate actions, and build healthy relationships.

- The common denominators of successful psychotherapy are a focus on process (patterns), solutions, the future, and skill-building. Learning how to do things well and spending time on developing and working toward realistic goals can equip you with the resources to cope with all that life brings, good *and* bad.

Chapter 3

DIMENSIONS AND SYMPTOMS OF DEPRESSION

IF I WERE TO PRESENT YOU with a problem, let's say a business-related one, such as how to increase efficiency in your department, wouldn't you first need some background information on the department (its purpose, its expectations, its relationship to other departments, its hierarchy, its personnel)? I hope your answer is yes. You'd want relevant background information so that you could focus your attention on the problem areas you identify. That is, you would go *from a general view* of the department *to a specific focus* on key problem areas.

I use the same sort of "from general to specific" problem-solving approach in addressing depression. By reading this chapter and the next one, which is even more specific about symptoms and the underlying patterns of thought and behavior that generate them, you will, I hope, identify some of the specifics of *your* experience of depression. Recovering from depression can seem an overwhelming task if all you are aware of is feeling lousy and utterly bewildered about where to focus your self-help efforts.

THE EXPERIENCE OF DEPRESSION

Whether you call it feeling down, feeling blue, being miserable with your life, feeling trapped, being negative, or seeing things darkly, the experience of depression can make life seem too much to cope with and not all that worthwhile, anyway.

Depression is truly a universal experience; it is a part of *everyone's* life at one time or another and to one degree or another. Why? Because no one escapes the hurts of life that trigger normal depressions. Depression is normal when someone dies, or when you have to move and start over, or when your friends tell you off. You may not see it in other people, especially if you have only casual relationships with them, but I can guarantee you, everyone suffers the hurts of life. It is not the "sign of mental health" to never get down. The real sign of mental health is how long it takes to get back up again. The word "resilience" captures the spirit of what I'm describing. And the starting point for being resilient is appreciating this fact: *you are not your depression; you are more than your mood.* Knowing this point is one way people manage to keep going during tough times and eventually bounce back from them.

Is your depression a "normal" one, or isn't it? Obviously, you need to make some determination so that you're not unnecessarily self-critical. And whether it is normal or it isn't, the most important thing is to identify what it's about. Then you can do something to move beyond it. The remainder of this chapter will consider the many different ways depression can surface. The intent is to help you enlarge your view of yourself so that you can apply realistically the self-help strategies offered throughout the book. You may want immediate solutions, but a focus on "quick fix" answers is usually part of the problem. It leads people to try formulaic answers that don't really apply to their individual circumstances.

Since depression has different causes and different symptoms in each person, you must be able to recognize what's going on in *your* particular case. What follows are numerous examples and lots of information to help you figure out where you will need to concentrate your efforts.

DIMENSIONS OF DEPRESSION

I have found it useful to identify patterns in the symptoms my clients present to me according to the different dimensions of experience. These dimensions are aspects of *all* experiences, good and bad. In regard to depression in particular, these dimensions include:

1. Physical symptoms;
2. Behavior problems;
3. Distorted thinking;

What Makes You Think You're Depressed?

Purpose: To characterize your individual experience of depression in order to determine where your self-help efforts can best be concentrated.

How do you know you are depressed? What are the symptoms or patterns you are aware of that lead you to believe you are depressed? List these in your notebook BEFORE you read on. Later, you'll learn about other symptoms of depression that you can add to your list if you discover they exist in you.

4. Mood and emotional difficulties;
5. Troubled relationships;
6. Specific situations that seem to trigger episodes of depression;
7. Spiritual or symbolic meanings attached to depression;
8. The personal history that led to lifestyle patterns that seem related to depression.

When you learn about your unique way of experiencing depression, you can better address the most relevant issues associated with it. Otherwise, you may delay feeling better by focusing on unimportant issues. For example, if your depression usually surfaces in specific situations, such as when you attend social gatherings or go home to visit your parents, then relying on drugs (even prescribed antidepressant medications) that must be taken every day and that operate solely on a physical basis is generally not a well-matched solution. Let's consider each dimension and its related symptoms separately so that you can better identify the central dimension(s) of your own experience of depression. For each dimension I discuss, I will start with a vignette that illustrates some of the key points.

THE PHYSICAL DIMENSION

The Case of Evan

Evan woke up with a start. As was his all too predictable pattern, he immediately strained to hear if there were any unusual sounds that might have awakened him. "All I hear is the sound of Cindy breathing deeply as she sleeps next to me," he thought. "Dammit, I'd give anything to be like her and be asleep right now." Satisfied that nothing unusual was going on, Evan looked at the clock. He realized that he didn't need to get up for nearly two hours; that just made him angry with himself. Moments later, his mind raced and spun as ideas about his work collided with things he planned to do that day and with events from yesterday. "Why am I spinning all this stuff around in my head when I should be asleep? Another day of the same damn thing—wake up way too early, lie in bed trying to fall back asleep, flash on everything in my life I hate, feel tired as hell all day from not sleeping, go to bed thinking I'm so tired I'll sleep great, and start the same damn cycle all over again tomorrow. Who am I kidding? There is something wrong with me—maybe I should see a sleep specialist or something."

Evan turned over, away from the clock that kept telling him how much sleep he <u>wasn't</u> getting. Thinking he had a sleep disorder and that a sleep specialist might help him somehow made him feel a little better for the moment. "I'll probably just need some kind of sleeping pill for a little while until I learn to relax more," he decided. When he finally got out of bed after a half hour of tossing and turning, Evan looked at Cindy and wished she was awake, too. A pang of guilt for thinking that passed through him and lingered as he looked at her sleep. Why should she suffer the way he did? He tried to remember the last time they had made love, but couldn't. It had been quite a while since he'd felt any desire for lovemaking. Another guilt pang.

His mind still racing along with a hundred different thoughts, none of which was very important when he evaluated it, Evan turned on the television and watched some old late-night or early-morning program on gardening. He thought that watching it would bore him to sleep. "I hate this; I wish I could sleep and wake up feeling rested and refreshed just once, instead of sitting here alone watching this crap while Cindy and the rest of the world snoozes on with not a care in the world." Evan learned a little more about pruning rosebushes than he cared to know that particular morning.

By the time Cindy got up, he could barely contain his irritation over her sleeping well and waking up cheerful. "God, I hate mornings," Evan said out loud to no one in particular as he shaved. "They're the worst part of my day. And today is going to be rotten—I can tell already. But, then, most days are." Evan pushed himself through the morning routine of shaving, showering, dressing, and mumbling a few words to Cindy, and then headed to work. He was tired already, and dreaded the prospect of a full day of work on so little sleep. His anxiety level rose as he thought of all the things he was expected to do. He put on his socially acceptable but totally phony smile as he entered the office, and proceeded to carry out his tasks for the day. At the end of the day, on his way home, Evan realized he'd forgotten to follow up on his idea for scheduling an appointment with a sleep specialist. "Maybe I just have a different sort of metabolism that I have to learn to accept," he said to himself, most unconvincingly. His thoughts turned to the evening news and what Cindy had in mind for dinner, even though he didn't much feel like eating.

Too early the next morning, Evan learned about the joys of growing his own tomatoes.

DISCUSSION OF EVAN'S CASE

Evan shows some of the classic physical signs of depression: early morning awakening (one form of the different insomnias commonly experienced by depressed people), rumination, fatigue and lethargy, feeling worse in the morning, diminished sex drive, anxiety, and a decreased appetite.

As you can see, most of Evan's symptoms are of a physical nature. Beyond what Evan shows, there are other common physical symptoms of depression: excessive sleeping (unlike Evan's insomnia), excessive appetite (unlike Evan's diminished appetite), a marked change in body weight associated with the change in appetite, vague physical complaints that don't have any detectable cause, or exaggerated physical complaints that do have a known basis.

The physical symptoms of depression are most often what first lead an individual to seek help from a physician. In fact, it is the family doctor or the general practitioner who is most likely to first encounter the depressed person.

It is the knowledgeable and experienced doctor who is able to identify symptoms of depression and make appropriate recommendations.

Pause and Reflect #7

Mind, Body, and Mood

The evidence indicates that most depressions are not physically (that is, genetically or biochemically) based. Then why does depression have such clearly physical symptoms? The temptation can be to treat physical symptoms physically, as with medications. Is this always a reasonable approach, or can it distract one from more salient problems?

My response: Depression has often been called a "whole body" disorder, which recognizes the obvious physical signs of the condition. As integrated units, what we think affects how we feel emotionally and physically, and vice versa. The fact that there is a physiology to everything we experience is evidence of a strong mind-body relationship. Beyond that, many people find it easier to deal with a concrete physical symptom (such as a stomachache) than with an abstract emotion (such as discontent at work). Thus, treating the physical manifestation alone can mean missing an opportunity to address the underlying emotional issue. Ignoring the physical signs, though, may be even worse. It is wise, then, to consult a physician and make sure there are no physical causes for your symptoms, and to evaluate the appropriateness of antidepressant medications for your particular problems.

Many depressive symptoms can be associated with dozens of different physical problems. Also, depression can be a side effect of many medications. The first thing to do always is get a thorough physical examination and report openly to your doctor your symptoms and concerns. It is possible that your depression has a physical origin.

THE BEHAVIORAL DIMENSION

The Case of Danny

On his way home from work, Danny made a point of stopping to buy Valerie some flowers. He felt bad about the fight they'd had that morning. He struggled to remember what had started the fight, but, as usual, he couldn't. He'd been a bit grumpier than usual that morning, but over the years Valerie had learned Danny wasn't Mr. Sunshine in the morning. She was quite experienced at keeping neutral what little conversation he tolerated while mostly just giving him some quiet company. Suddenly Danny remembered what it was Valerie said that had ignited the interaction. Valerie mentioned, all too damn casually to suit his taste, that she'd be stopping to see her friend Judy after work. Judy had just got some new furniture and wanted Valerie to see it.

Danny was aware of thinking, "Her priorities stink. There are a million things that need to be done around the house, and she's wasting time going to see furniture. She's never around when I need something, but just let one of her friends call her for something stupid like seeing furniture, and she's right there." Thinking this now puzzled him. "Is that really the way I felt this morning? Is that why I flew into a rage?" Danny didn't remember thinking <u>anything</u> this morning after Valerie announced her intentions. He was aware only of rage. He didn't even realize he was screaming at her until she ran from the kitchen to the bedroom and locked the door. He quickly decided he didn't have time for her hide-and-seek games, so he left for work, slamming the door on his way out as his only goodbye. He couldn't have known that Valerie was huddled in the corner, crying—again.

Driving to work that morning, Danny wove in and out of traffic, making plenty of obscene, angry gestures to all the rotten drivers on the road. While he was stopped at a light, some sadness caught up to him, and he shuddered and started to cry. He became angry with himself and tried to control it, but this crying episode was a lot like the others; it seemed to come on him suddenly, from out of nowhere. "Too bad it never leaves as suddenly as it comes," he thought. After a short while, the tears stopped, still just a curiosity to Danny. He decided to get a quick breakfast, but when the "quick breakfast" wasn't quick enough, he demanded to see the manager. He was actually disappointed that the manager seemed a kid, probably just a little older than the kid who'd taken his order. He was hoping for a more formidable opponent. He yelled his piece, finally got his food, and wolfed it down. No one was unhappy to see him leave.

When Danny got to work, things went from bad to worse. Incompetent co-workers, incompetent supervisors, stupid company policies, ridiculous bureaucratic procedures, all apparently glowing in neon that only Danny had the "perceptiveness" to see. Never much for paying compliments, he couldn't think of a single positive thing to say to anybody this day, though he thought he should try. When nothing came to mind, he demanded not to be disturbed, closed his office door, and opened his bottom drawer. Way in the back, well out of view, was a bottle. He muttered, "Relief is on the way!" He didn't quite feel right about his source of "relief," but decided he owed it to himself and everyone else to try to mellow out a little. That was also when he thought about picking up some flowers on the way home. He cried only one other time that day, and again just for a little while. He was a bit calmer after that.

DISCUSSION OF DANNY'S CASE

Danny is probably not the guy you would want to spend your summer vacation with. Yet when he's not raging about, he is truly a nice guy. What is this Dr. Jekyll–Mr. Hyde thing that happens to Danny? He shows many of the patterns often seen in depressed individuals: temper displays, aggressive behavior, the acting out of feelings in ways that are impulsive and may even be at odds with the way one really feels, perfectionist behavior, substance abuse, and crying spells. There are other behaviors that are common to depression: marked changes in the activity level (usually a decrease), slowed movement and slurred speech, agitated and anxious actions (pacing, knuckle-cracking, and the like), passive "giving-up" (no longer trying to change things for the better), and suicide attempts. Keep in mind, *no single behavior is an indicator of depression*, but it may be noteworthy as a possible signal of trouble.

Danny is clearly showing a gap between his emotions and his behavior. Can he learn to be more self-aware, self-controlled, and accepting? Yes, and to do that he'll need some help in coming to terms with his anger and how he uses it as a tool to try to manipulate others.

THE SITUATIONAL (CONTEXTUAL) DIMENSION

The Case of Linda

The telephone rang several times before Linda, deeply asleep, was conscious enough to realize it was ringing. She silently cursed whoever it was who had the audacity to wake her up, particularly so early on a Sunday morning, when she could have slept late. When she heard her father say hello in his inimitable bark, she realized it

Pause and Reflect #8

The Behavior-Feelings Link

How would you describe the relationship between behavior and feelings? Does your behavior consistently reflect your feelings? Why or why not? Think of a few recent situations where your behavior did not seem to reflect your feelings. What feelings did you really have? Can you learn to express your true feelings more directly? How would it help you to do so?

My response: There is a strong but imperfect relationship between behavior and feelings. People can say and do things they don't mean, especially under certain conditions, such as when they are fearful and angry. Strong emotions can lead people to react impulsively, losing sight of the goal and behaviors that would be best for reaching the goal. Describing your true feelings more directly and in a timely way to trusted friends provides an opportunity to vent. Then internal pressure doesn't build up to levels so intense that you lose sight of your goal or what constitutes appropriate behavior in later situations.

could only have been he. Who else would call so early? Who but her dad could be such a royal pain in the backside even from where he lived, over a thousand miles away? When he feigned innocence and asked, "Oh, did I wake you?" Linda wanted to reply with as much sarcasm as she could, but instead she meekly answered, "No, I was just getting up." Not that he would have cared if he had awakened her, anyway. He firmly believed that when a father calls his daughter, no matter the time, she should be thrilled to hear from him. Genuinely thrilled. Linda learned years ago—unfortunately, the hard way—the harsh price of not meeting his expectations. He could be really nasty. She asked him how he was.

Dad ignored her polite inquiry and announced that he intended to come for a visit. Linda wished that just once he'd ask if she had the time or the interest to see him, but he never asked. He announced. Linda's heart sank, but she tried to sound happily surprised. "How come, Dad? You were here just a couple of months ago." When he replied that he could use the rest, Linda's immediate response, kept strictly to herself, of course, was "So could I."

Then she felt guilty. She wondered whether other young women felt the same way about their fathers. Was she a terrible person who

71

just couldn't get it together to be around her dad? Immature, maybe? Or emotionally screwed up?

But she didn't really see herself that way. Not deep down. She reminded herself that she was a quite successful and competent woman in every other way. She lived alone and did it well. She managed her dating relationships effectively, staying out of risky situations and avoiding guys who were bad news. She supported herself completely and, though not wealthy, lived comfortably. She had good friends and was physically in excellent shape from a steady regimen of good diet and regular attendance at her dance class. Her job was going well, and, given the hectic nature of running an office for four busy professionals, she had plenty to be proud of. It truly puzzled her that she could handle every part of her life so well except for her relationship with her dad. Somehow, he made her feel so small, so insignificant, that she hated being around him. His fierce temper kept her from raising any subject he didn't like, and he certainly didn't like talking about his relationship with her. Daughters do what fathers say. They do it happily and without a fuss. Period. End of discussion.

Linda hung up after mumbling some affectionate words she didn't feel at all. And then the world went ugly for her. With two weeks to go until he came, a week of him being around, and with a recovery period of at least a week after he left, she figured she was going to spend the next month feeling deeply depressed. How she hated being so weak around him! Fantasies of telling him off, even fantasies of physical violence against him, floated through her mind. At one moment she enjoyed the fantasies and felt a little better, but the next moment she felt worse, admitting to herself that she was far too wimpy around him to do anything but cater to his every whim. Every spanking he had given her as a child, every shouting match they'd ever had, every embarrassment he had ever caused her flashed through her mind. She decided to stay in bed that day, too depressed to go anywhere or do anything. When Monday morning came, it took all the energy she could muster just to call in sick. Her father would most surely have disapproved of her irresponsible decision, she realized. She berated herself in his absence, and then took the entire day to decide whether she was going to pick him up from the airport on time or make him wait for her a while. She put off deciding until later.

DISCUSSION OF LINDA'S CASE

For many people, episodes of depression are associated with specific triggers. These can be certain people, particular places, distinctive objects, and special times (like certain seasons, holidays, anniversaries, and so forth, or even times of the day, week, or month).

Many people manage life well until they find themselves in a context that overwhelms them. Linda does a good job of managing her life until she has to deal with her father. For whatever reason—and you can guess dozens—Linda becomes powerless, helpless, and passive in her interactions with him. Nowhere else in her life does this occur. On the contrary, she is happy with the life she has created for herself. But she experiences depression for extended periods of time if her father enters her life even for a brief visit. She demonstrates well how the sense of control over her life that generally keeps her out of depression falls apart, triggering depression, in a particular situation.

Whenever depression is so clearly situational, the chances for recovery are especially great. Learning to manage the troublesome situation competently is the straightforward solution for preventing the "victim" mindset that so often leads to depression. That includes learning to create emotional distance from the anniversary of a loved one's death or the date of a relationship breakup or other such painful experience. Old triggers can be "disconnected" by the creation of new skills and experiences.

One type of situational depression is worthy of extra attention. The condition known as seasonal affective disorder (SAD) has been identified in many depression sufferers living in northern climates. SAD sufferers typically lapse into depression with winter's shorter days and don't recover until spring. There is considerable evidence that SAD is a biologically based depression: the diminished light of winter days prevents the necessary stimulation of certain neurotransmitters. For SAD sufferers, the amazing cure is as simple as some extra hours each day spent in normal activities near a special fluorescent light. Consult a psychiatric specialist (referred by your physician) if you think this may be relevant to you.

Purpose: To discover the strong relationship between situational influences and your behavior so that you can eventually create situations to bring out your best behavior.

Make a point of watching a few <u>Candid Camera</u> episodes (they're usually available for rent at video stores). You'll observe what happens to usual responses when you throw in a new factor. This is a funny show about pattern interruption, and the interruption of patterns is what I suggest as essential to your self-help program. What role does circumstance play in behavior, feeling, and thought? What situations could you create to bring out your <u>positive</u> feelings? Novel situations are excellent teachers.

Use the suggested outline below to help you identify situations that amplify your strong points.

SITUATIONS THAT AMPLIFY YOUR STRONG POINTS

Situation	Skill(s) It Amplifies
Example: Taking a class	Ability to learn
	Ability to relate to others
Planning a party	Ability to organize and plan ahead
	Ability to stay within a budget

THE SYMBOLIC DIMENSION

The Case of Beth

Beth woke up unusually slowly. For reasons she couldn't immediately comprehend, it was taking her too long to get her eyes open and focused and her mind into its usual sharp awareness. She felt some fear, but didn't know why. When she finally opened her eyes, she was startled to see that she was not in her bed. She didn't know where she was for a frightening moment, and then the sudden realization that she was in a hospital bed was confirmed by the page for Dr. Andrews that boomed over the public address system. A nurse appeared the next moment, and immediately provided every bit of orientation Beth needed. "You are in University Hospital on the fourth floor. You were attacked and beaten up. You'll find lots of cuts, bruises, and swelling in different places, but no bones are broken, there are no terribly serious injuries, and you will undoubtedly recover completely. You'll be here for a few days until you're strong enough to go home and we've had a chance to make sure you're okay."

Beth immediately felt some relief at knowing where she was and hearing that she would recover completely. Then, as if punched in the stomach and having the breath knocked out of her, she was bombarded with frightening and overwhelming images. She slowly tried to move, and cried out involuntarily from the pain. She lay still, and felt unreal while the fragmented memories began to surge through her awareness. Pulling into a tight space in the parking garage near the gym. Wanting to enjoy a good workout. Grabbing her gym bag and locking the car. A man's scream that sounded crazy and murderous. Turning to see who screamed. A man with a mad and tormented expression on his face coming right at her, grabbing her, knocking her down, beating her . . . Waking up here.

Beth shuddered. She tried to remember more, but it had all happened too quickly for her mind to record the incident in detail.

And then came the most painful question: Why? "Why did this happen to me? Why did this crazy man beat me up?" She searched for a reason, and eventually came up with several. "Maybe he mistook me for someone he hates. Maybe he was drunk or high on drugs and looking for a fight. Or maybe . . ." Her body went limp at her next stream of thoughts. "Maybe I shouldn't have been there. Maybe I shouldn't have been going to the gym. Maybe God is punishing me for being at the gym. Maybe I should have been at home, cooking dinner for my husband and daughter. Maybe God is punishing me for not being as good a wife and mother as I should be."

As she thought this, Beth sank into despair. She believed in God, and though she did not regularly participate in an organized religion's practices, she was strongly influenced by her belief that God has a plan for each of us, including lessons He wants us to learn from the things that happen to us. "This attack must be a lesson," she concluded. Beth became utterly immobilized by the enormous implications of her realization of the "meaning" of the assault. It meant she was a bad person, a person marked by God for suffering. It meant she was a failure as a wife. It meant she was a failure as a mother. How could she ever go on, knowing these things about herself?

Days later, though Beth's body was healing quite well, it escaped the attention of no one who saw her that she was deeply depressed. They assumed it was a natural aftermath of the trauma she had suffered. She barely ate, her sleep was wracked with nightmares, and she hardly spoke. When she did speak, she mumbled apologies to God and made promises to do better for Him and for her family. Her husband and daughter were puzzled by all the religious references in her conversation, but they said nothing about it. The two of them agreed that a few more days' rest in the hospital would probably be good for Beth, and mentioned the idea to her doctor. The doctor agreed that Beth could benefit from more recovery time, but when Beth was told she'd be spending a few more days in the hospital, she lost all the color in her face and asked aloud when God would be finished punishing her. She saw a dark cloud hanging over her head that would probably never go away.

DISCUSSION OF BETH'S CASE

Beth's terrible experience, the physical assault, led her to do what we all do when something unexplainable happens: seek an explanation. Unfortunately, the one she settled on involved punishment by God for her perceived shortcomings. Her symbolic interpretation of the "meaning" of the attack led Beth to blame herself, devalue herself, and consider herself a totally contemptible, utterly worthless human being. When your interpretations of life experiences lead you to be harsh and unforgiving with yourself, depression is sure to follow.

Beth showed many symptoms of depression arising on the symbolic dimension, including destructive thoughts, recurring nightmares, bothersome images, and arbitrary but believed explanations of the "meaning" of depression. Many, probably even most, people have a symbolic way of thinking about their depression. Do *you*? Some may think of it as a black cloud engulfing them, as Beth did. Others describe feeling trapped in a cage, or being chased by a vicious animal, or being publicly humiliated, or being on an emotional roller-coaster, or other such meaningful symbolic representations of depression.

How you represent the *meaning* or the *symbolic form* of your depression is your unique way of relating to it. Your representation may play a big role in the treatment process; consider treating someone who views the depression as a punishment from God versus treating someone who sees it as a raincloud. Both are hurtful, but can you predict which would be easier to overcome?

THE EMOTIONAL DIMENSION

The Case of Jim

The desert, especially while in full bloom, had always been Jim's favorite place to go on vacation. "Lord knows I need to get away now more than ever," Jim told himself. He was trying to build some enthusiasm for this trip. It didn't work, though. His mind always seemed to spin back to a review of the last eight months. He knew Marcy had been unhappy with him at some level; she shuffled around the house with a creepy, defeated look that Jim hated. He found himself gradually withdrawing from her and taking his frustration out on her two young children. "I never should have got involved with a divorced woman with children," Jim said to himself for the millionth time. "I should have known better."

While he absentmindedly finished loading his truck with camping supplies for his weekend getaway, Jim recalled Marcy's parting words as clearly as if she were saying them to him right then. They hurt every bit as much as when she'd said them. He didn't want to be so hurt ever again, not after this mess and after his gut-wrenching divorce from Bobbi years earlier. Jim had suffered horribly until he let Marcy reach out to him. He had spent years virtually alone, doing nothing but going to work and coming home. And being depressed. Feeling that he would never smile again. Feeling he would never

77

make a relationship work with anyone, even a single friend. Jim felt he was a useless human being.

At work, Jim managed to avoid others. He would hear other people laugh and tell jokes, and it could make him cry sometimes when he was alone that he couldn't find anything funny in their stories. He often would get angry at the superficiality of such people, how insensitive they were to his suffering. Didn't they know he was in emotional pain? Didn't anyone care enough to want to help him? How could they be so happy when he was so miserable?

Then Marcy came along, out of nowhere, it seemed. They met awkwardly, dated awkwardly, and then all of a sudden professed undying love to each other. Very confusing. Things were great for the first couple of years, but then Jim's feelings changed. Why? He didn't know. But Marcy could tell. And Jim could tell that she could tell. He knew from those defeated looks she so often had about her. They made him wonder why he could feel so indifferent to someone so nice.

Jim knew he needed this vacation. He needed to try to spark some life in himself again. Either that, or just give up totally and fade away forever. He didn't seem to care about anything anymore. He had been reprimanded by his supervisor for his declining work performance—and had felt even worse when he realized he didn't care that he'd been reprimanded. He felt like saying to his supervisor, "Pardon me, but you've obviously mistaken me for someone who gives a damn," but he couldn't do more than think it. He wished it amused him to think it, too, but it didn't. Nothing did.

Packing the truck with supplies fatigued Jim. He felt sad that he was going by himself, and for a moment thought about not going at all. Sometimes he could really drive himself crazy by feeling one way one minute, and feeling the opposite the next minute. Like going camping and staying home. Like living and dying.

With a push from someplace inside—he wasn't sure where—Jim climbed into his truck, started it up, and left. He tried again to convince himself that he was going to have a good time in his favorite place. For a fraction of a second, he almost believed it.

Hours later, Jim did everything just right to build a comfortable campsite. He scanned the vast horizon and saw no evidence of another human being—just cactuses, desert shrubs, and a dark, clear night sky with an unbelievable number of stars to gaze at. Jim looked up, took his rapid fill of the remarkable sight, and promptly became even more depressed as he realized that he wasn't feeling any better there. He was guilty that being there didn't make any difference; he still felt rotten. "If this doesn't help, <u>nothing</u> will." That thought scared him and made him feel even more hopeless than when a part of him still hoped the desert would cure his pain. He made a small fire and cooked some food, but, too preoccupied, he burned it. After he ate the little that was edible, he looked around and sat and listened to the silence. The thought passed through Jim's mind again and again: "If something bad were to happen to me out here, it would be a long time before anyone found out about it."

DISCUSSION OF JIM'S CASE

The intense emotional suffering of depression is the chief reason for its official categorization as a "mood disorder" by the mental health profession. In Jim's case, he showed all of the worst symptoms associated with depression: ambivalence (mixed feelings that can prevent you from moving forward in life), the loss of gratification, the loss of a sense of humor, feelings of inadequacy, the loss of emotional attachments (being apathetic or uncaring about things), sadness, excessive guilt, anger, the loss of motivation, the inability to experience pleasure (called "anhedonia"), utter powerlessness and hopelessness, and extremely low self-esteem.

This kind of intense emotional suffering is what leads people to have thoughts of suicide, just as Jim did. No suicidal person I have ever treated really wanted to die. Rather, he wanted to escape what seemed to be the unbearable pain of living. Suicide is a horribly desperate thing to do. People can and do recover from depression. There is no recovery from suicide. I'll say more about suicide in Chapter 5. What I want you to know now, however, is that things can and will get better. And when they do, you really should be here.

THE RELATIONAL DIMENSION

The Case of Henry

Henry sighed and took one last look at his drawings. Satisfied that his client would be happy with this latest architectural triumph, he rolled up the plans and placed them in a cardboard tube for safe-keeping. Then he carefully placed the tube in its own corner of the rack, which held at least half a dozen other such tubes.

When Henry opened his office door, he smelled the bacon from breakfast still lingering in the air. Alice had already left for the day,

LEARN BY DOING #10

In and Out of Touch

Purpose: To help you learn that your feelings are not always accurate nor are they always the best part of experience to focus on.

Do you think it's possible for people to pay too much attention to how they feel? When, if ever, is "get in touch with your feelings" bad advice? For example, if you focus on how you feel about standing in line at your bank, does that enhance the experience? When are your feelings an appropriate, life-enhancing focal point, and when are they an inappropriate, life-diminishing focal point? List at least a dozen specific contexts for each. Use the outline and examples below to get started.

Examples of Situations That Are Enhanced by Focusing on My Feelings	Examples of Situations That Are Diminished by Focusing on My Feelings
Deciding whom to date	Standing in line at the bank
Expressing appreciation for others' consideration toward me	Having to set limits appropriately with the children
Deciding what to do with time off	Giving a presentation at work

and neither of his teenage daughters was at home. He didn't know where they were, and he felt a little guilty that he didn't care more about where they were. "Well, they never talk to me much, anyway," he thought. "They've always been Alice's daughters more than mine."

This was one of those times when working at home was a disadvantage. Finishing an important project in midmorning created a sense of completion that made it difficult to launch right into another project. It felt better to enjoy the sense of completion for a while before starting in on more work. "Besides, no one is home, and the silence is so nice, I think I'd like to just enjoy it awhile." Henry loved solitude the most. Having Alice and two normal, and therefore rambunctious, teenagers in his midst at all times had grown tiresome to him long ago.

Henry didn't feel that he could talk to them about anything of importance. They were very superficial, in his judgment, and paid much too much attention to trivial things. Henry wished they could see the depth to life that he could, but they seemed infinitely more interested in finding ways they could better decorate the house or which fashions to wear. How he wished he could share with them his insights about existentialism, his views on political ideologies, or his experiences with exploring higher states of consciousness! But as soon as he mentioned philosophy or another such preoccupation, his magic worked: people disappeared. It had always been that way, if he was honest with himself about it. All through his life, from grade school to college, Henry had been considered the odd guy out. While others played and socialized, Henry read books by obscure European writers on even more obscure subjects. Other people were simply a mystery to Henry.

Somehow, Alice had been attracted to this quiet, pensive man. Henry was awkward in his responses to her interest, but Alice was gentle and persistent and eventually won him over. Henry couldn't have known that part of Alice's agenda was to get him to "lighten up" so that she'd have a more complete husband. Defeated in her efforts, she had given up long ago and left Henry to be the deep and one-dimensional recluse he had become. She was aware that she avoided real contact with him and that this frustrated him, but she felt it was an act of self-preservation, necessary so that she'd not get lost in the deep space of Henry's soul.

Henry sat for a long moment in the living room and looked around his house. He lived here in every sense of the word. He worked here, read books here, balanced the family budget here, and spent what little leisure time he had here. Henry usually went out only to pick up or deliver building plans or attend the unavoidable meetings with his clients.

Henry had established in his own mind long ago that he was a loner. He convinced himself that being a loner was acceptable, although he wasn't all that sure it was. But other people seemed so crude and unappealing to him that he thought it inevitable that he'd always be a loner. Even the people he met who were well educated and were leading seemingly sophisticated lives invariably surprised him with their superficiality. If he had to go to a party (for political reasons at work, of course), he would immediately try to find some-one like himself—someone willing and able to discuss the complexities of life. It always turned out the same, though. He would interrupt the pleasantries people were exchanging and turn the topic of conversation to something he considered more substantial. Occa-sionally, he'd get polite interest, but the conversation would always dwindle quickly and return to the mundane.

There were many times when Henry had tried to make friends. He often thought it would be nice to have some good friends, but it never seemed possible. Henry sometimes wished he could be as superficial as everyone else, but most of the time he just accepted loneliness as the price for having a superior intellect.

Henry began to feel anxious about having spent so much time thinking over and analyzing his lifestyle. He abruptly decided that other people were simply not worth the time and energy, considering how little, if anything, they contributed to his life. He went to the bookcase and scanned it for something to read. He finally settled on Ayn Rand's The Virtue of Selfishness.

DISCUSSION OF HENRY'S CASE

Henry's solitary world is an example of how powerful a force our relationships (or lack thereof) are in shaping our self-image and mood. Henry shows the inner conflicts and stresses of a person who isn't comfortable either alone or with others. He is socially withdrawn and isolated, often wishes to have contact with others, but remains socially apathetic. He is highly critical, finding nothing redeeming even in the people closest to him. (Can you imagine what effect he has had on his daughters' self-esteem? One hopes they have learned not to blame themselves for their father's limitations.) Henry has such a narrow range of communication skills that he is unable to share personal feelings and insights. He is so rigid in his style that, despite years of rejection by others, he has not learned what it takes to build a relationship with someone else, nor how to manage the transition from superficial first contacts to deeper bonding over time.

Beyond the poor skills that are proving hurtful to Henry, there are other patterns to this relational dimension that can lead to or maintain depression. Perhaps the most common is adopting a "victim" demeanor, whereby you put yourself at the mercy of whatever the other person dictates instead of operating as an equal. Likewise, if you are highly dependent on someone and are unable to provide well for yourself, then you invite victimization. Another common pattern is to seek approval from others to the point where you let them take advantage of you. Finally, acting like a martyr or in a self-sacrificing manner may mean you take too much or too little responsibility for others' thoughts or actions. This is a primary pattern of depression discussed at length in later chapters.

The relational dimension is often at the heart of an individual's

LEARN BY DOING #11

Specifics of Interpersonal Skills

Purpose: To teach the principle that relationships have roles and strategies. "Social skills" is a global term that needs to be broken down into specific things you can say and do that are likely to enhance your relationships and self-esteem.

If an alien from another planet landed on Earth and required you to explain how human beings relate, how would you do so? Make a list of factors that constitute good interpersonal skills, and then define each in terms of real behavior. For example, "attentiveness" is an important part of good communication. It involves eye contact, listening without interrupting, communicating respect to the other person by not making devaluing remarks, and other such behaviors. Use the example below to get your list started.

GOOD INTERPERSONAL SKILLS

Skill	Associated Behaviors
Attentiveness	Making eye contact, listening without interrupting, and accepting nonjudgmentally the other person's inherent worth
Acknowledgment, appreciation	Noticing others' efforts to be helpful or nice and commenting on them positively
Empathy	Recognizing others' circumstances, imagining what they must be like, and acknowledging, in a respectful manner, how these people must feel

depression, as you know from all I said earlier about the interpersonal model of depression. Feeling trapped in a bad relationship, getting rejected by a loved one, being isolated from the closeness of a good relationship, suffering the death of a highly valued person, seeing yourself act as a turn-off to others when you want acceptance or approval, and other such people-related issues are some of the most emotionally charged situations we encounter. Their potential as sources of depression is a direct result. Learning to manage relationships well is *vital* to overcoming depression and preventing its recurrence. Much more will be said about this later.

THE THOUGHT (COGNITIVE) DIMENSION

The Case of Anne

Anne did her typical stumble out of bed. She elected not to look in the mirror while she brushed her teeth, because she was reasonably sure she wouldn't like what she saw. When she eventually had to look, she was pretty sure her eyes were conspiring to form bags beneath them. Worry did that to her. Her family and friends used to kid her about how they could always tell when something was wrong in her life just by checking "the bag sign," as it came to be known. Anne never liked her eyes anyway, but she especially hated their transmitting secret messages she couldn't seem to contain.

Wearing a tattered old robe that she should have thrown out a long time ago, Anne self-consciously stepped out on her porch to look for the morning paper. After searching for several seconds longer than she thought she should have to, she saw the paper wedged in a bush on the side of her driveway. She was sure the delivery boy threw it there just to irritate her. Anne thought she must have a magnet of some sort that attracted abusive people to her. The examples were everywhere: cashiers who short-changed her in the grocery store, drivers who cut in front of her on the road, service people who showed up late—that sort of thing. She felt that such people were deliberately taking slaps at her for one reason or another, and it frustrated her to tears sometimes not to know why. All she could conclude was that she must be a pretty worthless person to be treated like that so often.

She took the paper inside and sat down with it at the kitchen table, as was her habit of late. She sipped some juice between page flips until she got to the "Help Wanted" section. As she gently touched the area under each eye, she began to search. Anne knew it was a waste of time to look again, but begrudgingly acknowledged that it was the responsible thing to do. She had looked in the paper every single day for the last three weeks, ever since being told her previous position was not going to be renewed in the company's annual budget. She was <u>always</u> getting passed over in one way or another, or so it seemed.

Sure, she had her own house, no small feat for a single woman.

And, yes, it was nice that she had a new car and a loving family and a wonderful boyfriend and a healthy savings account, but . . . well, none of it mattered, because right now she needed a job. She had never been unemployed for more than a month, and she even had a promising job offer pending right now. No matter, though. Everything in her life was terrible, because every day started with an insensitive paper boy and a "Help Wanted" section.

Something caught Anne's eye and caused her to look more closely. A new job listing—and it actually sounded like something! There was a fraction of a second's excitement, which was immediately overcome by doom-and-gloom predictions: "I'll never get this job. I'll bet they've already hired someone and are just listing the ad not to violate any laws. I'll bet they won't hire a woman. I'm never even going to be able to get an interview." Anne hesitated for a moment and then for another. She wanted to call to get information about the job, but felt it wasn't worth the bother; she knew she wouldn't get it anyway. An hour later, she was still at the kitchen table, trying to decide whether to call the number. In the meanwhile, she ate several small breakfasts and thought life was grossly unfair.

Then, in a moment of surprise optimism, Anne did call the number. A suspiciously pleasant woman answered the phone. Expecting the woman to turn unpleasant when she stated the purpose of her call, Anne felt a twinge of relief as the woman asked a few questions about her background and abilities. Anne understated her case deliberately. She didn't see any reason to push. After a few minutes' exchange, Anne was asked whether she'd like to set up an interview time. She hesitated, then agreed. She hated herself for those little hesitations, but saw herself make them all the time.

The interview was scheduled for that same day. Anne was thankful for that, or she might have had too much time to think about it and back down.

She showered and went to her closet to pick out something to wear. She pulled out no less than a dozen outfits, carefully considering and then rejecting each. A half hour later, she was still in her closet. Today was a little worse than usual. Normally, it took her "only" fifteen minutes to decide what to wear. Finally, she found something less intolerable than the rest and put it on. Realizing she'd spent valuable time looking for clothes, Anne shifted into high gear, grabbing a résumé and her purse and racing out the door, brushing her hair as she hurried along. In the car, she put on makeup and perfume as she drove, an ability she had perfected over the years. No near-accidents today—a good sign, she thought.

She arrived two minutes late and was greeted by the woman

attached to that suspiciously pleasant voice she had heard earlier. The woman handed Anne an application form and invited her to sit comfortably at the table in the corner to complete it. Anne sat down, looked around, and wondered whether this might be her next place of employment. She couldn't decide whether she liked that or not.

She handed in the completed application and was surprised when, after only a couple of minutes, she was called into the interviewer's office. This was a woman Anne thought she recognized, then realized she didn't. She seemed friendly, but Anne felt she was looking right through her. Anne shifted in her chair several times while the interviewer cleared her throat and reviewed the application, then the résumé. She nodded several times, which Anne took as a bad sign. Interviewers always nod a lot before they decide they can't stand you.

After a few questions, the woman and Anne shared some polite exchanges about the job and some information about the company. The interviewer let her know there were others to be seen, and Anne gathered herself together and left. She felt terrible about the interview; she was sure the woman disliked her, even though she had acted friendly. Friendliness, she believed, was just an interviewer's defense. She was sure she wouldn't get the job, and immediately became more depressed than at any point in the last three weeks. She wondered how long she could handle the abuse life was dishing out to her before she'd have to give up. The thought of suicide passed through her mind, but the image of no one bothering to come to her funeral caused her to reject it, for now, anyway. Anne drove home and was so preoccupied that she did not notice whether she stopped at the stop signs on her street.

When she got home, she sat, expressionless, in front of the television and flipped channels with her remote, unable to decide what to watch. Cable TV, lots of channels, nothing to watch.

Several days later, Anne got the call. The job was filled; thank you for applying; we'll keep your résumé on file for future reference; good luck. Anne was numb as she hung up the phone.

There was no way for Anne ever to know that the personnel director's niece had been hired without even having a formal interview.

DISCUSSION OF ANNE'S CASE

Of all dimensions of experience that most influence depression, the cognitive dimension is among the most potent. Your thoughts, ideas, beliefs, and perceptions are powerful factors underlying depression, simply because *how you think* and *what you think* determine so much of *what you do* and, therefore, what you experience.

Thinking involves making meaning out of life experiences, establishing connections between seemingly unrelated things, and countless other activities associated with shaping our experience. What has been shown to be true beyond a shadow of a doubt is that depressed people often make errors in thinking, what experts call "cognitive distortions." These errors lead to faulty interpretations, inappropriate reactions, and the pain of depression. Can you pick out some of the distortions in Anne's case?

Anne showed many typical depressive symptoms in her thinking: negative expectations leading to a sense of hopelessness ("I'll never get this job . . ."), negative self-evaluation (". . . all she could conclude was that she must be a pretty worthless person"), negative interpretation of neutral events (". . . the delivery boy threw it there just to irritate her"), suicidal thoughts, indecision, a "victim" mindset in which she was always the loser, worry and rumination (spinning the same negative thoughts around and around), and focusing on only the negative things in her life, to the near exclusion of the positive things.

There are other cognitive patterns associated with depression. In "global thinking," the person tends to think of "the big picture," missing the important details that would make the picture more accurate. This is one reason that depressed people often get so easily overwhelmed. If you think of breaking the patterns of depression as one big goal, for example, but don't understand that to do so will require many small steps, it may seem impossible to succeed. Global thinkers typically know *what* they want to do (or experience), but have no idea of the smaller steps that would make it possible.

Learning to think clearly, including how to separate what you make up in your head from what is really going on "out there in the world," is probably the most important skill to be mastered by a depressed person or a person at risk for depression. Many, perhaps most, of the activities I ask you to practice in the "Learn by Doing" sections are to help you approach situations with a more realistic—not depressed—way of thinking.

LEARN BY DOING #12

The Opportunity of a Second Chance

Purpose: To learn to think in terms of solutions. Recognizing that life situations tend to be repetitive, you can learn from past experiences the kinds of situations you don't handle so well. Then you can develop new responses that will work better, and have them ready for the next time.

Take the time to think of recent situations you know you didn't handle very well. Identify the specific thoughts you can remember having at the time that led you to do what you did. Deliberately change each of those thoughts, and then replay the situation in your mind with a new, successful outcome. It helps to use pencil and paper to correct your thoughts so that you can see them clearly in writing. How does it change your feeling about situations to replay them in detail with a successful outcome? The idea is to approach similar situations with better resources, rather than just focusing on what went wrong. Think in terms of solutions! Use the example below to get yourself started.

CHANGING SITUATIONAL RESPONSES

Situation	Previous Response	New Response
Example #1: Interacting with a boss who makes unfair personal attacks in the guise of constructive criticism.	Passively accepting unfair personal criticisms and remarks	Assertively refusing to accept personal remarks; refocusing the boss on work issues only
Example #2: Interacting with a job interviewer	Feeling too intimidated to ask what I want to know	Preparing a set of written questions to ask at an appropriate time

THE HISTORICAL DIMENSION

The Case of Marla

Marla sat nervously in the waiting area outside the school psychologist's office. She picked at her nails, pulled on her hair, shifted in her seat, and went through a sequence of other well-practiced nervous behaviors. She tried to figure out why she was nervous, particularly since this was the umpteenth time she'd been called down to see this guy, Mr. Lawrence. He was strange, but Marla liked him. At least he was nice to her. Not many people were.

Marla hoped she wouldn't cry today. She always got mad at herself for crying, yet she couldn't help it. Mr. Lawrence said she was in pretty bad shape and that some big changes would have to be made if she was going to continue in this school. Yes, she got all failing grades, and, yes, she skipped school and stayed home whenever school seemed too much to handle, which was most of the time. He had made her see a clinical psychologist, Dr. Mitchell, the type who talks to you about _all_ of your problems, not just school ones. She liked Dr. Mitchell, too, but he didn't seem to know how to do anything that would really help her. He always had her talk about things that happened to her and how she felt about them.

When Marla began to realize Dr. Mitchell felt as powerless as she did to do anything to help her, she stayed home for a week, crying and wishing she had never been born. Her mom didn't even know that she hadn't gone to school that week until the following week, when she happened to call the school about some administrative matter unrelated to Marla's school performance. When she found out, she did what she always did: she yelled at Marla, called her nasty names, said how much of a bother she was now and always had been, told her how much better her own life would be if Marla would either be a perfect child or leave home and go bother someone else.

Marla bit her lower lip when she felt the tears start. She hated her mother. She loved her, too, because, well, because she was her mother. But she really hated her. She hated her for marrying her father, a drunken and mean man who never knew the slightest thing about responsibility of any sort. Marla was only five when he left, but she remembered plenty from those years. She remembered the screaming, the door slamming, the times she got so afraid she would hide under her bed until things quieted down. She remembered seeing her mother with bruises on her face, and she remembered the times she would run up to her daddy when he came home. Sometimes he'd pick her up and hold her and say something nice to her. Other times, though, he'd bark, "Leave me alone! Go bother your mother!" and would push her away or, worse, slap her for bothering him. She never learned to predict on first sight whether today would be a slap day or a hug day, so she kept coming at him. Big mistake.

All of a sudden, Daddy was gone, and Marla found herself in a new home with another man Mom told her to call "Daddy." She couldn't understand, and wasn't sure she wanted to. This man yelled louder than her first daddy, though not as much. This man did something worse, though, when he yelled. He didn't just slap her; he hit her. Hard. She told her mom, but she never seemed to be around when he did it, so she was not inclined to believe Marla. Mom always took his side, and told her she deserved it, even though Marla knew she didn't. Life became a living hell. Every day, Marla wondered whether she would get hit for nothing—again—or whether she could escape his anger and be left alone in her room, her only sanctuary. She always felt this knot in her stomach when the school day ended, because then she'd have to go home. "Life is so unfair, and nobody loves me" was the sentence that ran through Marla's head constantly, and sometimes, when she looked in the mirror, she felt she deserved it. She was quite overweight—a fact that did not escape the less-than-sensitive boys in her school. She had to wear glasses, her skin was always breaking out, and her hair didn't even bear talking about.

The fact that Mr. Lawrence was nice to her was the only reason she would even see him. To find a nice man to talk to had previously seemed an impossibility. The only men she had ever had any real contact with were her two daddies, now both gone but too hard to forget. She hated them, hated what they did to her life. She was sure she'd never be anything important to anybody, which is why it was stupid to even try to learn anything or be any different. Mom didn't care what she was doing as long as it didn't bother her, and who else was there to care about her? On the basis of that thought, Marla decided Mr. Lawrence may be nice, but it was just his job. She gathered her things and quickly left his office, deciding it was a useless pretense. No one ever <u>really</u> cared about her, and no one was going to.

Later that night, when her mother was reading a magazine, she distractedly asked Marla whether she had seen Mr. Lawrence that day. Marla said she had. Her mother turned a page and said nothing. Marla went to her room and sat on the bed for a few minutes, waiting for something more, which never came. Again.

After a while, she heard her mother go to bed. She went to her closet, got down a small overnight bag, packed a few things, and sneaked out of the house.

Two days later, Marla's mother received a phone call from the police in a city over a hundred miles away. They said they had Marla; she had been found sleeping in the bus station. Embarrassed, relieved, and angry, Marla's mother pulled out her schedule and tried to figure out when she would have the time to go pick Marla up.

DISCUSSION OF MARLA'S CASE

In this era, when so many families break up and children seem an expendable commodity, the biggest losers are the children. It is no coincidence that young people are the fastest growing group of depression sufferers. Marla's situation may shock you if you believe in the sanctity of the family or parenthood. The sad truth, however, is that Marla is typical of millions of today's young people. What will her future be?

Understandably, Marla is already a chronically depressed person. Her history is one of neglect, of emotional and even physical abuse. She has had two rejecting and hostile males in the important role of "father," and she has a mother who is so self-absorbed as to be nearly unaware of Marla. Marla's history clearly explains her current depression, and unfortunately makes safe the prediction that she will continue to be at risk for depression unless there is intervention.

The typical patterns related to depression include: a history of significant losses (loved ones dying or leaving the family), painful and uncontrollable events that victimize the person (arbitrary punishments, abandonments, humiliations, abuses of any sort), inconsistent demands and environments (being rewarded one day for something that brings punishment the next), and a survival-based existence that never allows for the development of sophisticated and effective ways to meet life's challenges. When you're struggling merely to survive, it's nearly impossible to do much else.

Marla is so consumed with anger and hate, both for herself and the world around her, that it may be quite some time before she can believe that there are good and loving people out there. She has never yet experienced any such people unless they were paid professionals.

If experiences that provide you with a sense of well-being, a sense of safety and personal worth, and specific life skills are lacking in your

LEARN BY DOING #13

Values Learned, Values Missed

Purpose: To discover the specific skills you are missing as a result of what you were or weren't encouraged to experience in your development.

In your own personal history, what things were you taught to value? Devalue? If you were taught to think or act one way about communicating feelings, education, career, family, and so forth, then you learned some patterns for doing those things. What are the things you <u>didn't</u> learn? For example, if you learned to be a good caretaker of others, you probably didn't learn to take very good care of yourself. List as many as you can of the specific things you did and didn't learn. Keep this list handy, because you'll be adding to it as we go along. Use the model and examples below to help you get started.

VALUES I WAS TAUGHT

What I Learned to Value	What Was Overlooked
Taking care of others	Taking equally good care of myself
Keeping my feelings to myself	Accepting and expressing my feelings as an important part of myself
Work defines me	Learning to relax and enjoy leisure time

background, you are at risk of developing life patterns that hurt. It isn't that you want to hurt or need to hurt. It's that you don't know how to bring about the kinds of positive experiences that matter. If you want to break the patterns of depression, then learning now what perhaps you should have learned a long time ago will be your path to obtaining relief. Identifying what you as an individual need to begin to believe about yourself, and your responsibility for your own happiness, is the first step in the process.

Focusing on the pain of the past is *not* a solution. It may lead you to develop a deeper understanding of why you are the way you are, but an emphasis on explaining the past or the present does not create new views or skills for better managing the future. A knowledge of Marla's past explains her feelings and perspectives, but doesn't fix what's wrong with them. When you focus only on the past, you unintentionally focus on problems, not solutions. I'd like to suggest that you'll get farther with a greater emphasis on solutions.

EVALUATING YOUR EXPERIENCE OF DEPRESSION

As you can see from the different examples and symptoms described in this chapter, the problem of depression can take many forms and be caused by many different life situations.

How depressed you are is only partially determined by the number of symptoms you are experiencing. While specific symptoms may or may not be present in you to some degree, the intensity of the experience of depression is a purely subjective appraisal. It is comparable to the concept of a pain threshold. Some people manage to endure a great deal of physical pain and rarely, if ever, seek the services of a physician or dentist. Others seek medical or dental intervention at even a slight twinge of discomfort.

Since depression is so individual a matter, so must its treatment be. If you truly want to break the patterns of depression in your life, you will need to be skilled in identifying where your lifestyle patterns

LEARN BY DOING #14

Signs of Improvement

Purpose: To help you recognize your symptoms of depression and the dimension(s) on which they may tend to cluster, and to define the specifics of how you will know when you are improving (beyond just a global "I feel better").

Go back to the original list of symptoms that you associated with depression in the "Learn by Doing #7" on page 65 and now add to the list, if you find it appropriate to do so. Then categorize each symptom according to the dimension on which it's found (physical, behavioral, cognitive, etc.). What dimension(s) seems most prominent in your experience? Why do you think this is the case?

On a piece of paper, rank each symptom on a scale of 1 to 10 (1 easy, 10 difficult) as to how easy or difficult you think it will be to resolve. Next to each symptom, state <u>specifically</u> how you will know when it is improving. How will things look? What will you be able to do that you can't do now? How will your feelings change?

If you have difficulty being specific, that may tell you something about why things have not yet gotten better.

Use the table below to help yourself get started.

SYMPTOMS, DIMENSIONS, AND SIGNS OF RECOVERY

Symptoms	Dimensions	Rank (1–10)	Signs of Improvement
Sleep disturbance	Physical		An increase in the amount of uninterrupted sleep
Indecision	Cognitive		Making decisions, small and large, more quickly and with fewer mistakes
Irritability	Affective		Enjoying interactions more, much less snapping at others, more enjoyment of humor
Social withdrawal	Relational		Participating in social activities, engaging with others one-on-one more consistently, creating more social opportunities

make you vulnerable. Self-help is possible when you aim at the proper target.

SUMMARY OF KEY POINTS . . .
AND WHAT THEY CAN MEAN TO <u>YOU</u>

- Physical disorders can produce symptoms of depression, as can certain medications, making it necessary to first have a *thorough* physical examination. You may think it's just "all in my head," but common sense dictates that you first consult a physician to rule out physical causes.

- Stress is a common denominator of depression. It would be great if you could learn to recognize when you are stressed and take steps to reduce your stress level *before* it becomes debilitating.

- Depression takes many different forms and has many different causes. You don't have to waste valuable time looking for *the* cause, because there is likely to be more than one. How someone else experiences depression may have little relationship to what you're going through, so try not to take your comparisons to others too seriously.

- Symptoms exist on different dimensions of experience, each affecting some aspects of your lifestyle. Not all are generally in conscious awareness. For example, some people will focus on the physical symptoms, while others will tune into how those affect their ability to relate to others. There's more that goes on with you than you notice. It is important to recognize as many of the ways depression affects you as possible in order to intervene as comprehensively as you can.

- The cognitive, behavioral, and relational dimensions appear to be the most significant in influencing the course of depression. Learning to think clearly and behave and relate to others effectively are critical to minimizing your depression.

- Personal history establishes lifestyle patterns, but focusing on the past is far less important than making changes in those patterns for the future. Your goal in recovery from depression should be to take the steps today that will improve all of your tomorrows. Spending an inordinate amount of time analyzing your childhood or reflecting on all your past hurts is not the best way to break the patterns of depression.

Chapter 4

PATTERNS OF DEPRESSION

W HEN A DEPRESSED CLIENT comes to see me, it is with the hope that I will be able to say or do something to help. You have a similar hope in reading this book. By now, you are aware of my emphasis on the need to design treatments based on individual needs and differences. Since you are designing your self-help approach with variations of the ideas and methods presented in this book, it's important that you learn about the patterns of thinking, feeling, and behaving that can give rise to depression. With the help of this chapter, you can evaluate your experience by assessing to what degree, if any, you follow a particular pattern that seems to lead to your problems with depression.

The patterns I describe in this chapter represent ways people organize their experience and structure their personal views of "reality." What differs, often dramatically, from person to person and culture to culture is the way in which people view even the most fundamental things in life, like family structure, the role of men and women, work, love, *whatever*. Many of the patterns we develop bring us happiness, satisfaction, a sense of purpose, and other good things. Some patterns, though, lead us to make bad choices, demonstrate socially inept behavior, and form inadequate responses to life problems.

The goals, then, are to identify the things you don't know how to do that lead to consequences that hurt you, and to learn new ways of thinking, feeling, and behaving that will help you. You can learn to avoid creating problems (through bad choices or the ineffective handling of situations) and you can learn to manage problems that are not of your own creation (such as getting laid off when the company goes bankrupt or losing someone you love through death).

Let's go again from general to specific, and first consider the forces that shape people's individual patterns.

SOCIALIZATION AND PERSONAL DEVELOPMENT

From the moment you were born, and your parents turned to ask the doctor whether you were healthy and what your gender was, society, in a variety of powerful and dramatic ways, began to shape your life. Society has countless expectations for each of us regarding how we are "supposed to" behave as members. Your family is one of many representatives of society, but it is certainly the most prominent external force in shaping your individual experience and, consequently, your personality. The family, and the larger society of which it is only a part, communicate their expectations in a variety of ways, sometimes through clear, direct, and specific instructions about how to behave in a given situation, sometimes more indirectly.

Throughout our lives, we are rewarded for doing some things and are punished for doing others. There are experiences we are encouraged to seek out and those we are taught to avoid. So, too, there are subjects we are told are all right to talk about, and those we are taught not to talk about, and these also play a large role in how we perceive the world around us.

If you think back to the family in which you grew up, and the things you were encouraged to do and think about, the activities that your family did together, and the subjects you were taught to think of as important, you'll discover a lot about the source of your particular view of the world. The things that you were *not* exposed to, the subjects that were never talked about, and the things that you didn't even know existed until later are all just as powerful (maybe even more powerful) in shaping your perceptions. For example, when I was growing up, my family placed a strong value on taking frequent trips. We would travel all over the country to see different attractions. To this day, I have a strong appreciation of travel; I enjoy going to new places and seeing new things. Friends of mine, however, were not raised with so strong an appreciation of travel. As a result, they don't understand why I seem to always be on the go and why I'm not content to stay

LEARN BY DOING #15

Family Rules

Purpose: To identify forces in your family background that helped shape your perspectives.

What were the rules that existed in your family? Which rules were stated and which were implied? What things were you taught to value? How did you know what was okay to say or do? How did you learn what _not_ to say or do? You can write your responses in table form, using the outline and examples below to get started.

Family Rule or Value	How the Rule or Value Was Communicated	How My Response Was Rewarded or Punished
Value: Travel	Family trips were planned and taken frequently; trip taking was "modeled" for me.	Going along cooperatively and expressing enjoyment and interest were rewarded as desirable responses.
Rule: Work first, play last	Direct statement of the policy	Play was not allowed until assigned tasks were completed.

home for my vacations, as they do. For me, travel is "normal." For some of my friends, it isn't.

It is a general truth that the things we grow up with we consider to be "normal," and these become unquestioned parts of ourselves. It's often the things we grow up *without*, however, that can become main issues in our lives. Grow up with love, for example, and you're less likely to crave it or abuse it. Grow up without it, and it can become your life search—sadly, too often not even recognizable when it's right in front of you.

The immediate family is the primary agent of socialization in a child's earliest years. Later, other socialization agents assume increasing levels of importance in the child's world. These sources of experience and feedback are friends, family members outside the immediate nuclear family, the media (especially television), the school and teachers in particular, religious institutions, and other representa-

Pause and Reflect #10

Nature and Nurture

What is your reaction to my statement that depression is, for most people, a learned phenomenon? What are the implications of identifying it as a learned phenomenon as opposed to believing it is a medical or biologically based "illness"?

My response: From studying the changes in the prevalence of depression, as well as depression in other cultures, I find it clear that depression is more related to experience than to biology. The chief implication is that if it can be learned, it can be unlearned. A genetic disease can't be prevented, nor can a presumed biochemical imbalance be forever managed with antidepressants. Simply put, recognizing that depression is a learned phenomenon for most people brings it back into the realm of being a soluble problem.

tives of society the child is exposed to. Each and every one of us is exposed to forces that continuously shape our perceptions, feelings, and ideas. And these forces require each of us to develop ways of thinking and responding, ways that will work for us or against us in our handling of different life situations.

When you have learned patterns that work against you, depression can be a predictable consequence. In saying that, I'm suggesting that the patterns that you learned through your individual and cultural background have helped create the depression that led you to buy this book. *In order for you to overcome depression, you will not only need to identify the key patterns that have caused the state of distress you're in, but you'll need to develop patterns that will help you gain good feelings about yourself and your life.*

I hope that you are reading between the lines at this point and are aware that I'm saying much of what depression is about is *learned.* Therefore, not only can depression be *unlearned,* but you can teach yourself to prevent future serious episodes and to manage more effectively whatever episodes do occur so that they are less hurtful.

I suggest that depression is, for most (not all) individuals, a byproduct of faulty learning. When I say "faulty learning," I am *not* blaming you. I am directly stating that *you are the way you are because*

99

LEARN BY DOING #16

Learned Values, Changing Values

Purpose: To discover forces beyond your family that shaped your values and world view.

Beyond your immediate family, what are the most prominent influences on the development of your particular value system? With pen and paper, create one column called "Source," another column called "Value Taught," and a third called "How I Express That Value." What I would like you to do is be very specific about where you learned the value, what the value was, and how the value shows up in your everyday behavior and thinking. In doing this exercise, you will discover that some of the values that you hold work very well for you, and others end up working against you to one degree or another. This puts you, then, in the position of being able to modify your values over time in order to produce more satisfying life experiences. Use the table and examples below to get started.

Source	Value Taught	How I Express That Value
Piano teacher	Persistence	In learning any new skill, I recognize it will be awkward at first, but practice will improve my skill.
Baseball	Being a team player	I will put a project's success ahead of my own ego, diminishing my role if it will help achieve the goal.
Religion	"Golden Rule"	I trust others too easily and sometimes get taken advantage of.

that's how you learned to be through all the socialization forces mentioned above. That your background has led you to develop the patterns you now have is simply a fact. The past is your past. Neither you or I can change your past. However, there is much that I can say and a great deal that you can *learn to do* to change your present and your future for the better. As you will see in the next chapter, the future is not merely "more of the same." If you take the time, as you are doing now, to learn all the things you can about yourself and

Table 2. Examples of Value Polarities

1. Achievement vs. simply "being"
2. Emotional expressiveness vs. emotional containment
3. Being more emotional vs. being more logical
4. Materialism vs. spirituality
5. Being connected to others vs. being isolated
6. Being other-oriented vs. being self-oriented
7. Being task-oriented vs. being people-oriented
8. Being a conformist vs. being an individualist
9. Being competitive with others vs. being cooperative with others
10. Maintaining tradition vs. making changes
11. Taking risks vs. being safe
12. Seeking depth vs. seeking variety in experience

about handling life situations more effectively, then your depression can become a problem of the past.

There is one core aspect of your makeup that is more significant than the others: your values. In fact, most of your other patterns are directly related to your value system. I would like to focus on your values as they relate to your inner life. Then, following the discussion of values, we can take a closer look at each of the patterns that most influence your experience of depression.

SOCIALIZATION AND THE ROLE OF VALUES

Thus far, socialization has been considered only from the standpoint of the developing child. In reality, interactions with other people as well as with the various institutions of society go on throughout your life. Consider the role of socialization in your first two decades. It is in your first twenty years, most experts agree, that the largest part of your entire personal value system is developed and integrated.

What is a value system? Your value system is a mostly unconscious but strongly internalized framework for forming judgments about, and reactions to, the events of your life. Through your value system, you make determinations about each and every experience you have, evaluating what is normal and not normal, good and bad, right and wrong,

LEARN BY DOING #17

How Strong Are Your Values?

Purpose: To recognize your strongest and weakest values, and how each influences the quality of your life through the choices you make.

Go through each of the values listed in Table 2. Assign a number, on a scale ranging from 1 to 10, that reflects how strongly (10) or how weakly (1), you believe, you hold that value. How do you know? Specify the behaviors you engage in that reflect the value. The more extreme your numbers, the more easily you can identify which values represent your greatest potential strengths and greatest weaknesses. Use the outline below to help organize your thoughts.

Value	Its Relative Strength	Behaviors That Reflect That Value

acceptable and unacceptable, important and trivial. All of us *must* make judgments about our experiences in order to have a meaningful way of relating to them. For example, we each make judgments about other people because such judgments give us an organized way, *even if it's an incorrect one,* for responding to them. In short, making judgments is necessary in order to formulate a plan of action.

On the basis of your value system, you are likely to seek out one type of desirable experience, thereby precluding another type of experience. You develop certain capabilities that seem important or worthwhile, and you ignore others viewed as less necessary or valuable. You can't be everywhere learning everything! If, for example, you were learning how to cope with a difficult family environment, then you weren't learning how to relax and enjoy easy, comfortable relationships. This is a simple but significant concept, particularly in viewing depression as often arising from incomplete or incorrect learnings. *The things you don't know how to do can cause depression,* as you will see from examples in this chapter. Ultimately, mental health is the ability to adapt your abilities skillfully to the varied life situations you face.

VALUE POLARITIES

It may be useful to think of a value as existing on a continuum, with opposites found at the polar extremes and with lots of space between to represent different views about that value. I could describe many values that an individual may hold. Some are more powerful than others, though, in affecting your outlook and responses. Table 2 on page 101 lists several of the values that can play a central role in the experience of many depressed individuals.

As you look at the value polarities above, take some time to consider how each of the values is relevant to you personally. Think about the values you hold and how deeply you hold them. Consider, for example, the sixth value continuum, "Other-oriented vs. self-oriented." No one is completely other-oriented, nor is anyone entirely self-oriented. However, an individual's socialization history can lead him to be too intensely one or the other. Such an imbalance can create problems in his life.

For example, consider the way many women in America have been socialized. Despite the gains in equal opportunities for women, many women are still socialized to be other-oriented. Mothers frequently advise their daughters to be good wives, good mothers, and good daughters. Such value-laden advice essentially says, "Your worth comes from what you do in relation to other people, not from who you are as an individual." This value is very different from one that says, "Create and pursue your own independent dreams; they are as, or more, important than marrying or having children."

Relate this value to the eighth continuum, "Conformity vs. individuality." If a woman is taught to be a good wife and a good mother, to meet those expectations successfully she would have to conform to the demands of roles that she did not create, ones that may not fit her very well. After all, let's be realistic: not everyone is good spouse or parent material. To suppress or override dimensions of yourself in order to obtain approval from others places your self-esteem in their hands. It is difficult, if not impossible, to develop truly healthy self-esteem under such circumstances.

Considering the role that values play in processing all of your life experiences, it is easy to see how socialization may create patterns that put you at risk for a variety of negative experiences, including depression. For example, based on what we know about the value that says, "Be other-oriented and conform to the expectations and demands of others" in traditional female socialization, is it any wonder that women are diagnosed as depressed nearly twice as frequently as men? How can you feel good when too much of your self-esteem rests on other people's reactions to you? The value polarities of an "other-orientation" and the "need to conform" highlight how the values you are taught can lead you to seek out life experiences that may ultimately work against your well-being.

Each of the values listed in Table 2 on page 101 is neutral, neither inherently positive or negative. Rather, each derives its value only in relation to the many aspects of your life. Consider, for example, how a typical man in this culture is socialized to be achievement-oriented, having been taught from an early age that his worth is determined by his accomplishments. It should be no surprise, then, when he has high professional expectations and works hard to achieve them, putting even his relationships with his wife and family second to his work. And as long as circumstances permit him to express his need to achieve, his value of "achievement" can earn him great rewards in the forms of approval from others, financial success, professional status, and so forth. If, on the other hand, circumstances change, a crisis may ensue. If this hypothetical man is unable to continue achieving, for whatever reason, then the central focus of his life is lost, and depression inevitably follows. The significant point here is this: *Values can create rigidities that put you at risk for depression if those values are challenged in some way.*

Each of the values listed in Table 2 can represent an entire way of life. Periods of crisis in an individual's life that may show up as acute, serious depressions usually occur with the failure of the value system on which the person has based his life. You can predict the crisis proportions of a man's life when he has been forever climbing the career ladder, and suddenly his career is squashed by a layoff or a lengthy illness. And you can easily predict the probable outcome for a traditional female who completely builds her life around others (her husband, her children), who then leave her. If such individuals are able to deal effectively with the situation at hand, adjusting in a timely manner to the changes forced on them, they are much less likely to become depressed.

Let's consider a woman named Lucy, who is forty-five years old and

LEARN BY DOING #18

Identify Your Vulnerabilities

Purpose: To identify risk factors in your life based on imbalances in your values. Here is a true opportunity for prevention, not just "mop-up."

Go through the values listed in Table 2 and the relative weight that you assigned to them in the previous "Learn by Doing" exercise. Now I would like you to evaluate where your vulnerabilities lie according to your lifestyle. For example, if you are "all work and no play," valuing achievement and professional accomplishment more than anything else, then being unable to work for whatever reason would represent a potential crisis in your life. Go through all your other values and identify specific circumstances relating to each value that could pose a threat to your sense of well-being. By identifying your areas of vulnerability, you are in a better position to choose whether or not you want to do something to protect yourself from each vulnerability, or whether you simply want to acknowledge it and maintain your current lifestyle. Choice is better than no choice. Use the outline and example below to help organize your thoughts.

Value I Hold	Situations That Represent Risks to Me
Work, productivity	Vacations (can't relax)
	Layoff (can't work)

---

has been married for twenty-five years. Lucy has raised three children to maturity, and has been very successful, by her own standards, at being a good wife and a good mother. Can you predict what will happen when Lucy finds out her husband is leaving her for another woman? That would pose an overwhelming threat to the stability of Lucy's world. Having devoted her entire life to her husband and children, never having worked outside the home, Lucy may have little or no experience in effectively meeting her own needs (financial, professional, social). When her husband leaves her, the crisis is in full swing.

A therapist may advise Lucy to "get on with your life and start to do things for yourself." Of course, such advice would be technically correct, just as advising any depressed person to "cheer up!" is technically correct. Such "technically correct" advice, however, is not likely to be

Pause and Reflect #11

Personal Wishes in the Real World

The emphasis on values in this section is meant to highlight how finely balanced your awareness of your values must be with the actions that you take in life. Consider your internal experience when you respond to a feeling or a situation in terms of how you think you "should" feel or what you think you "should" value when, in reality, you don't feel that way. Being clear about what your values are and living according to those values but also balancing your internal beliefs and wishes against external realities are very important aspects of feeling good.

My response: It is difficult but necessary to keep track of the line that separates your feelings from your actions. When people act only on the basis of their feelings, they may say or do things that are at odds with the larger goal. For example, you may not feel particularly interested today in your child's drawings from school, but you can look at them and say nice things about them. Why should you act in a manner so inconsistent with your actual feelings? For the well-being of your child. Sometimes you have to put aside your mood and feelings in order to be there for others, placing their needs ahead of your wishes. Other times, you need to say what you feel ("I'm angry you're so late and didn't bother to call") in order to reach the larger goal of having others be considerate of your needs and wishes.

useful. This is *not* because Lucy doesn't want to change. Rather, it is because she doesn't know *how* to change. Lucy doesn't know how because her life has been based on the deeply held value of taking care of others to the point of being unable to meet her own needs. A history of self-care simply does not exist for her.

If you examine each of the values listed in Table 2, you can see how emphasizing experience at only one end of a continuum can lead to depressing circumstances. It can happen when you discover a deficit in your abilities based on the value and experiences represented at the other end of the continuum. This is precisely what I mean by "experiential deficits," imbalances, and faulty learnings as a common basis for depression. You can prevent episodes of depression when you learn to anticipate your vulnerabilities ("risk factors") for depression, because you can then seek out and develop a more balanced way of living.

Well before depression hits, the risk factors that lead up to it are usually in place. Too often, people notice and respond only to the most obvious triggering event for an episode, and never see the invisible risk factors (such as their values) that made them vulnerable in the first place. This point has tremendous preventive value. It is imperative, therefore, to examine your values in order to determine the strengths each permits you, as well as any associated limitations that may put you at risk later.

In order to live life well, you must acknowledge your values and seek to maintain a lifestyle that reflects them consistently. Sometimes, depression arises from situations where we disappoint ourselves by saying or doing something that violates our own values or how we think we "should" be. To feel good, it is also important to acknowledge the value of experiences that lie outside the boundaries of your previous experiences. Learning to do so is how you can actively develop a greater degree of flexibility. *Maintaining balance in your life means being able to change effectively with the changing times, comfortably adjusting to circumstances as the need dictates.*

Also remember that the values you learned early in your life may have little to do with living life well *today.* For example, assuming that once you marry someone, he or she will *always* be there for you is an older, albeit better, concept of marriage, but one that doesn't hold up so well today in light of divorce statistics. You can't assume someone will always be there. Rather, you will have to find someone who shares the values and skills that help make an enduring marriage possible.

Do your values fit with current realities? I'm a firm believer that when what you're doing doesn't work, you have to adjust to the reality of the circumstances and do something else!

OTHER PATTERNS OF YOUR EXPERIENCE

Thus far I have focused on the role of your values in shaping your experience. There are other patterns that also play significant roles in day-to-day living. In this section, I describe some of those patterns.

THINKING (COGNITIVE) STYLE

HOW DO YOU THINK?

The cognitive theories of depression presented earlier describe ways of thinking that lead us to respond in patterned ways to the everyday demands of life. Your thinking style can be described in a number of ways, one of which involves whether you tend to think in abstract or in concrete terms.

Abstract thinkers are able to conceptualize and relate to less defined things that do not currently exist in their immediate frame of reference, such as a concern for world peace. They're also able to sift meanings and principles from experience, and can recognize parallels and similarities in seemingly unrelated or dissimilar experiences. For example, they can apply the need to take risks to board games as well as to career moves. In contrast, concrete thinkers tend to focus only on what is well defined and immediate, and are not as likely to see similarities in seemingly unrelated events.

How abstract or concrete you are plays a big role in how you experience yourself and others. It influences such things as how readily you learn from experience, how precise your goals and actions are, and how clear your thinking is. I live in California, where some therapists speak of "sharing energy," "being grounded," "being connected," and "having space." These and other such abstract phrases seem to mean something to some people, but they are utterly meaningless to those who require greater definition and reality-based explanations. In another example, politicians talk about "patriotism," "doing the right thing," "the liberal or conservative agenda," and other such airy concepts. Those are poorly defined abstract terms representing lofty ideas rather than real experiences.

Often, clients will present vague, poorly defined goals that are so abstract as to be missing any connection to "real life." Clients who want to "self-actualize" or "discover their essence" are not likely to do well in treatment, because they have no concrete definition of what is supposed to happen. Abstract thinking can be wonderful, but *not* when your well-being is on the line.

Clients may say, "All I want is to be happy," but that is too poorly defined a goal for me to accept. I have to find out what we're really talking about. What does "happy" mean? How would you know if you were? What would be different? What could you do or experience that you can't do or experience now?

If your usual way of thinking is in patterns of abstraction, the absence of concrete and well-defined thought processes might call for treatment. If, on the other hand, you tend to be so concrete as to miss similarities among different experiences, as well as differences among similar experiences, that may also be a deficit requiring attention.

There is evidence to suggest that depressed people tend to be more concrete in their way of thinking. This may show up when the individual suffers a specific problem, gets help solving it, but is then unable to apply the solution to other similar problems. For example, consider someone who is unable to set effective limits (be assertive) in his relationships with others. A therapist may provide guidelines and techniques for him to practice in setting limits in a specific relationship, such as his marriage. But because the discussion about limit-setting revolved around his marriage, and did not refer to other associations, the fellow totally misses the opportunity to set limits effectively in other troubled relationships, such as with co-workers or other family members.

I encourage you *always to think about how the effective patterns you learn in one situation may apply in similar situations.* Keep in mind that the tendency to overgeneralize—to use the same pattern that worked in one place in every similar place—is also evidence of concrete thinking. For example, feeling and acting helpless as a child growing up in an abusive home may be a realistic response to that environment, but it makes no sense to act as if you are helpless everywhere, even as an adult. Such a "one size fits all" approach is an example of concrete, noncritical thinking.

ARE YOU A GLOBAL OR DETAILED THINKER?

There is another thinking style I'd like you to identify. Are you a "global" or a "detailed" thinker? This involves your ability to break full (global) experiences into component parts, and your ability to use the details to see the "big picture." Metaphorically speaking, it examines whether an individual is able to "see only the trees and not the forest" (detailed) or "the forest and not the trees" (global).

Depressed people tend to be global in their approach to life's problems. For example, you may take all the problems that seem to exist in your life and combine them into one large, overwhelming, and paralyzing depression. *Effectively breaking down and prioritizing problems and sequencing your problem-solving attempts is the best way to make life manageable.* If you ever find yourself thinking or saying things like "I can't deal with *all* of this," or "My life is a *total* mess," or "*Nothing* I do is any good," then you're making global statements. These are common ways to work *against* yourself by getting lost in your feelings instead of focusing on solving specific problems. Any time you feel overwhelmed to the point of giving up, you are in a global mode and need to become more specific and focused about your plan of action.

Global thinking leads to a paralysis of will and a loss of motivation. The same pattern surfaces in many ways besides depression; one of them is procrastination. If you find yourself constantly thinking about *all* the things that you have to do, feeling overwhelmed, and then never doing *any*, or very few, you are showing evidence of global thinking. Again, you keep yourself from taking *any* action by thinking you have to deal with *everything at once*. ("The whole house needs a thorough cleaning from top to bottom. It'll take *forever*—so I'll just sit here and flip channels!") *Learn to break down the things that you need to do into smaller, more manageable actions.*

Another way that global thinking shows up is in the self-critical comparisons you may often make between yourself and others. For example, when you see another person's success, you are observing the final product of his sustained effort over time. The "detail" person, who recognizes and understands the sequence of steps necessary to achieve something, can appreciate the amount of work and effort that went into that success. The global thinker tends to see only the finished product and gives no consideration to the time and effort that went into it, so he feels overwhelmed and depressed at being "unable" (in his mind) to succeed similarly.

The things you want (happiness, success, a good relationship) are possible for you, but if you don't know the steps for getting them, they will seem impossible to attain. Just because you don't know how to reach your goals at this moment doesn't mean you can't learn the skills to achieve them. Therapy often involves teaching clients how to break a global experience ("a good relationship") into manageable steps in order to show the specific sequence needed to achieve a particular outcome.

Let's consider an example. A friend tells you he's been using his computer to get all kinds of great information to stay current with trends he follows in business. He talks about the Internet, the World Wide Web, and his on-line service.

Let's assume you are not yet computer literate. You don't have a computer, you don't know why you'd want one, wouldn't know what computer to get, how to turn it on, how to get connected to an on-line service, or how to access information. How do you feel as you listen to your friend? Most likely a bit overwhelmed and inadequate.

Could you take the necessary steps to learn about computers? Yes! Are there people you know who can get you up and running and "cruising the web" in a matter of hours? Yes! In so doing, you'd be going from a global "computers scare me" to a detailed "here's what I use my computer for." Being global about computers can be overwhelming and frightening. Being detailed in your knowledge of how to use them for your specific needs is exciting. The former is depressing; the latter is empowering.

I use the example of learning about computers, but the same is true of writing a book, building a home, getting a college degree, developing friendships, building a career, and doing just about anything else you may want to do. The fact that *you* don't know how to do what others do *cannot* and *should not* be (globally) interpreted as "The other individual is competent and I am not." That is distorted thinking, and it's depressing.

It is vital to your sense of well-being to invest the time and energy—if it is important enough to you—to find out from capable sources the necessary skills and steps to bring about the results you desire. It bears repeating that not knowing *how* to do something is quite different from assuming you *can't* do it. You can overcome your global thinking by *learning specific steps in an organized sequence that can lead to desirable out-*

comes. If you don't know how to do something, learn from someone who does and also has the ability to teach it in detail. Often, people who are good at doing something don't really know how they do what they do. They're not holding out on you; they just don't know how to explain their methods or thought processes.

The best people to learn from are those who can be specific about what they do and can effectively teach it. That even includes how to overcome depression, which is a good reason to read Kathy Cronkite's fine book, *On the Edge of Darkness: Conversations About Conquering Depression.* Cronkite was able to get many well-known and insightful people to describe the ways they overcame their problems with depression. You can learn valuable things from those who were generous enough to share their experiences.

HOW DO YOU EXPLAIN LIFE EVENTS?

A third aspect of your thinking style relates to what is called "attributional style." Attributional style, as you may remember from the first chapter, is the patterned way you explain to yourself the events in your life. For example, in your explanations of negative events, if you typically blame yourself, respond in a global way, and believe that your circumstances cannot change over time, then depression is a predictable consequence. On the other hand, if you recognize that negative things are not always the result of your personal shortcomings, that lousy circumstances can and will change, and you limit your conclusions to the specific situation at hand, then you are far less likely to experience depression. This highlights the necessity for you to be able consistently and skillfully to recognize whether something is or is not in your control, whether it's temporary or permanent, and whether it will affect only one area or many areas of your life.

ANXIETY AND ATTENTIONAL STYLE

ARE YOU FOCUSED OR DIFFUSE?

Some of the most troublesome symptoms of depression are agitation and anxiety. Anxiety is probably the most common co-morbid condition to exist with depression. Anxiety impairs the ability to focus and think clearly. It can get so physically uncomfortable that people want to crawl out of their skins. To cope, they often turn to drugs or alcohol.

Bad choice. *Drugs and alcohol can and do make depression worse.* Whatever substance someone uses to manage his anxiety may calm him to a limited extent. But it's an emotional Band-Aid and has these liabilities:

1. Drugs mask the problems in real need of help.
2. Drugs delay or even prevent your developing more effective and sophisticated strategies of self-management, making repetitive hurts more likely.
3. Drugs can create physical addictions at most, emotional dependence at least;
4. Drugs affirm your sense of being out of control and barely managing, hardly a boost to self-esteem.
5. Drugs can stimulate or aggravate the same neural pathways as depression.

Drug abuse by depression sufferers is all too common. More than one person in four (27 percent) who suffer major depression have an alcohol or drug problem or both. This figure is more than double that of the general population. Often, the person can end up getting help for a drug problem, but the underlying depression is not addressed at all. This is a pathway to relapses.

Never underestimate the role of drugs in your day-to-day living, whether they are ingested with a casual afterwork "happy hour" drink or with an early-morning cup of coffee. Biochemistry *does* matter, which means so does your use of drugs, and so does your diet. Take the time to learn how. If you find yourself anxious and unable to cope or maintain a meaningful level of concentration without abusing alcohol or drugs, then it is important to take steps to achieve a greater ability to relax and concentrate.

Come back to the question of the quality of your attentional style and find out how weak or strong your ability to concentrate is. If you are having difficulty focusing on what you read as you go through this book, or if you have a difficult time remembering what you just read, then your attention span may have been affected by your depression. No, you are not losing your mind, and no, you are not hopeless. But you will need to take steps to master the anxiety or discomfort that is disrupting your ability to concentrate.

Anxiety can take different forms, just as depression can. For most people, anxiety generates rushes of fear and adrenaline, making it difficult to relax, sit still, pay attention, get comfortable, or sleep well. Instead of taking drugs or drinking, some people try to keep busy all the time. Having a steady supply of work or chores to do keeps them

LEARN BY DOING #20

Learn to Relax

Purpose: To encourage you to calm yourself and create a sense of personal comfort that can help you focus your problem-solving skills. I can't say enough times how important such calming and focusing skills are!

I have created a series of audiotapes designed to assist you in developing the skills of relaxation and positive states of mind. (The tapes are described in Appendix C of this book.) Each one addresses a different aspect of the most common problems associated with depression.

You can obtain other relaxation tapes from a bookstore or library to take home and use to practice relaxing. Be forewarned that relaxation tapes vary dramatically in quality. If the tape that you have purchased is not to your liking after the first few plays, or doesn't seem to help you relax, then obtain another. Don't assume that you can't relax just because a tape doesn't help you. Assume the tape is at fault, and get some others to try.

Practice sitting quietly and relaxing with your thoughts at different times throughout the day. At first, you'll probably notice how your mind wanders and nothing much useful happens. Notice, though, how your ability to relax and focus improves with practice. Learning to sit quietly while focusing on positive ideas and meaningful perspectives can be a wonderful source of good thoughts and feelings.

focused on something safe and external, making it easier to avoid the anxiety-provoking thoughts they'd have if they slowed down long enough to notice them. The problem with such a coping strategy may be apparent to you: you can't stay perpetually busy and continuously avoid yourself. Eventually, you have to stop and be with yourself. The better goal, then, is to learn how to be with yourself in a way that's both calming and effective in recognizing, correcting, and even preventing anxiety-provoking thoughts.

There are various relaxation and self-correction techniques that can be helpful, including hypnosis, meditation, visualization, and guided imagery. These methods can teach you to take your wandering mind and train it to focus in a specific direction. Movement-based focusing exercises, like t'ai chi, or more vigorous approaches, such as physical exercise (running, swimming, martial arts, bicycling), are also invaluable in helping to reduce anxiety and build focus. These skills require consistent practice, so you may want to enlist the aid of a spouse or friend to help you get on track. Once you start, the positive results will most likely speak for themselves. You'll feel good!

I am an especially strong fan of clinical hypnosis as a focusing aid, having worked with this valuable tool all my professional life. Hypnosis involves relaxing and focusing on helpful ideas. It is about building useful frames of mind. Contrary to common misconception, hypnosis *enhances* your sense of control, rather than diminishing it. I know of nothing more empowering than learning to manage your feelings, your body, and your actions according to your own wishes. (If you choose to learn self-hypnosis, make sure you see a *licensed health professional with good clinical credentials* who uses hypnosis, and not just a "hypnotist." You can get a referral in your area by calling the American Society of Clinical Hypnosis at (847) 297-3317.) With the regular practice of any of the techniques I've mentioned, you can increase your amount of focused relaxed time. As you do so, you will enhance your ability to relax and manage your anxiety. You can also expect an improvement in your sleep and level of physical energy.

Trying to help yourself is considerably more difficult when anxiety impairs your ability to learn effectively. Self-management skills for handling anxiety and agitation will be valuable to you during difficult times. Furthermore, such skills hold great preventive potential by reducing your negativity and stress when you practice them on a regular basis.

SELF-ACCEPTANCE

DO YOU REJECT PARTS OF YOURSELF?

One of the truisms in the world of psychotherapy is "The harder you try to control a part of yourself, the more you are controlled by that part." A pattern I commonly see is that depressed individuals take parts of themselves they define as negative and try to "get rid of" those parts. The harder you try to get rid of a part of yourself—as if that's possible—the more that part consumes your energy and attention.

Recently I treated Emma, who seemed to be one of the sweetest, kindest, most gentle women you could ever meet. Emma reported that most of the time she was, in fact, gentle and kind and considerate. But every once in a while, seemingly without cause, she would become enraged, sometimes endangering her family by throwing things or becoming violent with them. Emma's background involved two parents who placed strong value on their daughter's being sweet and good. They devalued Emma's expression of other basic emotions, particularly anger. Their attitude was "If you have nothing nice to say, or if you can't be pleasant, then say nothing."

As a result, Emma took part of herself—namely, "angry feelings"—labeled them "bad," and spent a great deal of her energy trying to suppress them, regardless of the context in which they arose, even appropriate ones. So, instead of being able to recognize and accept anger realistically as a basic emotion of *all* people, and instead of learning how to recognize anger and deal appropriately with her angry feelings, Emma would continually strive to suppress her anger. When it would reach the intense level at which she could no longer contain it, it would erupt in dramatic and powerful ways.

Can you predict what Emma feels about herself when she erupts, especially when she endangers her family? You're right—she feels self-hatred, despair, and depression. Whenever you label an existing part of yourself (anger, sexuality, appetite for sweets, jealousy, competitiveness, insecurity) as "bad" and attempt to get rid of it, you are denying its inevitability, and you are probably destined to fail. If you attribute your failure to personal weakness, and not to the inappropriateness of your goal, you can end up feeling pretty bad.

Whether one tries to eliminate an appetite for sweets that leads to eating binges, or whether one tries to suppress sexual feelings and then acts out in sexually irresponsible ways, the point remains the same: trying to suppress basic and natural parts of yourself is a strategy destined to fail. A far more realistic response is to accept the reality and the inevitability of such parts, and learn whatever positive value they may have in your life. For example, anger is a basic and necessary emotion. It is an important feeling that can lead you to defend yourself, set appropriate limits on others, motivate the action to fight injustices, and ventilate frustration. Clearly, anger has positive potential. To express your anger, though, it is neither necessary or acceptable to throw tantrums and abuse others verbally or with acts of violence.

If you accept the inevitability of angry feelings, your more realistic tasks will become clear: learning to recognize anger at its earliest stages (when it is simply irritation, for example), and learning to respond to it realistically by choosing *whether* to express it and *how* to express it constructively (by talking out differences and creating new ways of dealing respectfully with others).

The necessity of accepting and making good use of all of your parts is basic to managing your life in a responsible and satisfying way. In some cases, the better goal is *not* to change yourself, but to put yourself in situations that define your parts as valuable. For example, if you are a "free spirit" and want and need a lot of freedom to make personal choices, but you go out and join the Army because you want a steady paycheck, you are *not* creating a good situation for your self-esteem! Or if you want monogamy in your intimate relationship and then you date someone who does not value faithfulness, you are making a mismatch that can only become a source of pain. When you can realistically identify and accept different parts of yourself, then you can choose the environment you either enter or create in order to have the support for those parts of yourself.

PERCEPTUAL STYLE

DO YOU SEE MOLEHILLS OR MOUNTAINS?

It has long been observed that many depressed people magnify their negative experiences and simultaneously minimize the positive ones. For example, "catastrophizing," or converting small problems (or potential problems) into major crises, can cause a great deal of unnecessary discomfort. "Putting things in perspective" means recognizing that your feelings are in some way out of line in proportion to the situation at hand. You may be making mountains out of molehills or making molehills out of mountains (exaggerating or minimizing what's going on).

Do people often tell you that you're making too much of something? Maybe you are! Or maybe they are making too little of something because they don't want to have to deal with it. Always be as objective as possible. Use feedback from objective sources and trusted others when it is feasible to do so.

Conventional wisdom has always suggested that depressed people distort things in a negative direction, fueling their own bad feelings. (One wry observer said that "depressed people look at the world through crap-colored glasses.") To a large extent, that's true. But it's also true that in many situations the depressed person's judgment is remarkably accurate, not distorted. It isn't an all-or-none phenomenon.

The psychologist Lauren Alloy of Temple University has described a phenomenon called "depressive realism." Contrary to the conventional wisdom suggesting that depressed people always distort things in the negative direction, Alloy demonstrates that many depressed people, in fact, see *some* things more realistically than nondepressed people. It appears that many "normal" people distort their perceptions in a positive direction in order to feel good! Their view of life through "rose-colored glasses" may lead them to be less realistic, yet produce greater happiness, than the more realistic depressive. "Normal people" can unrealistically minimize problems and dismiss them with a wave of possibly unfounded optimism. ("Nuclear annihilation? Holes in the ozone layer? Overpopulation? Don't worry—people are creative! People are survivors!") It raises an interesting philosophical question: Would you rather know the truth if it's depressing, or feel good?

Optimism about life experiences certainly feels better than pessimism or even realism. There is substantial evidence that optimists generally live longer than pessimists, suffer fewer health problems, have fewer mood difficulties, and are better performers on the job. However, optimism may involve more distorted perceptions than those of the "depressive realist." Bear in mind that these perceptions are context-specific. A person can be realistic about some things, yet be terribly unrealistic about other things. Likewise, you can be optimistic about some things yet pessimistic about others.

THE SELECTIVITY OF PERCEPTION

Another aspect of perceptual style worth noting is the selectivity of perception. There is equal opportunity to see good alongside bad in almost every situation you encounter. Few situations are either entirely good or bad. And nobody's life shows only success or failure. To notice nothing but the negative is a distortion of perception, as is noticing only the positive.

Perceptions can be selectively distorted for better or worse. Whenever and wherever possible, seek information as objectively as you can in order to discount any automatic negative interpretations you may make.

People can get so caught up in their negative ideas and negative frames of reference (including negative interpretations, negative expectations, and so forth) that they essentially stop responding to external realities. Let's say that you make repeated attempts to win the approval of your parents, who always seem to withhold it. If you try and try and then try harder, and then try even harder, to get your parents' approval, and continually do things that *you* think should be rewarded, that is an example of what I call "internally generated experience." *You* tried to do things *you* thought would please them. *You* made those things up! Those are *your* thoughts, *your* ideas of what they'll respond to, not theirs. Being internally oriented does *not* orient you realistically to your parents. You are not asking the most important questions: Do these people even *have* the ability to offer approval? Or is expressing approval something these people can't do? What do they value, if anything, related to my capabilities, that would lead them to give their approval? Will they give approval only for my doing things it would hurt me to do? Unless you realistically assess them, you will spend time and energy on things that won't work, and become more and more frustrated and depressed as a result.

Pause and Reflect #12

Truth and Consequences

Compare "depressive realism" and optimism. One may be more realistic and painful, the other more upbeat but unrealistic. What is the choice here? Is it more valuable to know the truth or to feel good? Why?

My response: Optimism feels better than pessimism, and when it involves an arbitrary question like "Is the glass half empty or half full?" I'd choose the optimistic response every time. Often, however, the questions are not so arbitrary, and a little bit of fact-finding will make it clear that one answer *is* more accurate than another. Personally, I'd rather know the truth even if it's hurtful than live in a happy make-believe world. So many of our world problems are getting worse because of the inability of many people to deal with them realistically (because facing reality isn't pleasant). Avoiding or minimizing problems in order to feel good just isn't an effective strategy for managing life. But when it's the issue of half full or half empty, I'm a strong fan of the more upbeat interpretation.

It is extremely important, as you can see from this example, to go outside yourself to *determine the objective reality of the situation before you become intent on a goal you have generated internally*. Simply put, what goes on in your mind may be *irrelevant* to what's going on out there in the real world.

LOCUS OF CONTROL

WHO'S IN CHARGE?

Whether you believe you have control over events in a given situation strongly influences how you will feel there. As the learned helplessness model described earlier suggests, if you feel you are a victim of circumstances, meaning you were hurt by circumstances you couldn't seem to do anything about, then depression is likely. Feeling victimized by seemingly uncontrollable circumstances is called an "external locus of control."

Pause and Reflect #13

If It's Real on the Inside, Is It Real on the Outside?

Why do you think people respond so much more to their internal feelings, perceptions, and desires than to external facts? What are the benefits and liabilities of being this way?

My response: People are not rational creatures, though we clearly have the potential to think and act rationally. It requires effort to put aside feelings and impulses in order to determine their appropriateness. It is more difficult to seek information beyond what falls into your lap, and easier to stay with the familiar.

The chief benefit of being subjective in your approach to life is that you get to explore and develop a true appreciation for all your unique and special parts. The chief liability, though, is that you can too easily get lost in yourself at the expense of knowing and dealing effectively with "reality."

If, on the other hand, you are able to assert some control over a hurtful situation, then the likelihood of experiencing depression is reduced. Feeling in control of a situation is called an "internal locus of control."

In general, developing and maintaining an internal locus of control in which you correctly perceive an ability to make choices and act on those choices can effectively minimize episodes of depression. The key, though, is to be accurate. If you think you have control and you really don't ("I'll make my boss give me a promotion"), you can be at risk for depression because of what is called an "illusion of control."

When you are unclear about the issue of control, it can mistakenly lead you to attempt to control things that neither you nor anyone else can control (the illusion of control). Or it can lead you to *not* try to control things that *are* controllable (learned helplessness) if you were to look at the situation more objectively. Thus, learning to make clear judgments regarding the controllability of each situation you face is a vital skill to develop. Only then can you respond effectively to the many situations life presents to you every single day. The issue of locus of control is so important that it is given much more detailed consideration in Chapter 9.

TEMPORAL ORIENTATION

ARE YOU PAST-, PRESENT-, OR FUTURE-ORIENTED?

Each individual forms a relationship with the dimension of "time." How you relate to time is also a learned pattern that affects your view of yourself in particular and life in general. Some people are taught to deeply value traditions, and thereby stay close to all that has gone on before. This encourages a stronger relationship to the past and so is called a "past orientation." Others are taught to set goals and continually strive to reach them. They are taught to live life with a focus on how each day's actions can help bring about the desired goals. This is called a "future orientation." Others are bombarded with so many things to keep up with on a daily basis that nearly all of their attention is focused on moment-to-moment experience. They're scrambling just to get by. When they are schooled in the philosophy of "live now, be fully present in this moment," they develop a "present orientation."

Depressed individuals tend to have a past temporal orientation, meaning they dwell on the past. Do you continually review past hurts, past failures, and past episodes that were painful? As you rehash the past, of course, the past extends painfully into the present. Simply put, thinking about past hurts causes hurt *now*. Likewise, if you use the past as the reference point not only for thinking about your present but also for predicting your future, then you are contaminating your own future.

If you do not yet have the ability to grasp that *the future does not have to be a reflection of the past,* then it is understandable that you would have only negative expectations. Sometimes the ability to envision positive changes is so grossly impaired that it leads to the most serious problem associated with depression; namely, suicide. Suicidal individuals erroneously believe that their past and current experiences of pain are what lie in store for them. From that distorted perspective, then, suicide may actually seem a rational alternative. I suppose it is, in extremely rare circumstances. But far more often, it's just a lousy way to die.

One of the greatest gifts of nature is our ability to imagine and actively bring about many things that do not yet exist for us. Obviously, I believe deeply in the capacity for people to change (yes, that means you, too), or I would not do what I do for a living. Nor would I invest my time and energy in writing this book about change.

Focusing on the past is like trying to drive a car forward by looking backward. The ability to create positive and realistic expectations is vital for overcoming any hopelessness you may be experiencing. Do not be so tied to either the past or present that your vision of the future is clouded. There are too many important things you haven't yet experienced. I focus in detail on the ability to create a positive future for yourself in the very next chapter. I consider it the most important skill of all.

COMPARTMENTALIZATION SKILLS

HOW ABOUT A PLACE FOR EVERYTHING
AND EVERYTHING IN ITS PLACE?

Another important skill for maintaining good mental health is the ability to distinguish different aspects of your experience. This is the ability to "compartmentalize." Some individuals may experience a hurt or disappointment that has profound effects on every aspect of their lives. Others who experience a hurt or disappointment limit its effects to only part of their lives.

Picture a building with many different rooms. Each room is a compartment connected to the building yet separate from the other parts. What goes on in one room does not directly affect what goes on in another room. Think of yourself now as having *lots* of different rooms. Compartmentalizing effectively keeps the hurt from growing in size and intensity within you.

Here's a real-life example of what I mean. I saw a depressed young man named Ed, not long ago, who reported that he sometimes got into arguments with his girlfriend, Christie, with whom he was living. Sometimes the arguments would take place in the early morning, right before each independently went off to work. Ed said that although these arguments were rarely about anything important, he would get so upset that he would be unable to put his hurt and angry feelings aside and function normally. He sometimes got so upset that he would call in sick to work, and then spend the day in bed, rehashing the argument and magnifying his fears that Christie would leave him. In short, Ed would work himself into a frenzy and then despair over his inability to cope with something as trivial as an argument.

The fact that a small issue or a small difference of opinion could trigger such a strong reaction shows us that Ed had a low ability to compartmentalize. Christie, on the other hand, was clearly better able to separate her personal life from her professional life. She apparently could limit the effects of their morning argument so that it did not interfere with all the other things she had to do throughout the day. Christie was a good example of what I mean when I say *you are more than your feelings, you are more than your history, and you are more than any one aspect of your total self*. Christie knew she was more than her relationship with Ed. Ed needed to develop a similar perspective. The ability to compartmentalize allows someone to tolerate a failure without "feeling like a failure," or losing without feeling "like a loser." _Some_ is not _all_.

Consider a different sort of example. It is known that for many depressed individuals, early morning is usually a difficult time of day. Once the positive momentum of action is initiated, the day gets easier and easier. By evening, people usually feel better. It is interesting to note how some depressed individuals can report to me that "mornings are the most difficult" (representing high compartmentalization), while others tell me that when they have a difficult morning, it "ruins the _entire_ day" (an example of low compartmentalization). Can you distinguish the difference between "a bad morning" and "an entire day ruined"? Can you separate different aspects of experiences, so that one bad interaction with someone doesn't ruin your entire day, or one bad feeling doesn't trigger a whole depressive episode?

Learning to separate different portions of your experience will be an important skill to develop, especially since some of what I advocate is that you learn to separate distorted thoughts or distorted feelings from your choice of actions. You would be compartmentalizing your feelings in order to respond effectively to the situation at hand. Your

LEARN BY DOING #23

Identify Your Patterns and Level of Balance

Purpose: To actively identify your patterns for organizing internal experience and note how they cause or contribute to your depression.

Go through each of the patterns presented in this chapter. Identify in specific terms how each pattern relates to your thinking, feeling, and behavior styles. Then identify the specific areas in which you recognize imbalances. Use as many of your experiences as possible to show that the pattern really is a reflection of how you usually do things. Use the outline below to get started.

Pattern	How I Manifest It	Areas in My Life Reflecting an Imbalance
Abstract thinking		
Concrete thinking		
Global thinking		
Detailed thinking		
Internal or external attributions		
Permanent or temporary attributions		
Global or specific attributions		
Focused attentional style		
Diffuse attentional style		
Self-rejection		
Magnifying style		
Minimizing style		
Internal locus of control		
External locus of control		
Past orientation		
Present orientation		
Future orientation		
Low compartmentalization		
High compartmentalization		

feelings would be one factor to consider, but *not* the only one. While many of my colleagues are still (over)emphasizing the importance of "getting in touch with your feelings," I would like to advocate that you learn when it would be best to "get *out* of touch with your feelings"! *To have choices* about when to get in touch and when to get out of touch with your feelings, you need to compartmentalize different aspects of your experience. You have to be clear that you really are more than just your feelings, important as they may be at times.

Of course, *any* imbalance represents a potential hazard. It is possible to overcompartmentalize experience. For example, some individuals become so intent on handling things logically that they are completely out of touch with their feelings, having overcompartmentalized them. The goal, as always, is *balance*. Balance in your ability to compartmentalize creates the option for you to get into or out of a particular experience.

Given the importance of this topic, I devote an entire chapter to it, Chapter 10.

SELF-ASSESSMENT OF SIGNIFICANT PATTERNS

You now know that as you develop one aspect of yourself through repeated experiences, it is typically at the expense of developing other aspects of experience. You are in a better position to appreciate my emphasis on deliberately creating experiences that can provide you with internal balance. In order to function in a healthy and balanced way, you must learn to do those things whose *lack* of knowledge now causes you distress. Now, instead of your depression being a mystery to you, you can start to recognize the patterns that bring you down. Lots of ideas for generating changes are provided throughout the rest of the book.

I hope that, as your self-awareness increases, you will recognize where imbalances exist in your life. Then you can take the steps to broaden your range of experiences and thus overcome any current depression, and prevent recurrences as well.

Consider another example. If you recognize that you are too dependent on others in general (too "other-oriented"), or on another individual in particular, that dependency may be "an accident waiting to happen." If you need other people to be around to the (imbalanced) extent that you are uncomfortable when you are alone, then, even though others are present, you are at risk of an acute depressive reaction should the person you depend on be unavailable. Here is an opportunity for prevention. If you know that you are extremely uncomfortable being alone, you must take *active* steps to learn to be comfortable alone. (Perhaps you can push yourself, slowly but surely, to go places and do things by yourself, reminding yourself that you're perfectly capable of doing things alone.) This does not diminish the worth and importance of having other people in your life. It simply redefines your relationship with them as one of equality rather than of dependency. It means *wanting* to be with others, not *needing* to be. Similarly, it is worth noting *any* patterns you observe in yourself that diminish your ability to function effectively and completely. You can then make a plan of action to improve yourself in these areas.

In this chapter, I have described patterns that are the foundations of your experience. I hope you will consider how each of them applies to you, helping you identify those areas in which you excel and those where you have vulnerabilities. This can show you where you should focus your efforts to break the patterns of depression. And it can suggest important ways for minimizing the risk of future depressive episodes.

SUMMARY OF KEY POINTS . . . AND WHAT THEY CAN MEAN TO YOU

- Lifestyle patterns can lead you to manage life situations well or put you at risk for depression. Life is redundant in so many ways that it would be helpful to have new skills to face difficult situations that may repeat themselves.

- Your socialization history determines the range and quality of the patterns you develop. You have learned to do some things well, but not others. What you didn't learn before, you can learn *now*.

- Your value system is the single most important factor in determining your thoughts, feelings, and behaviors. It leads you to seek out or to avoid specific experiences that shape your views. Your values aren't right or wrong; rather, the issue is how they affect your choices whether the results enhance or diminish your quality of life.

- Your value system creates vulnerabilities that represent risks for depression. For example, if you value work and achievement above all else, or closeness to others, you are at greatest risk when you can't work or when others leave you. By recognizing your vulnerabilities, you can take preventive steps (like preparing emotionally for retirement or learning to be more comfortable alone).

- Your thinking style dictates the range and quality of your perceptions and may be described as abstract, concrete, global, or detailed. Each influences how you perceive and respond to life experiences.

- Attributional style concerns your explanations of life events that may work for or against you. Do you see bad times as caused by you or by others? Are they temporary or permanent? Do they affect your whole life or just part of it?

- Attentional style is what determines your ability to concentrate on and absorb meaningful ideas. Focusing and relaxation skills are valuable tools for building your ability to pay attention and learn.

- Self-awareness and self-acceptance are necessary for you to place yourself in situations that bring out the best in you. You can modify how you express parts of yourself, like anger, but you can't get rid of such parts. Often the best strategy is to put yourself in situations that reward you for who you are rather than punish you. The very trait that one person criticizes you for is the trait that someone else will appreciate.

- Depression can lead to selective perceptions that involve amplifying the negative. It's important to start amplifying the positive in your awareness. Even when your first perception of something is negative, push yourself to find and comment on at least a couple of its positive aspects.

- Perceptions regarding "control" dictate whether you see yourself as a victim or master of experience. Being a victim is a reliable path to depression. So is trying to control the uncontrollable. With the help of later chapters, you will learn to read more accurately where the control really is in a given situation.

- Temporal orientation refers to a concentration on the past, present, or future. Preoccupying yourself with past hurts diminishes your ability to focus on positive possibilities. Strive to focus on creating a positive future and to avoid rehashing the past.

- Compartmentalizing is necessary if you are to effectively address different areas of your life without letting one interfere with another. Remember the image of a building with lots of different rooms. You can learn to open and close doors to your best advantage.

- Any imbalanced (extreme) pattern puts you at risk for depression. The goal is to achieve balance by developing each part of yourself more fully. The exercises throughout the book are to help you "exercise your muscles" that have been underutilized for far too long.

Chapter 5

BEYOND ONE DAY
AT A TIME

THIS CHAPTER MAY WELL BE the most important one in the book. I focus your attention on the one factor that controls, more than any other, what will happen in the rest of your life. It is the single factor that helps determine whether you will recover from depression, how long it will take you to recover, whether you are likely to participate in therapeutic homework assignments (those provided in this book or given by a therapist), how complete your recovery will be, and whether you are more or less likely to suffer further episodes of depression. The all-important factor I'm talking about is "expectancy." Expectancy refers to your perceptions about the future in general and *your* future in particular.

Clear and realistic thinking about the future influences every aspect of the treatment of depression. You cannot expect to recover unless you identify and address your beliefs and your expectations. Here's why. If you believe a self-help book cannot truly be of help to you, and thereby *expect* no benefit, why would you bother to read it or participate in the activities it encourages you to do? Why seek out a psychotherapist if you believe nothing can change? Negative expectancy can lead you to do the same old things in the same old way, somehow hoping you'll miraculously get a different result. "Nothing can help me" is a statement of negative expectancy. It squashes any motivation to even try. If you believe "nothing can change; I'm trapped," another statement of negative expectancy, why expend any time or energy on learning to do things differently?

Let's put the concept of expectancy into real-world terms. You may remember that in January 1994 the city of Los Angeles was rocked by a major earthquake. At the epicenter, in Northridge, destruction was extensive. If you had gone to Northridge soon after the quake, you would have observed that many people were already busy repairing their homes and putting back together the broken pieces of their lives. Other people beat a hasty retreat, picking up and moving to other parts of the country. Some people sat on their front porches, head in hands, bemoaning their fate, sinking deeper and deeper into despair and even depression.

How would you explain these different responses: bouncing back, leaving town, giving up? In a word—expectancy. If you believe that "an earthquake happened, it's over, and now it's time to get on with fixing things up," then you have an expectation that *life can and will return to normal.* This is an optimistic and motivating perspective. If instead you believe, "Why bother to fix things? It's just going to happen again," then you have the negative expectation that any effort you expend in moving forward with your life will be wasted, lost to your pessimistic prediction of further disaster. There is no reason to repair bridges, freeways, buildings, homes, or lives if you believe "It's just going to happen again." And, of course, no one can assure you that it *won't* happen again, so you may feel justified in having negative expectations.

As you can see, I'm no longer talking just about expectancy. I'm also talking about your mood, your level of motivation, your resiliency in reacting to hardship, and your willingness to take new risks, especially intelligent, well-calculated risks. To be willing to do something different to improve your life always involves some risk. Expectancy is clearly at the heart of all that may be possible in the face of difficult or painful life circumstances.

The Case of Mel: Waiting to Die

When I came out to my waiting room, I was immediately struck by the sight of my new client, Mel. A physically large man—very tall and obese—Mel dwarfed his wife, Betty, who sat with her arm linked in his. Mel's eyes were closed, and he did not open them when I introduced myself and extended my hand in greeting. Betty took my hand, and the look in her eyes told me volumes about her struggle. She politely introduced herself, then Mel, who still made no move to acknowledge my presence. His deliberate refusal to greet me was a powerful indicator of Mel's emotional pain.

Getting him to stand up and follow me into my office was only the first of many challenges. Betty stood first and gently pulled on Mel's arm, offering a nonverbal command to stand. After a while, he did. I silently wondered how she had managed to get this huge man out of the house and to my office. I watched Mel closely, waiting to see when he would open his eyes to find out where he was going. He never did.

Betty nudged him along and led him slowly to a large armchair in my office. She signaled Mel to sit. He fell gracelessly back into the chair, his eyes still closed. Here was this deeply troubled man I was supposed to help, and he had yet to make a sound or even establish eye contact with me!

After only a moment, in a tired voice, Betty began an obviously oft-repeated monologue. She described Mel and all he had been through. Watching Mel as Betty spoke, I could not help noticing the stream of tears that rolled down his cheek. I gingerly placed a tissue in Mel's fist; he passively accepted it but didn't use it. Betty noticed Mel's tears and my little effort to comfort her sixty-year-old husband, but she just kept telling Mel's story.

He had had a serious heart attack not quite a year ago and had undergone immediate quadruple bypass surgery. From the moment Mel woke up after the surgery, his behavior was as I saw it now in my office. He rarely spoke or even opened his eyes. Each day, all day, he sat in a chair at home and cried.

As Betty continued her narrative, I asked occasional questions, directing them to Mel. But he made no effort to answer, so Betty answered for him.

Mel had been seen by several psychiatrists and psychologists, two of them while he was still in the hospital. His total lack of responsiveness frustrated them all to the point where they withdrew from the case and referred Mel elsewhere. I hoped I could help him.

Betty went on with Mel's history. A hard worker all his life, Mel took great pride in his job as a factory supervisor. He had worked hard ever since he was a teenager, rarely calling in sick, reluctant even to take vacations. His marriage to Betty had been stable but a seesaw— lots of rough arguments, lots of tender making up. They loved each other deeply and were committed to each other.

Mel had had wonderful plans for their retirement, which was to start in about three years. They would take their motor home and travel all over the country at their leisure. Now, their dream seemed to belong to different people in a different lifetime, totally unrelated to the hell of the past year. As Betty described their retirement plans, Mel moved in his chair, as if positioning himself to say something, but he didn't.

CAN YOU MAKE A DIAGNOSIS?

What do you think was going on inside Mel that would account for his deep depression? Pause and answer that question before you read on. It's important, because your answer will show how tuned in you are to the main theme of this chapter.

Ready to go on? Did you answer that Mel was just feeling sorry for himself, or that he was unable to adjust to the reality of his heart attack? Do you believe he was unable to deal with issues of his own mortality? All of these are reasonable ways to explain Mel's depression.

Are any or all of these explanations correct? The answer is "yes, but . . ." Yes, they were issues for Mel, but they were not central to what was going on with him. A fundamental pattern I introduced you to in the previous chapter, "future orientation," was the culprit here. Future orientation is the ability to relate to the future as though it were as real and immediate as whatever is going on right now. And, as I will describe shortly, this ability is not common. What was Mel's future orientation?

The most response I got from Mel in that first meeting was a grunt or a nod. I sensed he was listening, though, but that he couldn't or didn't want to expend the effort to talk to yet another "shrink."

At our second meeting, I asked Betty to stay in the waiting room, and I saw Mel alone. I didn't ask questions or require that he respond to me in any way. Instead, I described some of my clients, their problems, and how their mistaken ways of looking at things had caused them pain. I emphasized the common theme of people so caught up in concerns of the moment that they inadvertently made bad decisions for the future. I told Mel about one fellow who dropped out of high school so that he could buy a flashy car; I described a young woman who planned to marry a bad-risk fellow just to get out of her parents' house; I told lots of other "going nowhere" stories. After hearing several of these accounts, Mel opened his eyes and looked directly at me for the first time. He said, "I'm going to die." Then he closed his eyes and started to sob uncontrollably.

Does that tell you most of what you need to know about Mel? Whatever the other details of his life, his depression clearly stemmed from the belief, continually spinning around in his mind, that his life

Pause and Reflect #15

A Life Frozen in Time

If you wanted to keep your life exactly the same as it is now, how would you do it? What would you do to stay in the same frame of mind? Work at the same job, keep the same relationships, do the same everything? How would you avoid meeting influential new people—become a recluse? How would you stop learning new information—stop reading the papers and watching the news? How would you keep yourself from trying new things? The things you want to do or have are most likely possible, but not if you continue to do the same things in the same ways.

My response: When you come to accept a little more readily that life is always changing, and that new situations are always approaching, you can shift from doing what is familiar but doesn't work very well to doing new things that may feel unfamiliar but are more likely to succeed.

was over. With no future, in his mind anyway, Mel was sitting in a chair literally waiting to die. Now, if _that_ isn't depressing, what is?

If Mel thought about the future at all, it was overrun with images of his being dead or nearly dead. He knew that his heart was bad and death could come at any moment. To him, that meant he couldn't go anywhere or do anything because of the unknown (but surely negative) effect it would have on his heart. So Mel sat and waited.

Now come with me into the often distorted world of depressed thinking. Why didn't Mel's cardiologist assure him that he was fully recovered from the heart attack? He did! But Mel, deciding that doctors don't tell the truth about dying patients, didn't believe him. Why didn't Mel read the good news in books and magazines about living a normal life after a heart attack and bypass surgery? He made a feeble attempt to do so, but the fact that other people played tennis, took trips, went back to work, and _lived_ only depressed Mel more! Why? Because _they_ might be able to do those things, but Mel was sure _he_ couldn't. Why didn't a doctor explain to Mel that he would have greatly reduced the risk of another heart attack by becoming physically active and eating carefully, rather than sitting around day after day and getting fatter? Because Mel _knew_ that "his number would come up" _no matter what he did._ His expectancy was an entirely negative one that said, "Why bother? Nothing can make any difference."

Because reason and logical persuasion were initially so ineffective with Mel, I decided to approach things differently. I wanted to create a direct experience that would help Mel step outside the limits of his distorted thinking. After several sessions, at which Mel openly discussed his belief that his life was over, I gave him a homework assignment designed to disrupt his pattern of sitting around, waiting to die. To motivate him to do the assignment, I pointed out that I thought it was unfair that Betty had to check on him constantly to see how he was. To Mel's surprise, I chastised him for his insensitivity to Betty, allowing her to call out to him from wherever in the house she was just to check on his well-being. I told him that the least he could have done was save her the effort by keeping a timer with him and every fifteen minutes announcing, "I'm still alive." Somberly, Mel agreed that this was fair to Betty, so he accepted the task assignment. It became the turning point in treatment. He could not help absorbing the repeated self-suggestion that he was still alive! His tolerance for sitting passively and waiting to die diminished sharply in the days after this pivotal session. Sometimes the assignments I give people seem a little strange, but now you see how they can bring about valuable perceptual shifts, helping people to see things differently. Eventually, Mel was able to start redefining his future, gradually approaching it with a therapeutic dose of hopefulness.

By shifting his perspective from "I'm as good as dead" to "I'm still alive," Mel was able to accept the challenge to use his life—however much of it he had left, whether days or decades—in a positive way. He and Betty began to take short cruises to pretty places, and little by little Mel worked up the confidence to travel in his motor home. As far as I know, you'll find him in some trailer park somewhere enjoying his "second shot at life," as he calls it.

LIFE WITHOUT VISION

One of the most troublesome aspects of the human makeup is our limited ability to anticipate the consequences of our actions. If you consider the state of the world today, turbulent as usual, you see the evidence of human shortsightedness nearly everywhere. For example, we all seem to realize on some level that our planet's natural resources are irreplaceable, yet we continue to abuse them. For the sake of short-term convenience, and our emphasis on our own well-being and profit, we thoughtlessly pollute our water and air, and hunt entire species to

Pause and Reflect #16

Trees and Elephants

The loggers in the Pacific Northwest are enraged with environmentalists who want to protect endangered species and old-growth forests. The loggers complain, "What about us? Who protects our jobs and families?" Many have bumper stickers on their trucks that read PRESERVE SPOTTED OWLS—STUFF THEM! The loggers want to do what they're trained to do and what they've done for generations—harvest timber.

The ivory carvers of China are enraged with environmentalists who want to protect elephants from extinction. The carvers complain, "What about us?" They want to continue carving ivory, since that is all they know how to do. Yet, in just the last decade, elephant populations have been cut in half. Some researchers estimate that the elephant will face extinction within the next two decades if dramatic steps are not taken to protect it from ivory poachers.

How do you get across the message to such people that they are simply delaying the inevitable? When the last elephant dies, carvers will be out of work. When the last timber is cut, loggers will be out of work. A career change will be forced on them. Should they wait until that time, or change now while there are still trees and elephants? How should you handle things when your personal desire for comfort or security conflicts with external realities?

My response: Every day in my clinical practice I see the disastrous effects on people who respond to problems with avoidance or denial. They've said, "It's too scary," or "Maybe it really isn't as big a problem as I thought." These are strategies destined to fail. To delay or refuse responding to problems because they seem too complex or are too personally threatening is a poor choice. Regardless of how you feel when addressing important and emotionally charged issues, the discipline and strength of facing and resolving them is what builds character and prevents things from getting worse. Feelings aside, what's best in the long run?

extinction. For short-term satisfaction, we risk disease and death by smoking cigarettes, taking drugs, and finding countless other ways to abuse and destroy ourselves. For short-term comfort, we avoid dealing with critical issues we'd prefer not to think about, almost ensuring that they'll get worse over time. Long-term negative consequences seem to be so far removed from people's focus on the now as to be invisible. Then, when they come about, they are the basis for human anguish.

Why are people so shortsighted? Why do we make reckless decisions at the moment only to suffer terrible consequences later? "Gee, it seemed like such a good idea at the time" is one of the things I hear almost hourly; it is meant to explain obviously bad marriages, wildly impulsive business decisions, bad financial decisions, and self-destructive and socially irresponsible behavior. Where is people's foresight? Why don't they know and act on the knowledge that it's not a good idea to have an affair with the boss's wife? Why don't they know and act on the knowledge that having unprotected casual sex with a stranger or taking unknown designer drugs is potentially fatal? There are a lot of reasons, but in general much of human misery could be prevented with some high-quality forethought. So let's consider its value.

In their important book *New World, New Mind*, Robert Ornstein and Paul Ehrlich presented a strong case for the notion that the inability to anticipate consequences in a useful way is, at least in part, a product of biology; specifically, neurology. Ornstein and Ehrlich observed that the human nervous system is organized to respond to the novelty and intensity of a stimulus, and that habituation ("tuning out" of routine or ongoing stimuli) occurs in each of our sensory systems in response to our immediate environment. Thus, the novelty of a sensational murder trial can dominate national headlines and television while far more profound events are taking place: more animal and plant species are becoming extinct, more people are dying of starvation and in war, and more people are being born, adding to an already overpopulated planet. These significant events have become so commonplace that they go relatively unnoticed in comparison with the drama of a trial.

I believe that Ornstein and Ehrlich have made an important point in a context seemingly unrelated to therapy, one with profound implications for the mental health profession. Mental health professionals have frequently stressed the importance of "getting in touch with your feelings." We have encouraged people to "get the most out of life today," even if, over the long run, that advice leads to higher divorce rates, the painful breakup of families, the violation of traditional legal and moral standards of behavior, and countless other examples of short-term gain achieved at the expense of long-term decline. The mental health profession has unwittingly facilitated the cultural emphasis on immediate gratification at the expense of a higher quality of life. It has encouraged personal satisfaction at the expense of social responsi-

LEARN BY DOING #24

Marketing the Now Philosophy

Purpose: To identify—and learn to resist—the ever-present and potentially depressing message to "live now," emphasizing "now" as more important than "later." In some contexts it is, but in others the future matters more than this moment.

For at least two weeks, make a point of noticing—even writing down—the advertisements that catch your attention, whether on television, radio, billboards, or in newspapers or magazines. How do these ads encourage you to pursue instant gratification in one form or another? Identify the goals such ads lead you to believe you can quickly accomplish. Weight loss? Beauty? Health? Muscle tone? Love? Sexiness? Physical relief from medical problems? A good night's sleep?

Why do these ads work so well? Are they realistic in what they promise? Many people do not think critically about such seemingly mundane communications as ads, yet advertising shapes beliefs far more readily than you may realize.

People come to expect instant solutions to complex problems, and by underestimating the complexity of the problems, they attempt simplistic solutions that will likely fail. What does that have to do with depression? A great deal, because when you try to solve a problem and fail, you can easily (though incorrectly) convince yourself that the problem is unsolvable, and then feel hopeless and depressed as a result.

bility. (And still, as a clear sign that we're on the wrong path, the rate of depression in all age groups keeps rising.)

The emphasis on "here and now" and "living one day at a time" is a philosophical position with potentially dire consequences. The mental health profession will have to accept its share of the responsibility for helping to establish hazardous values and perspectives for society, presumably in the name of fostering "mental health." Noted psychiatrist and social critic Thomas Szasz once commented that if the East Coast has the Statue of Liberty, the West Coast should have a Statue of Responsibility. I wish *I'd* said that.

When we consider the emphasis on immediacy, as well as the mental health profession's extraordinary preoccupation with clients' childhood experiences as the focus of therapy, it is easy to appreciate

Pause and Reflect #17

When Enough Is Enough

Imagine having an unlimited opportunity to tell someone of hurtful incidents in your life. At what point, if ever, would you decide to stop focusing on the past and start thinking about a different and better future? Be specific about how you would know when it was time to stop looking backward. Spot the error in the common lament of my depressed clients: "I won't be happy until my parents treat me better when I was a child!"

My response: There's no doubt that being able to express your feelings is important to your well-being. There is also no doubt that people can get "stuck" in their feelings. The line I want you to walk is the one separating a useful venting of your feelings from a useless "spinning around the same old stuff" in your head. Find the point to go from venting to action as soon as you can.

why people become so intensely oriented to the past and the present while grossly misrepresenting or underestimating the future. And there is no human condition in which this is more apparent than in clinical depression. *Of all the important factors underlying depression, none is more powerful or wider in scope than your orientation toward your own future.* Thus, it is vital that your orientation be a positive, realistic, and motivating one.

The ability to think about the future in positive terms is called, simply, "optimism." Optimism that is realistic is motivating and helpful on many levels, including mood. Martin Seligman, in his excellent book *Learned Optimism,* presents a cognitive approach to building optimism based on its many benefits. I strongly encourage you to read his book, which provides yet another means to look to the future in meaningful ways.

It is unfortunate that people are not routinely taught to be future-oriented. Thinking in terms of eventual consequences, of how to extrapolate current conditions into future probabilities, is necessary to survival. You are not born with this ability. Ideally, you learn it as you mature. Those who have a well-developed future orientation practice it automatically, like walking or talking. But this happens only if parents or other significant people in your life serve as examples and encourage you—perhaps even force you—to develop the ability. They do so by requiring you to plan ahead, predict the specific consequences of your actions, and have a variety of specific goals—short-term, intermediate, and long-term. Too few people sense the importance of specific goals, because they are caught up in day-to-day living. (Do you know the old line "It's hard to remember you came to drain the swamp when you're up to your neck in alligators"?) Or they may learn to be future-oriented in one area, like career planning, but not in other areas.

WHEN YOU FOCUS ONLY ON NOW AND THEN

Often depressives continually review old traumas, including rejections, humiliations, disappointments, perceived injustices, and, in essence, all hurtful things from the past. Furthermore, these individuals rely heavily on past experiences as the reference point for interpreting both the present and the future. Even when a depressed individual focuses on what is going on now or anticipates what is going to happen, he does so by simply extending the past into the present and future. I often hear depressed clients say such things as "I'll never have a good job. How do I know? Because I've never had one." Or "I'll never have a good relationship. How do I know? Because I've never had one."

Since a cornerstone of depression is the inability to develop a more positive future by focusing excessively on the negative past, it is inadvisable, perhaps even harmful, for anyone to immerse you in even more of the past. Therapists who say, "Let's continue to talk about your childhood," session after session, are doing you a disservice. An overemphasis on the past limits, and may even prevent, the development of a positive orientation to the future. When you're depressed, you already know how to focus on the hurts of now or of your past. How to build a future that is more satisfying and beneficial is the more relevant task at hand. Thus, I strongly urge that we start to reconsider the conventional wisdom that suggests therapy must invariably focus upon your past.

It is not coincidental that the psychotherapies which have proven themselves to be the most powerful and consistent in treating depression not only de-emphasize the past, but actively encourage setting realistic goals—establishing a future orientation—and expending consistent effort in the direction of reaching those goals.

The key point is that you want things to be different *tomorrow*. You want to know that your future holds positive possibilities, and that it is not going to be more of what is and has been painful. But unless you develop the skills to think about the future realistically (using the exercises of this chapter) and have a specific plan for *actively creating* the means to change possibilities to realities, you can get stuck in the "one day at a time" philosophy. Unless you have a compelling vision of the future, life *is* just a series of nows. And when now is crummy, depression is nearly inevitable.

SUICIDE—THE MOST LETHAL PART OF HAVING NO VISION

The Case of Jeff

I had to keep Jeff on the phone until the police got there. Every passing moment seemed to me to last forever—a paradox of feeling my adrenaline racing along in slow motion. Jeff kept telling me between sobs that "I have to" while I kept saying, "Put the gun down; there's no need to kill yourself." He was breathing hard, almost gasping. It took me only a moment longer to realize that I was, too. Jeff told me his wife had just left him for someone else, his grownup kids were scattered all around the country, leaving him lonely, and his job was "grunt work." After a few beers, he had concluded he would be "better off dead." I listened to him describe his pain and isolation, and let him know that, as bad as things seemed right now, they could change if he'd let me help him. On my second telephone line, my secretary was told that the police had arrived. She passed me a note that said, "They're there." I knew the next few minutes would mean life or death for Jeff. My stomach was in knots.

I encouraged Jeff to go outside and walk around to clear his head a little before making such an irreversible decision. From the couple of sessions we'd had, I believed Jeff trusted me enough to listen. After a moment's hesitation, he put the phone down and went outside. Immediately, I could hear the commotion. What seemed an eternity later, though it was actually less than a minute, a police officer got on the phone and said, "We got him. He's okay. Where should we take him?" When my head stopped spinning, I arranged for Jeff's hospitalization. Although it was not an easy journey, Jeff, supported by good staff in a safe environment, and provided with sensible approaches to treatment, soon found his way out of his personal hell. His life now is very different from what it was that day, and Jeff smiles and says that's just fine with him.

How can someone get so overwhelmed, so pained, that the finality of death seems a tempting solution? Jeff didn't really want to die; he just found the depth of his despair too much to bear at the time he called me. Life *can* get objectively brutal from time to time, but other times people simply react subjectively *as if* life is brutal. In either case, the result is often a sense of futility, hopelessness, and depression.

Learning to distinguish the objective from the subjective can prevent such feelings, however.

The negative expectations for the future that characterize depression are the essence of hopelessness. Hopelessness can lead you to believe that the future is entirely uncontrollable and holds no possibility for anything but more pain and anguish. There is no better predictor of suicide than a person's degree of hopelessness. To a man who believes that the future holds no positive possibilities, but only more unbearable pain, suicide can actually seem a reasonable option. The inability to create realistic images of a positive future, in conjunction with a global cognitive style (where all of life's difficulties are responded to at once, rather than being "divided and conquered"), can create overwhelmingly painful feelings that lead a person to want the ultimate relief that suicide seems to promise.

Suicide has been called *the permanent solution to a temporary problem.* Why do people do it? I have worked with many suicidal people over the years, and it is obvious to me that these people did not truly want to die. Rather, their emotional pain was so great that they felt it impossible to endure any longer. Suicide is rarely the result of a wish to die. It is seen as the only way to end the suffering. When such seriously depressed people have the will and ability to develop a plan for a positive future and then commit themselves to the plan, their suicidal feelings dissipate. What seems hopeless rarely is.

Anyone who contemplates suicide is anticipating a future devoid of all hope, a future characterized by the same intensely painful feelings of this moment in the same, or even more hurtful, circumstances. Thinking of the future in this dark and limited way stifles the development of the positive motivation that naturally comes from wanting to attain worthwhile goals. Wanting to stop the hurt or wanting the depression to go away are not goals. They are merely wishes.

ARE YOU SUICIDAL?

If you are suicidal, I can assure you that the future holds unlimited possibilities, but your current way of thinking prevents you from knowing that. Because of your depression, you may feel unable to muster the effort to make things better. Or you may think your problems are permanent or unresolvable. Perhaps some aspects are, I'll grant you, but not *all.* You don't have to change your life all at once. Just making the first move on a specific path to improving your future

Pause and Reflect #18

Your Ghost of Christmas Future

Remember the classic story A Christmas Carol, by Charles Dickens? In this much loved Christmas tale, Ebenezer Scrooge is a miserable miser hated by all. With only cynicism in his heart, Scrooge is visited one Christmas Eve by three ghosts, the ghosts of past, present, and future. Only when he is visited by the Ghost of Christmas Future does he come to realize the dire implications of continuing on his negative path. Scrooge changes his ways for the better when he sees himself being remembered badly by everyone in the future, a fate he desperately wants to avoid.

Knowing you are on a hurtful path gives you an opportunity to say "This isn't where I want to go." It creates a chance for you to say "I'm not going to wait until it's too late. I'm going to do something now that will help me later." What do you want your future to look like?

will relieve some of your pain. In fact, you have already made a good start by reading this book.

If you feel desperately suicidal right now, let someone skilled help you to think beyond the immediate pain so that you can experience the relief that is definitely possible. Skip to Chapter 12 and *see a qualified professional at once!* Do not let the bad feelings of *now* prevent you from enjoying the good ones that are to come. You can't realize how temporary these bad times are until you're looking back on them later, wondering how you could ever have felt this way.

BUILDING HOPEFULNESS

Why try to move forward with your life when you've been hurt and feel so bad? Why try harder when you've already tried so hard? There's one compelling reason I can think of: what you have done so far hasn't worked. That doesn't mean you *can't* do what it takes to improve your life. It means only that the approach you used wasn't right for the results you wanted. Before you relive the frustration or pain of your failed attempts and give up, why not allow for the possibility that other techniques can work and that you can eventually master them? We are taught, "If at first you don't succeed, try, try again." I would add ". . . and when you try, try again, *do something different.*"

For you to break the patterns of depression, your expectations must be positive and realistic. Change is possible, and you can make good things happen in your life if you approach each situation intelligently and with some flexibility. Otherwise, you may keep doing over and over again what doesn't work.

Changes really do occur when you do things differently. As you develop more positive and realistic expectations in your life, self-destructive indifference and a lack of motivation will undoubtedly give way to an interest in learning how to achieve your goals.

WHAT DO YOU WANT FOR THE FUTURE?

If I could wave a magic wand and eliminate depression from your life forever, what would you do with your future? Think about it for a moment. Is there something you feel a need to experience, or something significant you want to accomplish? What is your purpose in life?

That is one of the most profound of all human questions. For some, life is filled with deep meaning and purpose. Others see life only in terms of day-to-day existence, something to get through, nothing in particular to strive for. Some people view life as simply what it is, and have no need for a purpose. Others feel depressed and empty without a strong sense of purpose.

Viewing life as purposeful can bear directly on depression. On one hand, everyday life can be overwhelming for those who read too much into random events. On the other hand, those who see little if any meaning in life's events may sacrifice the possibility of gaining insight into patterns that enhance their life, patterns that could also prevent or minimize future pain. Obviously, we need to find a balance between thoughtful consideration of what happens to and around us and the "analysis paralysis" that too careful a consideration of life can create.

We also need a sense of purpose to provide motivation and the will to endure beyond immediate suffering. I can think of no more gripping example of this observation than the psychiatrist Viktor Frankl's experiences in the Nazi concentration camps during World War II, described in his powerful book *Man's Search for Meaning.* If you saw Steven Spielberg's profoundly moving movie *Schindler's List*, then you

LEARN BY DOING #26

Many Purposes

Purpose: To discover the relationship between a sense of purpose and the behaviors it spawns.

Try to identify at least one sense of purpose in the people closest to you—family members, friends, neighbors, and co-workers. (Use the example below as a guide.) How do their lives reflect it? What about the quality of life for those who don't seem to have a sense of purpose? A fine book to help you focus more on life purpose is called The Spiritual Diet, by Diane and Jonathan Kramer.

Person	Purpose(s)	Behaviors That Reflect the Purpose
Parent	Raising and caring for children	Being available to children emotionally. Volunteering time and energy to meet children's needs. Patiently teaching and reteaching, if necessary, key life skills. Demonstrating affection.

have at least some frame of reference for appreciating how barbaric and inhuman the concentration camps were.

Frankl, a skilled and insightful observer, couldn't help noticing how individual prisoners reacted in dramatically different ways to the brutal conditions. All were starved, beaten, humiliated, living continuously with the prospect of a horrible death that could happen any moment based solely on a camp guard's whim. Yet some people managed to endure and survive while others did not. What made the difference? Frankl's answer to this question is "a sense of purpose."

For Frankl, the purpose was created the moment he was separated from his beloved wife at the start of their imprisonment. He developed an intense desire to live so that they could eventually be reunited. Hope kept him going, as did the conviction that the current horror would end and permit the longed-for reunion. His belief was that the horrible conditions were transient, not permanent. Having a goal allowed him to endure the painful circumstances.

In daily life, the value of the long-term goal over short-term difficulties is evident. How do you get a college education? The value of the degree allows you to endure boring lectures and the stresses of final exams and term papers. (People say to me, "Me go back to college? I'm forty-six! If it takes me four years to finish my degree, I'll be fifty!" Then I ask, "So how old will you be in four years if you *don't* get a degree?") How do you raise a child with self-esteem? The goal of having a child with a healthy self-image virtually precludes your calling the child names or humiliating or ignoring the child. How do you motivate an employee? The goal of the person feeling good about himself and the job overrides any impulse to insult the person or question his heritage when he makes a mistake. A sense of purpose in each and every interaction—with others *and* yourself—can lift you out of the destructive feelings of the moment. This is a vital skill to master.

DO YOU HAVE PURPOSE IN YOUR LIFE?

What drives you? Many of my depressed clients seem to have little or no sense of purpose or meaning. Consequently, they have no future that compels them, no goal that pulls them along. The day-to-day routine is their whole life, not only a part of it.

Lee—A Case of Finding Other Purposes in Life

Let me illustrate the point with the case history of a man who came to me complaining of deep depression. This forty-four-year-old, very successful real estate developer was literally worth millions. I had first seen Lee about a year earlier, when he was experiencing difficulties in his new marriage. Using some of the techniques I taught him, he quickly resolved those issues.

Lee was back now, telling me that, for the first time in his life, he felt lost. He had nothing left to fight for professionally, financially, or personally. His business, bank account, and marriage were all doing well. He had fought all his life to get to this point of success. Why wasn't he happy? His need to achieve was a basic part of his makeup. Now, he was being pushed to retire by his new wife, who wanted to do little else but travel. With his achieving days all but over, in his view, and having achieved his original goals, he was experiencing depression. Lee thought he "should" be happy now, only to find it was not in his makeup to sit back and do nothing for

LEARN BY DOING #27

Solid Foundations Built on Quicksand

Purpose: To identify the relationship between a person's sense of purpose and the risk factors of depression.

I have a friend who is a brilliant researcher at a prestigious university. He is a well-known author and teacher who works nearly eighty to ninety hours a week. He is competitive, achievement-oriented, and takes his work very seriously. Predict under what circumstances this man is at greatest risk for an emotional crisis. What specific steps could he take now to prevent such a crisis? List them.

Can you see how his personal value system, emphasizing only professional achievement, makes him emotionally vulnerable to situations in which he cannot achieve something? He has few close relationships and a difficult time just relaxing. He would greatly benefit from getting some balance in his life through more contact with others and enjoying time away from work.

What are _your_ vulnerabilities, and how can you plan your life to achieve greater personal balance? Develop a structured means for doing so by writing out things you can do that reflect a balance. For example, if you almost always put other people's needs ahead of your own, plan some things to _do_ on a regular basis that are meant to be purely self-nurturing; then _do_ them. Use the outline and examples below to get started.

My Strong Area	My Weak Area	Things I Can Do to Strengthen My Weakness
Achievement	Relaxing	Schedule at least one leisure activity per week.
Completing tasks	Tuning in to people	Ask someone to meet me socially for lunch or dinner at least once a week.

the rest of his life. Extensive traveling was not in his long-term game plan. He had never thought about <u>relaxing,</u> much less retiring. Do you see how an overemphasis on one aspect of life (in his case, achievement) can create a deficit in another (in his case, being able to relax more)? As you've learned, lifestyle imbalances can pave the way for depression.

In this particular case, our sessions focused on shifting Lee's self-definition from what he accomplishes to who he is. I had Lee go to several retirement communities and interview people there. Specifically, Lee was asked to identify ten people who were handling retirement well, and then ten who were not. He was asked to identify the specific factors that accounted for people responding well or poorly to the apparent lack of structure in their lives. Lee is a thoughtful man by nature, and it didn't take him long to realize that relationships matter a great deal to well-adjusted people. Lee had never been particularly relationship-oriented, because you can't "accomplish" relationships; you can only build them carefully and work at them consistently to keep them vital and healthy. Lee soon turned his attention to establishing closer relationships with his two grown children (from a previous marriage) and a more satisfying social life with friends. His depressing idea of "sitting around and doing nothing the rest of my life" soon gave way to "keeping my finger in the pie" and consulting, while leaving lots of spare time to pursue new hobbies and friendships. Now that he is over his depression, Lee is glad he is financially able to do the things he likes and still contribute personally and professionally to others in ways that are rewarding to him. He relaxes, he travels, and he has not fallen into an "all-or-none" trap.

How do you develop a sense of purpose? You find something you consider important enough to justify your time and energy. You do that by *trying* different things that seem important, not just contemplating them. You can't get attached from a distance. Today's world bulges with important issues, and your contribution *can* make a difference. Purpose is most powerful, though, when it is deeply personal. Investing yourself in being a more loving partner, a better parent to your child, or in a cause that is important to you—literacy, conservation—reflects one of the most important of all lifestyle antidepressants. *People who have a strong sense of being connected to something greater than themselves suffer less depression.* Whether it's marriage, religion, a school play, coaching your son's Little League team, keeping up your house, formal education—whatever it happens to be—is less important than developing a sense of attachment to whatever that something is. Only you can decide which relationships or activities can arouse your willingness to become involved. In order to do so, you will have to acknowledge that there are other people and things in the world as immediate and important as your depression. I know this is not as easy as you'd like, yet there is no one so powerful and so future-oriented as a person with a "mission." Explore the possibilities.

LEARNING TO THINK PREVENTIVELY

Often, people are so bogged down in addressing existing problems that they have too little time to notice opportunities for prevention. Teaching yourself to think ahead, anticipate consequences, and project beyond immediate gratification (or immediate pain) are fundamental skills for reducing the risk for later depression. Not all depressions are preventable, but many of them are when you have the ability to extrapolate circumstances or patterns in a realistic and detailed fashion. There really is such a thing as "cause and effect." I can often predict quite easily and accurately that if I engage in "this" behavior, "that" consequence is likely.

An ability to anticipate consequences and realistically assess probabilities has enormous preventive value in overcoming depression. There are many risk factors for depression. In the largest sense, life is a risk factor; as long as you are alive, you face countless circumstances that are potentially hurtful. If you have relationships, you run the risk of losing them. Since you live in a human body, you face the prospect of injury, disease, or death. If you have a job, you run the risk of losing political and economic battles and of being fired or replaced. If you are alive, you face the inevitable difficulties associated with being alive.

One therapeutic goal, then, is to establish positive expectations— that your experience can change for the better—and another goal is to form realistic expectations, predictions, probabilities, and possibilities for all life events, good or bad. Only then can you carefully identify when it is safe to make an emotional investment or when a situation is too hazardous and potentially toxic to do so.

What follows is a case that illustrates how someone can make terrible decisions by being too focused on *now*, thereby missing preventive opportunities.

LEARN BY DOING #28

Hindsight and Foresight

Purpose: To facilitate your ability to anticipate the consequences of your actions.

Here's a structured way to start to develop foresight. It may seem like a lot to do, but take your time and keep the goal in mind.

Pick up a newspaper every day for a month or two. Go through the headlines and identify those stories which clearly reflect a negative event that occurred due to the lack of foresight. After you identify many such stories, pick at least two each day about which you can consider these questions carefully:

1. Could this event have been predicted and even prevented?
2. What insight and foresight could have prevented the negative event?
3. How soon into the situation could some application of forethought have prevented the event?
4. What situational factors prevented the individuals involved from anticipating what could go wrong?
5. What psychological factors kept the people involved from anticipating what could go wrong?
6. Was this situation unique or does it have relevance to other negative events that may be prevented with some foresight? Be specific.

When you have done this with impersonal news stories for at least a month, shift to personal events in your life. After you've done that for at least a month, go the final step. Predict people's responses in upcoming situations and see how accurate your predictions are. When your predictions are good most of the time, your confidence in your judgment will grow, as will your self-esteem.

Erica—A Case of
Distorted Sense of Future

Erica arrived at my office looking like a model for Saks Fifth Avenue. She was impeccably dressed, perfectly groomed, and extremely depressed. I'll omit the smaller details and just tell you that Erica had lost her job five years earlier and soon afterward was gripped by an overwhelming desire for motherhood. Her husband, Ray, wasn't sure he wanted to be a father. In any case, he wanted at least to wait until they were more financially secure. Somehow, Erica managed to convince Ray that they shouldn't wait. She became pregnant within a few months, and was now the mother of Bobby, her four-year-old son.

Erica pressed a handkerchief to her face as she spoke, quickly dabbing away the tears. She described Bobby as the cause of her depression.

"I wanted a baby so very much that I couldn't think of anything else," she said. "I pushed Ray into fatherhood before he was ready, and I feel guilty about that. But I feel even guiltier that I'm tired of being Bobby's mother!"

Erica repositioned herself and went on. "I know that must sound awful to you, but I can't help it. When I was pregnant, I felt like a queen. I was in heaven. When Bobby was born, he seemed like a miracle to me. During that first year, I held him every minute. I looked at him lovingly all the time. I was thrilled. I didn't mind that he cried in the middle of the night, and I didn't mind staying at home with him. On the contrary, I enjoyed it. But by the end of his first year, I was beginning to feel that I'd had enough of building my world totally around Bobby."

She started to cry harder and paused for a long time before collecting herself and continuing. "I couldn't believe I was feeling that way. I couldn't even let myself think it, much less talk about it to Ray or anyone else. What would they think? So for a long time I simply refused to pay attention to those feelings. But every time Bobby cried or messed himself, I got angrier and angrier with him. And I hated myself more and more for feeling that way. He's a good boy, and I love him. But, damn it, I feel trapped and have felt that way for three long years. I can't take it anymore. He was the cute little baby I wanted, but he isn't little and he isn't a baby anymore. Now he is forever asking questions and acting stubborn as a mule—and he can't seem to sit still for five minutes. I catch myself screaming at him, and I feel terrible about that. The problem isn't him; it's me. I wanted a baby, not a whirlwind. I mostly came here to find out whether you think it would help me, psychologically speaking, if I had another baby. What do you think?"

Are you cringing at the thought of Erica's having another baby? I hope so, because she illustrates how the distorted thinking of people trapped in depression can lead them to attempt solutions that will undoubtedly make their problems worse. Erica's "solution" is typical

LEARN BY DOING #29

Imagery: The Rocking Chair

Purpose: To create some future-oriented imagery that can motivate your taking positive action _now._

Relax, breathe slowly and regularly. Let your eyes close and take yourself forward in time to some point in the distant future. Imagine yourself very old, physically tired, but mentally alert. Picture yourself sitting in a big wooden chair, gently rocking on the porch of your home.

Imagine in detail sitting in the rocker and describing your life to a young child interested in this old person (you). How would you describe your life? In terms of random events? Purposeful accomplishments? Important relationships?

Review the things in your life of which you are most proud. What would you describe as your greatest sources of pride? Which of these required great effort and careful planning?

Next, review your life in terms of potential regrets. What would you most regret not having done? What reasons or excuses would you offer for not having done it?

Now, think twice before you decide that it's too late to do the things you would regret not having done. That rocking chair is many, many years away . . .

of people who tend to make the same mistake over and over, risking the same terrible consequences. This is the basis for one of my most important pieces of advice: when what you're doing isn't working, do something else!

Let's look at Erica's case a little more carefully. Erica loses her job and decides her next career should be that of "mother." She envisions a baby, cute and cuddly, that she can feed and water like a pet. Okay, you have to admit that she had a goal, and I've been talking about the importance of goals. So what's the problem?

The problem is that Erica's vision of the future at that moment of decision about motherhood was wholly unrealistic. She pictured a baby in her arms the next year, but she didn't anticipate the baby's developing into a child of nursery school age, or becoming a nine-year-old who might break windows and refuse to clean his room, or being an irritating adolescent who would sulk and openly and brazenly defy any attempts to communicate or be held accountable as a member of the family. (I like the bumper sticker that says HIRE A TEENAGER . . . WHILE HE STILL KNOWS EVERYTHING.)

In short, Erica's sense of the future was so limited, and her degree of self-knowledge in this area was so confined, that she made what I personally consider one of the most important of all life decisions—undertaking parenthood—in a wholly unrealistic manner. It's pretty well established that babies get older, and, barring catastrophe, eventually become adults. Why hadn't Erica thought about that?

My basic definition of future orientation emphasizes the ability to be so realistic and detailed about the future that the future seems almost as real as the present. Clearly, Erica's future orientation was not well developed. As a result, she felt trapped, hopeless, and depressed. I hope it is growing ever clearer to you how important it is to think ahead, anticipate consequences, and take preventive measures when possible.

Erica's tale has a happy ending. She had the right idea about needing a change in her life, but her idea that maybe it should be another child was obviously not the best solution. Over the course of a few sessions, we discussed how happy she'd been when she had a career and some professional goals to strive for. We talked about the possibility of her resuming her career, especially now that her son was old enough to be in preschool and would soon be in school. Erica had been distorted in her "all-or-none" view of having to be a full-time mother. She got excited at the prospect of resuming her career, and soon lost her resentful feelings of "being trapped." It took her a while to commit to that course of action and find a job, but she has done so successfully. Her feelings about her son are very different, now that he isn't her only source of activity or self-esteem. She says, "Being a mother is great, but I'm glad I have my career, too. I wouldn't want to be without either my son or my job." She is completely free of depression and feels "like my old self again."

HOPEFULNESS AND HOPELESSNESS

Considering the great emphasis I have placed on positive expectancy, it would be easy for you to assume that I advocate the positive value of hopefulness in the treatment of depression. In fact, hopefulness *is* a valuable ally when unrealistic hopelessness is a dominant theme in you. However, I am aware of no single pattern that is unilaterally positive or negative *everywhere.* Hopefulness is no exception.

Hopefulness is a positive and motivating force in the recovery from depression, especially when you are unrealistically hopeless, as in believing that you can never have a better job or a better relationship. At the other end of the spectrum, however, is hopelessness that is realistic (and hopefulness that is unrealistic). Consider, as an example, a woman who stays in a highly abusive relationship where she is the object of physical violence or emotional abuse. What holds someone captive in such a painful relationship? Sometimes it's economic dependence; sometimes it's poor self-esteem. Sometimes, though, the answer is "hopefulness." As long as the woman is hopeful that "he will change," she will probably stay where she is. As long as someone is hopeful on the basis of wishes, and not facts, that the job will get better, the relationship will get better, the person will get well, or the situation will improve, he is likely to stay "stuck" in a depressing situation.

Frequently clinicians encourage a client to "let go" of circumstances that the client feels unable or unwilling to release. These efforts to pry the person loose from negative circumstances may be met with massive resistance, which serves to maintain the destructive elements of the client's life. Often the person has become depressed as a result of staying in a bad situation (bad job, bad relationship) in which he is continuously being hurt, but he stays put because of the hopeful illusion that somehow "things will change."

To believe that your spouse will stop using drugs or alcohol, that your harshly critical partner will eventually become loving and affectionate, or that some other individual or circumstance will change is certainly hopeful, but it is your responsibility to evaluate the feasibility of your hopefulness. You have to be able to distinguish between inner fantasy and external reality.

It may seem unusual in light of everything else I've discussed in this chapter, yet it can be therapeutic to encourage in yourself a sense of hopelessness for a *specific* circumstance (not "life"), which *should* be recognized as unchangeable. However, even in such a case, there is a hopefulness that conditions will improve when you recognize the particular situation as hopeless and then take steps to extricate yourself from it. In such instances, you will discover that it is not your personal limitations generating the hopelessness of the situation; rather, it is the circumstances beyond your personal control. Thus, in the absence of self-blame, the likelihood of depression is diminished. These points are discussed in greater detail in Chapters 8 and 9.

Hopefulness and hopelessness cannot be separated; they are two sides of the coin. The unrealistic hopelessness for the appearance of positive conditions and the unrealistic hopefulness for the improvement of negative conditions are common themes that surface in the treatment of depression. A goal of treatment, then, is to understand that the future is not simply more of the same, and that you can take steps today that will result in changes, leading to the belief that life can be fulfilling and worth living.

Neither you nor I can change your past. But tomorrow hasn't happened yet. What would you like to have happen? What about next week, next month, next year, and all the years after that? The things you do now, today, lead to what happens tomorrow and all the tomorrows that follow. Use the skills you're learning to develop a positive and realistic future orientation. All the good things in your life will come from things you do both inside yourself and out in the world that make your life worthy in your own eyes.

A positive future orientation is the starting point for developing everything else you need to break the patterns of depression. Learn all you can learn, and you'll look back one day on how you turned your life around for the better. *Plan* on it!

SUMMARY OF KEY POINTS . . . AND WHAT THEY CAN MEAN TO <u>YOU</u>

- Expectancy refers to your perceptions about the future in general and *your* future in particular. *Whether* you think about the future and *how* you think about it will help determine the likelihood of your recovery from depression.

- The inability to anticipate realistic consequences for proposed actions and the tendency to follow immediate impulses can lead to hurtful—and depressing—circumstances. You have to resist the tug of your feelings when it is clear that they are pulling you in a destructive direction.

- Most people, for biological and cultural reasons, never learn to think ahead realistically. Developing that skill will require patience and perseverance.

- The importance of having goals that are short-term, intermediate, and long-term cannot be overstated. Learn to think about how the actions you take now either fit with or are at odds with your goals.

- Remember, realistic attitudes toward both hopefulness and hopelessness will provide the balance necessary to plan for the future.

Chapter 6

LIFE: IT'S ALL IN
THE INTERPRETATION

There's an old joke, not terribly funny but definitely relevant, about a man seeking the "truth" to the question of the meaning of life. He spends his entire life desperately searching all around the world for the answer to his urgent question. He talks to world and religious leaders, philosophers and poets. He eventually learns of a wise but reclusive guru, living at the top of a forbidding mountain in the Himalayas, who can give him the ultimate answer to his question. So he arranges to get all the equipment he'll need to make the difficult and strenuous climb to the top of the mountain. He spends many days braving freezing weather, avalanches, and rock slides. Physically exhausted, nearly delirious, he finally reaches the mountain fortress where the guru lives. Trembling with anticipation, he encounters the aged guru and humbly asks his question: "Oh, great wise man, what is the meaning of life?" The guru pauses, contemplates the question for what seems an eternity, and then quietly answers, "Life is a bowl of cherries." The young man is incredulous! He's astonished! He takes a step back and yells, "That's it? That's it? Life is a bowl of cherries?" The guru says, "You mean it's not?"

This joke illustrates the main point of this chapter: every human being on this planet comes to terms, in one way or another, with defining the meaning of life in general, and the purpose of his own life in particular. At the very start of this book, I introduced you to the well-known Rorschach Inkblot Test. You may recall that test subjects are shown a series of inkblots and are asked to describe what they "see" in each one. People see all kinds of different things: animals, people, and objects doing and experiencing different things. Each person will interpret the inkblot differently, on the basis of his own personal background and psychological makeup. The inkblots have no meaning in and of themselves. There is only the meaning that people "project" onto them. In psychology, this is known as the "projective hypothesis": when people face an ambiguous situation, they will inevitably project onto it a meaning that fits their frame of reference.

In a broad sense, life is an *experiential* Rorschach. Is there anything more ambiguous than life itself? The principle governing people's responses to a Rorschach is the same principle that governs their responses to life. They make meaning out of and respond to life experiences on the basis of their backgrounds, beliefs, and values. For example, out of all the professions in the world available to choose as my career, I chose to become a clinical psychologist. In my view, my job has the potential to make an important contribution to the well-being of people. However, there are many people who have no interest in psychology and place no value in psychology. I've had people say to me, "You're a psychologist? Why don't you get a *real* job?" Of all the things I could have been in life professionally, why did I choose to become a psychologist? My values of education and service, my emphasis on relationships, and my love of problem-solving made being a clinician a clear choice. Why do *you* do what *you* do? *Why* do you place importance on what you do?

Life offers all of us countless opportunities. Which opportunities we choose to pursue is clearly a reflection of our value systems and the things we've been taught to view as important. Thus, from the choices we make, both large and small, we are the ones who give our lives meaning.

Why is having meaning important? Why is it important to have a sense of purpose? Think about those times in your life when you felt useless or purposeless, and how it affected your mood and self-image. You have an opportunity now to carefully examine this process of making meaning out of the formless inkblot we call "life." You can evaluate whether the things that you have given meaning to in your life satisfy you according to the meaning you've given them, and, if they do not, you can change your life's direction. What is the purpose of your life? Is it to suffer and endure hardship? Is it to seek higher consciousness? Is it to relax, have a good time, and enjoy the ride? Is it to make money? Is it to raise children?

Pause and Reflect #19

Choosing a Life

Many people do not feel that they choose their career or lifestyle. They feel they have just "fallen into it." Do you think that it is a choice not to make a choice? Why or why not?

My response: It is definitely a choice not to make a choice. Every time you avoid taking action to change things for the better, you are making the passive choice to keep things the same. It is self-deception to believe "things just are the way they are." Even when you can't directly change circumstances, you can change your response to those circumstances. Whoever it was who said, "That which you are not striving to improve, you are choosing to let deteriorate," clearly understood this point.

The need to explain things in order to understand them is a basic human requirement. People want things to make sense, and they want and need to understand what's going on. When people are confused or uncertain, they are in an unpleasant internal state, an anxious state, one that can be changed only by attaining clarity and understanding. All the things that you experience, you can find a way to explain. If I ask you for an explanation of why you choose to live where you live right now, you could most likely give me one. If I ask for an explanation of why you treat your friends the way you do, you could probably explain your behavior. If I ask why you use your money the way you do, why you use your time the way you do, and why you react to situations the way you do, you can give me explanations.

DO YOUR EXPLANATIONS HELP OR HURT YOU?

Here is an important question that directly relates to your experience of depression: How accurate or realistic are the explanations you give yourself for the events of your life? You may be good at giving plausible explanations for your experiences, but there can be, and usually is, a big difference between "plausible" and "true."

Let's say someone gave you wrong information or bad advice on a course of action you had to take. You will naturally provide yourself with an explanation as to why that happened. Perhaps you'll conclude that the person was malicious, intentionally trying to deceive you; perhaps you'll conclude that the person was poorly informed himself; perhaps you'll conclude that you were at fault for not double-checking the information you were given.

Regardless of your conclusion, though, the point is that *you'll reach a conclusion about why things happened the way they did.* Through all the things that you do each day, you're continually engaged in a process of explaining to yourself about yourself, about others, and about events in the world around you. Each person develops a style for explaining things to himself. This is what is known as an "explanatory style" or "attributional style." Your explanatory style plays a huge role in how you feel. Consider the example in which someone gave you bad advice. If you conclude that was your fault for not double-checking the information, how will you feel? Compare that to how you would feel if you concluded that the person was poorly informed. And, finally, compare it to how you'd feel if you found out you were intentionally misled. Each interpretation generates a different feeling in you, doesn't it?

The feelings you have are closely related to how you explain the things going on *around you* and *within you*. Let me provide another example. Suppose a friend is going to pick you up so that the two of you can go someplace and do something fun together. Now, suppose that time passes, and your friend does not arrive to get you. With each passing minute, you do a lot of self-talk about this person's being late. You'll notice how, as a result of the things you say to yourself, your feelings change, quite literally from moment to moment. If at first you think of your friend as being insensitive and irresponsible, you'll find yourself feeling angry with him. If you think that perhaps something bad has happened to him, you'll naturally become concerned. If you suppose that your friend may have been in an accident, or somehow been physically injured, preventing him from arriving on time, you become worried, even frightened. If you think that this person doesn't care much about you and that's why he's late, you feel rejected, lonely, even depressed. When your friend finally shows up, forty-five minutes late, your first feeling on seeing him is probably one of relief. Then perhaps irritation, followed by all the other feelings that you've gone through in the forty-five minutes of waiting and wondering what was going on. This is a clear example of the relationship between your explanatory style and internal mood states.

It should now be apparent that *situations that are ambiguous represent risk factors for you.* Not everyone reacts to ambiguity in the same way. Some people form positive interpretations that lead to good feelings. Forming an explanation is a learned reaction, so if your reaction to ambiguity is one that sets you up to get hurt, it is time for you to learn to react differently. The first step in that direction is to recognize that your explanations are made up by you and you alone. They are merely interpretations. They are not facts until you have clear, objective evidence.

How you deal with ambiguity relates to a number of other patterns closely associated with depression. One such pattern is known as "dichotomous thinking," more commonly known as "all-or-none thinking." Different people react differently to ambiguity. The all-or-none thinker will tend to make extreme (and therefore unambiguous) a situation that is actually not at all extreme. For a person to see only black and white in a gray situation is a reflection of that person's need to exaggerate things in order to see them as "clearly" as possible. It means, of course, that the person isn't really responding objectively to what is, in fact, true or realistic.

I mentioned earlier that people generally do not like ambiguity and therefore need to assign meaning to life experiences. What happens when this principle is applied to a situation where the meaning is not clear or where no objective proof can exist? The person who is prone to

Pause and Reflect #20

Tolerating Ambiguity

Reflect on how you respond to ambiguity. When you are unclear about something, do you ask lots of questions in order to try to quickly gain clarity? Or do you let things remain unclear, passively assuming that answers will eventually emerge? This is what is known as a "tolerance for ambiguity." Do you tolerate ambiguity well in some situations (like a relationship) but become intolerant in others (on the job)? How would you assess your tolerance for ambiguity? The need for clarity is potentially very helpful in overcoming depression. The art of skillful living is to form accurate conclusions based on objective evidence, and not jump to arbitrary conclusions in order to avoid ambiguity.

My response: When I say that ambiguity represents a risk factor for you, I am alerting you to the depressing pattern of reading negativity (such as rejection or humiliation) into events that could just as readily be interpreted in ways that wouldn't hurt you. Before you conclude something is negative, gather facts to clear up any ambiguities. Don't assume, for example, what someone meant. Ask! Say, "I'm not sure how to interpret that. What exactly did you mean?" This skill has great preventive value.

extreme thinking will likely state his perceptions as if they are objective facts, even though they are not demonstrable or provable in any way. For example, we have millions of people in this country who believe in astrology, despite the fact that there isn't objective evidence that the position of the stars even remotely affects one's experience. Believers treat astrology as if it were an established fact. But, in the same way that astrologers cannot prove objectively the truthfulness and the reality of their beliefs, I cannot objectively disprove the reality of those beliefs. If I could disprove astrology, or if astrologers could prove it, it would then be a more settled issue. The same is true of countless other similar ambiguous beliefs.

If my client says, "The meaning of life is to suffer," how do I disprove that? How does he prove it? It's simply a belief system a person has, and it's obviously an *arbitrary* belief system. There is no real evidence for or against it that is able to answer definitely the underlying question about the meaning of life. So, people spend their money call-

LEARN BY DOING #31

Reacting in the Extreme

Purpose: To learn to recognize and self-correct "all-or-none thinking" when it surfaces in response to life situations.

Identify a recent occurrence in your life to which you now acknowledge you reacted in an extreme fashion. How did you (erroneously) perceive the situation that brought about such an extreme reaction?

Identify the thought sequence that led to your extreme reaction. For example, if someone gets a grade of B on an examination and then concludes, "I'm a failure because I didn't get an A," or if someone doesn't get a promotion at work and concludes, "I'm a loser," he is demonstrating the all-or-none thinking that is likely to give rise to strong negative emotions. Re-examine situations to which you find yourself giving all-or-none explanations. Your reactions may be reflective of dichotomous thinking and a low tolerance of ambiguity. If so, you've identified patterns to monitor and correct!

ing psychic hotlines, they buy books by people describing their history of UFO abductions, and they buy rare animal parts (such as rhino horn powder) to enhance their sexual potency (driving many species to the brink of extinction for no good reason). Where is critical thinking? How can people possibly believe in unprovable things that ultimately *dis*empower them, like astrology or problems that are said to be carryovers from past lives? (How can it be personally empowering to believe that your destiny is controlled by the position of the stars? Or by Karma? Personal empowerment comes from knowing *you make choices* and that those choices influence your experience.)

The phenomenon of dichotomous thinking can lead people to react to their arbitrary beliefs as if they were facts. If the person is not prone to depression, then that pattern is not serious. However, for you, someone who *is* prone to depression, it represents a potential hazard. It is more important to you than it is to those who are not depressed to *learn to respond as well as possible to the objective evidence that exists when it is available to you.*

You will have to learn to be a critical thinker, always monitoring and correcting thoughts and attributions that can hurt you. To do that, you have to be aware of what defines a situation as ambiguous; I want you to be able to smell ambiguity from ten miles downwind!

LEARN BY DOING #32

Ambiguity As a Depression Risk Factor

Purpose: To help you learn that your interpretation of an ambiguous situation may be negative and hurtful.

Consider the following three scenarios, and see what answers would most likely occur to you:

Scenario 1: Your boss holds a meeting at work and demands that almost everyone you work with be there. You are not told to attend the meeting. Why not? Write your one-sentence response.

Scenario 2: You apply for a job that you want very much. You are told you'll hear something in a week. Two weeks later, you still have not heard whether you're to be given the job. How do you interpret the apparent delay in processing your job application? Write your one-sentence response.

Scenario 3: You meet a close friend for dinner, and throughout the evening he seems distant. How do you interpret your friend's aloof demeanor? Write your one-sentence response.

If you believe that you are an undeserving person, for example, and that you don't deserve to be happy, rephrase that thought as a question: What does someone have to do in order to deserve to be happy? Obviously, there is no clear, unambiguous answer to that question. That question is as ambiguous as "Is astrology real?" or "Why do innocent babies die?" There is no clear, definitive answer. Your answer will be dictated by what your background has led you to believe, but it may not at all be a reflection of what's really true. Any answer you generate is only your projection to a question that is essentially unanswerable. Part of learning to break the patterns of depression soundly is to *learn to bypass, as best you can and as often as you can, ambiguous questions for which there is no one true answer.* Train yourself to recognize ambiguous questions quickly, and to avoid generating speculations that will put your emotions on a roller coaster.

Stop and really think about your reaction to such everyday situations. Is your reaction positive, negative, or neutral? On the basis of the principles already described in this chapter, it's possible that you have altered your responses from what they would otherwise have been. If you gave the typical response of a depressed individual in Scenario 1 in the Learn by Doing box above (the one in which the boss didn't ask you to attend a meeting), you are likely to think that your job is in jeopardy or that you are not a valued "part of the team." You would see your employer's action as a fault of your own rather than as a statement about the other person's experience. If your explanatory style is negative, then you are less likely to consider the positive possibility that your boss doesn't want to distract you from what you're doing or take up your time with something that has nothing to do with you.

In Scenario 2 (the one about the late word on your job application), you may have come to the conclusion that the delay is a bad omen for your job prospects. If your style is positive, then you are likely to interpret it as a nondepressing statement about the methods or relative inefficiency of this company's hiring practices. In Scenario 3 (the one about your friend being distant), if your explanatory style is negative, you are likely to interpret it as a rejection or as a statement of your friend's disregard. A more positive explanatory style would lead you to think that your friend is preoccupied with a problem that has nothing to do with you or that he is immersed in some internal experience, such as anxiety or depression.

As you are learning, optimism has a structure. When faced with ambiguity, optimists readily adopt a positive interpretation. It may not be any more accurate, but it certainly feels a lot better!

So, what's the point? Well, there are a couple of important points here. First of all, in learning about attributional style, you're learning that life offers us many ambiguous situations on a steady basis. All you can do is interpret each experience according to your belief system and background—in short, according to your projections. With a depressed individual, the projections tend to be negative and self-damaging, thereby feeding the negative thoughts and negative ruminations that fuel negative feelings. You are now learning that the interpretations (attributions) you make every single day, many times a day, all play a *very* large role in how you feel.

A preventive tip is to think ahead and do your best to recognize ambiguity in a situation *before* you go into it. Get used to asking yourself, "Where's the ambiguity?" Before you think something and make the mistake of noncritically believing it, get used to the task at hand. Where can you get objective evidence that either confirms or contradicts your interpretation? Does such objective evidence exist? Can you know in advance that there is no clear answer to your question, and that there is no objective information available? For example, in Scenario 1, you don't *know* why the boss hasn't included you in the meeting. You can certainly speculate on all kinds of possibilities: the boss is preoccupied and forgot, the boss doesn't like you, the boss has other plans for you, the boss knows the meeting topics don't apply to you, and so on. You can think of many reasons that the boss hasn't included you, but the reality is that the only person who knows why you weren't included is the boss. Yes, you may be able to obtain objective information, but not until you talk with that person to find out exactly what's going on—assuming that your boss will be truthful with you (another ambiguous assumption to evaluate).

In the second situation, the only information available to you about being hired is from the potential employer; you have no way of knowing what's going on in that company until you find out directly. So it's possible to alleviate your uncertainty by calling the interviewer to ask about the status of your job application. The decision to call is not a simple one, though. Part of what you have to consider is that even if the information *is* objectively available someplace (in this case, with the employer), will it work to your advantage or disadvantage to seek it? You may decide that it's driving you crazy not to know whether you're going to be hired, so you'll call to find out the status of your application. However, it is also possible that your call may annoy the person doing the hiring.

Now you have a new dilemma, a new ambiguous situation. Should I call or shouldn't I? Will I annoy that person or won't I? Maybe you feel that your rapport with the interviewer was good enough to permit you to make the phone call. The interviewer may be pleased by your interest and enthusiasm. On the other hand, you may have thought the person distant, difficult to communicate with. He may be irritated with having to answer your phone call. It now becomes your judgment as to whether to contact the interviewer.

In the third scenario, the only person who knows why he is being distant is your friend. Again, you have a choice. You can resolve the ambiguity by directly asking, "You seem distant. Is that right? If so, can you tell me why you are distant?" Now, you face the same range of choices as before. Will your friend be annoyed that you're trying to engage him on a level that he doesn't want to discuss? Or will he welcome the opportunity to put your mind at ease by acknowledging the validity of your observation and letting you know that it's nothing you've done; it's that he is preoccupied with a problem that he's not ready to talk about? The point is that you, as a critical thinker, *learn to weigh your options.* You learn to think of the possibilities available and to anticipate the likely consequences of each one. In short, you learn to think things through.

I would hope the following phrase, or some variation of it, eventually becomes automatic: "This situation is ambiguous. I could project negative stuff into it and make myself feel lousy, but rather than depress myself unnecessarily, I think I'll just tolerate the ambiguity until I get more information. I remember Yapko saying, 'Prevention when possible!' "

LEARNING TO TOLERATE AMBIGUITY

For the depressed individual, attributions dictate the quality and range of experience. If you're going to recover from depression and prevent future depressions, you'll need to *handle ambiguity* in as effective a way as possible. When you get into situations that in and of themselves do not have clarity (such as what the "right" career is), and you seek clarity, you may be setting yourself up for tremendous frustration and even depression. Recognizing ambiguous situations in advance is best, but a quick recognition when you're in one will help you avoid making arbitrary and hurtful attributions.

The same principle of tolerating ambiguity applies to many other value-laden questions. What is the best use of my day off? Is there a right way to live my life? What is the right treatment for my depression? Who is the right person for me to be in love with? How should I spend my Christmas bonus? Where's the best place to go for our vacation? Should I tell my colleague he may be fired? Should I remind my sister that Mom's birthday is next week? These are questions about what's "best" or what's "right." Not very many things in life are so all-or-none.

As someone prone to depression, you will have to judge each situation on its own merits. There is no single rule that applies equally well in all life situations. It becomes your task to recognize your strengths as well as the areas in which you are most vulnerable. Only then can you *regulate your actions according to the result you want, not simply according to how you feel.* When you learn to suspend making arbitrary attributions and, instead, look for clear evidence, you will recognize the situations that feel good and enhance you as well as the situations that feel bad and diminish you. Then you can choose to pursue the good ones.

I want to emphasize the necessity for becoming skilled in making attributions that are not simply projections which arise from your hurt and despair. Those feelings can too easily lead you to form such negative conclusions about life, relationships, or yourself that you can end up aggravating your own depression by noncritically believing them.

You need to get outside your own subjective interpretations of events and circumstances in order to evaluate them critically. You may be incorrect in your assessment. Or you may come to recognize that there is no opportunity to be objective because no objective information about the situation exists. To then arbitrarily adopt the most negative and depressing conclusion is simply self-defeating. In such cases, there is absolutely no more evidence for your negative conclusion than there is for any other.

TYPES OF ATTRIBUTIONS

There are specific ways to describe the characteristics of attributions you make. Often, in psychotherapy, my task is to teach my clients to "re-attribute" their experiences. That is, I want them to reach a different conclusion about some event, perhaps a less hurtful or more accurate one. Learning to characterize your attributions puts you in a better position to decide whether your attribution for some experience is appropriate. If it isn't, you can strive to re-attribute it.

INTERNAL-EXTERNAL ATTRIBUTIONS

One way to describe an attribution pattern is according to whether it is "internal" or "external." An internal attribution is one in which you conclude that whatever happened was your own doing. For example, if we reconsider the scenario in which you meet a close friend for dinner and he seems distant, an internal attribution is, "He must be angry with me," or "He thinks I'm dull and really doesn't want to be here with me." From such statements, it's evident that you're attributing your friend's aloofness to something about yourself. The focus of your attribution is an *internal* one to explain the negative situation.

The opposite type, the external attribution, is one in which you conclude that the situation happened because of something outside yourself. If you come to the conclusion that something is not going very well for your friend and he is brooding about it, you are attributing his demeanor to something that is going on with him rather than with you. If you are clear that you are not responsible for your friend's aloofness or his bad mood or his problems, it saves you from feeling unnecessarily guilty. It also allows you to be more emotionally available to him as a friend. On the other hand, you don't want to form an entirely external attribution if you really *do* have something to do with how he's feeling. How to resolve the ambiguity? You probably know the answer by now. Ask!

It bears repeating that a common but distorted way of thinking is to form internal attributions for negative situations. This is also known as "personalizing," or taking impersonal things personally. Every time you personalize a negative event by putting your feelings or self-esteem at the center of it, you place yourself in the position of having to react to it. That is how people ride "emotional roller-coasters"; they automatically form internal attributions for negative events, a reliable path to becoming overemotional and depressed.

STABLE-UNSTABLE ATTRIBUTIONS

A second pattern involves a "stable" or "unstable" attributional style. A stable attributional style was discussed in the previous chapter, where I talked about people's expectancy and their depressing view of hurtful situations in their lives as being stable, or unchangeable. When you view a condition as permanent, you are making a stable attribution. As you previously learned, the error in forming a stable attribution about some hurtful circumstances is to assume that they will remain the same when, in fact, they may realistically be expected to change.

Thus, another important skill is the ability to determine when a situation is unchangeable (stable) and when it is not, and whether it's for internal or external reasons. Only then can you make realistic decisions about whether to "hang on" or walk away from the situation. It is a common theme among my depressed clients to either hang on to things they should let go of (bad relationships, bad jobs, bad investments) or let go of things they should hold on to (pursuing an education, maintaining a relationship, finishing a project). Knowing when to hang on and when to walk away is an art clearly worth mastering. When is the appropriate time to let go? When the situation holds no *realistic* possibility for improving. To assess this accurately, you have to make sure it's not your depression leading you to believe it's hopeless.

With an *unstable* attributional style, the individual sees situations as having the potential to change. The perception that "things can change" relates very directly (as you learned in the previous chapter) to your level of positive motivation and your willingness to participate in your own recovery. On the other hand, it can also keep you trying under impossible circumstances, unrealistically believing that bad conditions will improve, while you sink deeper and deeper into depression. The reason I devoted the entire last chapter to expectancy was to help you make sure that your view of your future, based on appropriate stable and unstable attributions, is *realistically* hopeful.

GLOBAL-SPECIFIC ATTRIBUTIONS

A third way to characterize the patterns of your attributional style relates to global and specific attributions. You make global attribution when you believe that what you're experiencing in a given situation affects *everything* you experience. A specific attribution limits your conclusion to the situation at hand. Someone making a global attribution following a stressful job interview is more likely to say "I'm a loser" than he is to say "I'm not as good at job interviews as I'd like to be," a more specific type of appraisal.

You may recall the discussion in Chapter 4 on compartmentalization and see its relevance here. Part of developing a realistic and nondepressed attributional style is to be more specific about the things you are experiencing. That's especially true when what you're experiencing is negative. There's a world of difference between saying, "I don't do very well on job interviews," and saying, "I am a loser as a person."

Consider now your attributions about your own experience of depression. I ask you, "Why are you depressed?" How do you respond? If you say, in essence, "I'm depressed because I'm just no good at building a life for myself. I've always been depressed, so I guess I'll always be depressed. I'm just a total mess," then, as you can see, your attributions are *internal, stable,* and *global* in nature. In fact, there is a very strong relationship between this type of attributional style *for negative events* and the experience of depression.

In therapy, I regularly teach my clients to be more *external, unstable, and specific* in their attributions when bad times hit. In other words, I want to teach people that: (1) it isn't they, necessarily; (2) it is not always going to be that way, necessarily; and (3) it doesn't affect all that they do, necessarily. Sometimes the problem is the situation, and it's going to change, and it's only that one specific situation that's a problem. Learning to identify—situation by situation, interaction by interaction—whether the attributions are *objectively* internal or external, stable or unstable, global or specific, is critical to recovering from depression now as well as preventing future episodes.

PREVENTION WHEN POSSIBLE

I sincerely hope you will learn to think clearly enough about your life experiences to be able to use preventively the skills you are learning here. In this chapter, you have seen that you may project negativity into ambiguous situations, you may think in more extreme forms (such that your perceptions tend to be more black and white than gray), and you may, by that kind of extreme thinking, be putting yourself at risk for responding to situations incorrectly. You've also seen the different ways your attributions, or patterned explanations, can directly affect your mood and outlook. If you watch yourself handle a situation in a way that isn't effective, based on your inaccurate perceptions, you may come to the conclusion that you're no good or you're somehow not worthy. That's how you can unwittingly reinforce your depression.

You're now in a much better position to see the relationship between your general outlook on life and your explanatory style. Someone who views situations in a negative way and predicts that things will always be negative might be called a pessimist. A person who consistently views things in a positive way, who predicts positive things for the future, and who tends to see the positive in ambiguous situations is someone we could describe as an optimist.

Obviously, optimism feels better than pessimism! We remember the old metaphor of the glass that can be viewed as being half full or half empty. The amount of liquid in the glass, of course, is the same; the only difference is the person's viewpoint. The person who sees life as "half full" feels better than the person who sees life as "half empty."

Which perspective is "right?" Who knows? It is another ambiguous question, like "Is there a universal truth?" So much of life is ambiguous, and our response is so subjective, that many philosophers (known as "constructivists")—and therapists, too—have come to the conclusion that reality is "whatever you think it is." Their attitude is that "truth" is often unknowable, and that the real value of the person's life is defined in terms of personal happiness, success, love, and humanity.

Is reality whatever you think it is? For those who believe that astrology is real, it has meaning. The person who believes that all things happen for a reason will look for reasons for everything. For those who believe that dreams have meaning, their dreams have meaning. Those

Pause and Reflect #21

Let's Step Outside and Settle This

How do you feel about my saying that you will forever have to monitor your beliefs? Can you see how it will empower you to step outside your beliefs in order to consider their relative usefulness, rather than being confined within the beliefs and never having the ability to question their accuracy, worth, or role in your life?

My response: It may seem like a burden, at first, to have to monitor your thoughts and correct the distorted ones. As you will quickly discover, though, it becomes a habit you'll love because of all the problems it prevents and the wonderful sense of control it reinforces in you.

Your attributional style plays a significant role not only in your depression, but also in your level of productivity and your physical health. Attributional style affects mood, and mood affects physiology and behavior.

---

who believe life is burdensome find it burdensome. Your beliefs dictate the course of your actions and feelings. Since your viewpoint plays such a large role in how you feel, you will forever have to monitor your beliefs, and you'll always have to "step outside" them long enough to evaluate whether each belief is valid and works for or against you.

ATTRIBUTIONAL STYLE AND PRODUCTIVITY

Let's examine more closely the relationship between attributional style and the level of productivity. We can do so by considering the case of John, a client of mine.

The Case of John: Aiming for the Stars

John is a salesman, selling plumbing parts to building contractors. His success depends on his ability to sell as many plumbing parts as possible to all the contractors who build residential, commercial, and industrial buildings. Naturally, John would like to monopolize the market and have all contractors use only the parts produced by his company. The reality, of course, is that John has competition.

Other companies that manufacture plumbing parts would like to sell their products.

John is confident of the quality of his company's products, but he recognizes that competing companies can sell similar parts, although of lesser quality, at cheaper prices. John is so confident that his parts are superior in quality to his competitors' cheaper parts that he sets himself the task of making 100 percent of his calls result in orders for parts. John's ambition is noble but misguided.

John came to therapy feeling very discouraged about his work. He often found himself anxiously awake in the early morning, ruminating about whether he was going to make enough sales to earn the commissions he lives on. He was irritable at home, withdrawing from his wife and children, and was unable to relax and enjoy leisure activities. He was definitely depressed.

I asked him, "What factors influence whether or not a contractor purchases your parts?" John's immediate answer was "My ability as a salesman." I asked, "Is that the _only_ factor that determines whether or not you make a sale?" His automatic answer: "Yes."

From that exchange alone, you can see why John is so anxious and depressed. Take a moment and think about it before you read on. Realistically, what salesman of _any_ product successfully signs on all of his potential customers for his product? What is the effect of John's assuming full responsibility for a successful sale? Isn't it interesting that John sees no factors other than personal (internal) ones that influence his success as a salesperson?

I asked John whether any other factors might also influence a sale. He was puzzled. "Like what?" he asked. I said, "Isn't it true that other people sell a similar product at a cheaper price?" He acknowledged that but added defensively, "That product isn't nearly as good." I asked, "Aren't there some buyers who consider price and nothing else, who don't care about the quality of the product?" John reluctantly agreed. "Yes, I suppose there are some people who consider price alone." I then asked, "Isn't it true that there are some people who, when you happen to call on them, may have had a bad morning? Perhaps they've gone over their budget that very morning and they don't feel like talking to a salesman. Maybe they're concerned about a mountain of debts just when you're asking them to take on another expense." Hesitantly, John agreed. I went on, "Isn't it true that some people will not be responsive to you because they've already made a deal with someone else? They may not want to tell you about that because they'd rather avoid getting into a discussion about your parts versus someone else's." John agreed once again.

I continued to identify factors having nothing at all to do with

John's skills that could influence whether he would make a sale. You could almost see the light bulb turn on in John's head. All of a sudden, it became obvious to him that no salesman could realistically expect to sell to 100 percent of the market. Instead of blaming himself, he began to realize that there were many <u>external</u> reasons to account for his not being 100 percent successful. When he viewed his situation from that more realistic perspective, John actually became cheered by recognizing that he was successful in nearly 80 percent of his sales calls. John's more realistic expectation about his work permitted him to feel good about how much he did accomplish for his company.

This case illustrates how a person's attributional style affects his mood and outlook and, consequently, his productivity. John was making fewer sales calls to his previous customers and avoiding meetings with new ones. He attributed his avoidance to the fear of failure and of rejection. He was afraid that he might not be able to make a sale, yet making a sale was his only criterion of success, even though it was not entirely in his control. His internal attribution was getting in the way of the very results he wanted.

The relationship between attributional style and level of achievement is currently being examined in a variety of work and school environments. Why, for example, a child with a high level of intelligence and great academic potential will produce only poor grades may have little to do with the teacher, the classroom, or the other students. It may have a lot to do with the child's attributional style. He may not see any reason to learn; if he has no future orientation about the worth of an education, then his motivation to succeed will be marginal and his grades will reflect that. Or if he is afraid to make a mistake, generating a global attribution that says, "I'm stupid if I make an error," then his ability to learn is going to suffer. Martin Seligman discusses these issues insightfully in his book *The Optimistic Child*.

Similarly, if a worker doesn't see any opportunity for professional or personal gain (no promotion, no raise, no special recognition), why should he bother to perform? As you learned in the last chapter, good motivation is directly tied to a person's sense of a positive outcome. One way of thinking about your own level of motivation, then, is in terms of your attributional style. Your internal ("It's my fault"), stable ("I can't change"), and global ("I'm a loser") attributions will have a detrimental effect on your work output and level of achievement, because your motivation has been sapped or because you distrust your ability to succeed.

ATTRIBUTIONAL STYLE AND HEALTH

Attributional style also plays a role in your general health and well-being. One of the things now known about depression is its relationship to physical problems and illnesses. Often, in the earlier years of a person's life, illnesses take such simple forms as headaches, backaches, stomachaches, and fatigue. There is evidence to suggest that, as one ages, there is a steeper decline of physical health if depression isn't adequately addressed. Why depression affects health less in earlier years but more in later years is not well understood at this time. But the relationship between the decline in physical health and increased age is becoming more apparent from the data being gathered.

Your level of depression affects your body's immune system in ways that are now being studied in the relatively new field called psychoneuroimmunology. Research data show a relationship between people's outlook (their relative degree of optimism or pessimism) and their general health. The immune system is the body's natural defense system against disease. Depression seems to weaken the immune system, allowing illness-causing agents more readily to gain a foothold in your body. Overcoming depression will promote greater physical health to go along with your improved emotional well-being.

As the fatigue associated with depression dwindles and your energy starts to return, it would certainly be helpful to improve your relationship with your body in deliberate and healthy ways. I strongly urge you to get into an exercise program or some sort of physical training (walking, swimming, karate, fencing, tennis, *anything*). Using your body in active ways that help it get strong and harmonious with your feelings is essential to recovery from depression.

The fact that your mood plays a strong role in your body's natural defense system is an important piece of preventive information. So is the fact that your mood helps determine whether you are likely to guard your health and follow prescribed treatments. As you learn to avoid the pitfalls associated with depression, you can truly expect to feel better, physically and emotionally.

BREAKING YOUR PATTERNS OF ATTRIBUTION

Your levels of optimism and pessimism reflect the way you think about your life and the world around you. It's important for you to identify and avoid the hazards described in this chapter: dealing with ambiguous situations; thinking in all-or-none terms; personalizing things that aren't personal; viewing changeable things as unchangeable; and responding globally instead of dealing with specifics. *Without self-correction, you continually run the risk of accepting attributions that maintain pessimism and, consequently, bad moods, low productivity, and poor health.*

This chapter orients you to the nature of your own attributional style. It can help you to develop a tolerance for ambiguity when that's appropriate and necessary, identify relevant sources of information when they exist, and learn the arbitrary nature of your interpretations of life experiences. Your attributions can be the fuel for the despair and the negativity of depression. You're learning that you don't have to get attached to the hurtful ones as if they are real or "true."

I have not made a judgment about the relative worth of optimism or pessimism. Instead, I am making a strong case for your *judging each situation on its own merits,* learning to search out and make use of facts when they exist. I also encourage you to invest less of yourself in explanations—good *or* bad—that have no possibility of being proven. You can control your degree of emotional involvement with the different things that you experience. That way, you don't get too heavily invested in a viewpoint that is arbitrary and hurtful, and may eventually be proven false by further experience.

I strongly encourage you *to respond more to what's out there in the world around you than what is in your head, especially when what is in your head generates depression.* The things that you want for yourself, the peace of mind, the comfort of a well-run, well-balanced life—these are good things to want. And they are reasonable things to want. What you're slowly and deliberately learning, I hope, is that there are ways to get what you want, but only when you're not getting in your own way with arbitrary and hurtful explanations that hold you in depression's grip.

SUMMARY OF KEY POINTS . . .
AND WHAT THEY CAN MEAN TO <u>YOU</u>

- People have a need for meaning, a need for understanding. This leads you to interpret why things in life happen the way they do.

- When people face an ambiguous situation, they project meaning into the situation according to their background or frame of reference. Your personal history and range of experiences are all you have to draw on in making life decisions.

- Since life is ambiguous, the understandings and explanations that you have for the events of life are arbitrary, but they play a huge role in how you feel. So, instead of just letting yourself think anything, you have to exert some control over your thoughts and the choices you make based upon them.

- Situations you face that are ambiguous—that have no objectively true interpretation—represent potential risk factors for depression if you interpret them negatively. You can save yourself a lot of bad times by learning to instantly recognize ambiguity and restraining yourself from automatically making and believing negative attributions.

- It is essential for people prone to depression to respond as well as possible to objective evidence when such evidence is available. When you recognize a situation as ambiguous, strive to get facts to respond to so that you don't respond only on the basis of your feelings.

- Once you recognize the ambiguity that exists in a situation, you can weigh your options and anticipate the likely consequences of each of the options. I want you to know you have choices about *whether* and *how* to respond to things that happen in life.

- Learn to regulate your actions according to the results you want and *not* simply according to how you feel. Your feelings matter, but they can also get in the way of your reaching greater goals.

- Explanations or attributions for experience can be described as internal or external, stable or unstable, global or specific. You can learn to recognize your attributions and correct them if necessary.

- Depressed people most frequently make internal, stable, and global attributions for negative events. Optimistic people tend to make external, unstable, and specific attributions for negative events. When you face life situations, push yourself to form conclusions most likely to help, not hurt!

Chapter 7
HOW YOU THINK AND WHAT YOU THINK

Previously, I mentioned that certain styles of thinking and particular belief systems can cause or worsen depression. In this chapter, I will be specific about the ways of thinking and the beliefs that underlie depressive states. As you read about these common but potentially damaging beliefs, I hope you will become more aware of and objective about your own beliefs. Then you can be selective about which beliefs have merit and which are hurtful in given situations.

COGNITIVE DISTORTIONS

Along with other experts, Aaron T. Beck, M.D., a well-known psychiatrist who has studied the thought patterns of depressed individuals for more than thirty years, observed that depressed people frequently make errors in interpreting experience. Beck devised the approach known as "cognitive therapy" (discussed in Chapter 1) for identifying these distortions and correcting them. They are listed in Table 3, on the next page. Some are already familiar to you from previous discussion.

Each of the cognitive distortions in the table represents a way of interpreting information and experience that encourages depressed feelings. The cognitive model teaches that your emotions are directly related to your perceptions, and you are encouraged to deal with what goes on in your life as rationally as possible. Rationality means learning to think clearly and weigh factual evidence before forming conclusions, thereby keeping your feelings in line with reality.

Healthy doses of rationality, when practiced and integrated, can

Table 3. Cognitive Distortions

- All-or-none thinking (dichotomous thinking)
- Overgeneralization
- Mental filter (selective perception)
- Disqualifying the positive
- Jumping to conclusions
- Magnification (catastrophizing) or minimization (trivializing)
- Emotional reasoning
- "Should" statements
- Labeling and mislabeling
- Personalization

alleviate most episodes of depression and even prevent many of them. How? By keeping you from getting lost in the hurtful aspects of your distorted thinking. Just as I described in the preceding chapter, on attributions, the ever-present danger to a depressed person is the trap set by his own thinking. Let us therefore carefully consider each of the cognitive distortions.

ALL-OR-NONE (DICHOTOMOUS) THINKING

All-or-none thinking, as we saw, is the tendency to make extreme interpretations, seeing things as black and white, with little or no gray. Can you identify what is extreme about these examples? Getting a B on an exam and feeling like a failure; not getting a promotion at work and feeling like a loser; not getting unanimous approval and feeling like a reject. Whenever you let a small unpleasantness ruin an entire experience, you are showing evidence of dichotomous thinking.

You may recall from the previous chapter that extreme thinking is often related to a low tolerance for frustration and ambiguity. People like clarity and certainty; confusion is unsettling. A lack of certainty about the best response to a situation, or the meaning of something, can create a sense of urgency in you, a need to set things straight. In striving to reach a clear understanding as quickly as possible (to escape the frustration of uncertainty), you may make errors in judgment that will eventually prove quite costly.

Let's apply the principle to a real situation. Consider Katherine, who has been dating Steve for several months. Katherine feels it's important to get a commitment of some sort from Steve if she is to continue dating him. If Steve is unsure about his feelings for her, or about the wisdom of making a commitment at what he thinks is too early a point in the relationship, he will be unlikely to make any promises, and this leaves Katherine unsure about Steve's real feelings. If Katherine needs certainty, she is likely to increase the pressure on Steve for a commitment. The extra pressure she puts on him to eliminate the uncomfortable ambiguity of the relationship is just enough to make Steve feel that Katherine is too demanding and too urgent. That scares him. Steve tries to leave things a little looser, and Katherine interprets that as evidence that he doesn't really care. She further increases the pressure on Steve to commit, he becomes even more determined not to do so, and he breaks up with her. Katherine's discomfort with uncertainty led her to apply pressure to Steve to get clarity, but what she got was a breakup. Would the breakup have occurred anyway? Maybe—but maybe not.

Many life situations, perhaps most, are ambiguous by nature. Few situations are all or nothing. Adjusting positively to life means recognizing the many shades of good, normal, right, and moral. The idea that two individuals can live virtually opposite lives yet both be "right" represents a leap to higher consciousness. Such a leap, however, allows for greater acceptance of others. By being less extreme, you will judge others and yourself less harshly. When you make the critic living in your head "lighten up" a bit, you'll see more of what you do as being perfectly all right, even though it may differ from your original idea of "perfection" or from the way you did things before.

OVERGENERALIZATION

When you let one experience represent an entire class of experiences, you are overgeneralizing. For example, if you have ever reacted to an entirely new situation as if it were the same as a situation you've experienced earlier, then you've demonstrated the cognitive distortion of overgeneralization.

In the world of depression, overgeneralization surfaces when a person forms a broad conclusion and then noncritically applies it to all similar situations. If you have a negative experience, you can recognize that it was a negative experience of a *particular* type, or you can use it to overgeneralize about your worth as an individual ("I'm no good"), the value of life ("Life stinks"), and all similar situations ("It *always* happens like this").

Overgeneralizing involves not making clear distinctions between separate but similar situations in order to recognize how situation B differs from situation A. For example, if you suffer a hurtful experience in a romantic relationship and you conclude that *all* men [or women] are cruel or selfish, you are overgeneralizing. Why? Because you can't say what *all* men or *all* women are like on the basis of one person (or even several others like him who hurt you).

At the breakup of a relationship, some people decide, "You can't trust women [or men], so I will never let myself be vulnerable and fall in love again." They build their entire lives around that overgeneralization, and years later the irrational decision still holds. They are still alone, and now they are more miserable than ever. The solution is to learn to discriminate between situations, *for each situation is best judged on its own.*

Treating *all* men or *all* women as if they are the same is an obvious distortion; if you want to save yourself the agony of a breakup, you should learn to judge who is worthwhile being involved with and whom you would do well to avoid. There are many wonderful men and women out there, but there are also many men and women who are not to be trusted. Your job is to learn to tell them apart, considering each according to his or her makeup. Some tips to help you do so are provided in Chapter 11.

Pause and Reflect #23

Overcoming Prejudice

Are you prejudiced? In what ways do you think of or treat all members of a group as if they were the same? What experiences have led you to be prejudiced against yourself by overgeneralizing feelings of helplessness, negative self-worth, and other such depressive patterns? How do people overcome prejudice? What things can you do to explore the possibility that perhaps you are better than you realize? <u>Do them!</u>

My response: When you treat all of you as if you are the one part of you that you don't happen to like, you are prejudiced against yourself. When people act in a manner contrary to the stereotype, the stereotype weakens and eventually must be revised. I encourage you to act against your limited view of yourself as much as possible, going out of your way to do things inconsistent with your negative view of yourself. Take care, of course, not to do them blindly; use forethought and a viable plan. If you need help in formulating such a plan, then get it!

In addressing the beliefs that commonly underlie depression, you should be aware that it is the overgeneralization of these beliefs that leads to their noncritical acceptance. Without the ability to see differences, even between similar situations, you may end up responding to them as if they are all the same. Applying such a "one size fits all" pattern to life experiences means you will be more likely to make repetitive mistakes, thereby fueling your negativity, poor self-esteem, and depression.

Have you ever noticed how difficult it is for people to overcome their prejudices? Well, consider your poor self-image as a prejudice against yourself. If you have concluded that you are helpless or incompetent, *challenge that negative view of yourself.* Go out of your way to do things that can alter that view. For example, if you feel you cannot learn new things, attend a class in something that interests you and do all you can to make it a successful experience, even hiring a tutor if need be.

MENTAL FILTER

If you focus on one aspect of an experience to the exclusion of other pertinent details, you are using a mental filter. The uncanny ability of depressed individuals to focus on the negative only causes or exacerbates negative feelings. If you recognize that your first and most automatic reaction to situations or people is likely to be negative, challenge yourself *not* to stop there. Go out of your way to find aspects of that same situation or person that are at least neutral, maybe even positive. As you become practiced in going beyond focusing only on the negative, you will enlarge your field of vision to include the neutral and positive. For example, if a cashier shortchanges you in the grocery store, you may automatically assume that the individual is dishonest or is trying to take advantage of you. But now push yourself to think of his action as neutral (he was too busy, too distracted talking to another cashier) or even positive (he was rushing to serve you, overanxious to perform well). Notice the differences in your feelings when you make a negative versus a neutral or positive interpretation. This skill, like all the others in the book, requires practice. First, you must recognize how your behavior and thought affect your depression, and then you must go beyond your habitual way of doing things to break that pattern.

DISQUALIFYING THE POSITIVE

The tendency to reject positive input from others by devaluing its worth or ignoring its significance is called "disqualifying the positive." In general, we tend to discount anything that contradicts our existing belief system. "Cognitive dissonance" refers to our tendency to ignore, minimize, or twist new information to make it consistent with what we already believe. If you think of yourself as a nice person, for example, and you then do something mean to someone, does that change your self-image? No; you find a way to explain it away ("I was stressed out") but continue to see yourself as nice. The mechanism of cognitive dissonance keeps your world stable, leading you to respond to life in a patterned and reasonably consistent way. Someone whose belief system is negative will, predictably, discount the positive. Someone who is optimistic is just as likely to reject any negative feedback.

If your negative beliefs go unchallenged, the mechanism of cognitive disso-

nance can keep you depressed. For example, if you feel negatively about yourself and someone contradicts your self-image and tells you something positive but you reject it, then you are left with only the negative, and your self-image continues to be poor.

In order to break the vicious cycle, you can start with simple things. When someone pays you a compliment ("That's a nice dress"), say, "Thank you." Stop yourself from discounting the compliment ("This old thing? It's just something I've had for years"). You can let others appreciate you even if, at that moment, you do not appreciate yourself. Otherwise, you may as well tell the person who gave you the compliment, "I don't agree with you and I can't allow you to feel that way." The absurdity, of course, is that the other person already *does* feel that way!

You can even go a step further and examine why he gave you positive feedback. Is it possible that you could learn to judge yourself by the same standards? (How good would you feel if you could do that?) When you get a little more comfortable accepting compliments, you may learn to offer yourself some compliments that acknowledge your having done well in something. Eventually, as you become more experienced at accepting positive feedback, from others as well as from yourself, your view of yourself will grow more balanced and realistic. After all, there *are* things you do well. There *are* things about you that are really great. Learn to recognize and use the strengths and abilities that have been there all along and that you discounted. That is what developing your "personal power" is all about.

JUMPING TO CONCLUSIONS

A major error people make, whether they are depressed or not, is to take an incomplete bit of information and make up the missing material with their own thoughts. The result is that they reach a conclusion even though there are few if any facts to support that conclusion. Any time you form a conclusion about anything, I would encourage you to ask yourself, "How do I know?" Your response should be more objective than "It's a feeling I have." The goal is to minimize the subjective thinking that you use to interpret what goes on around you.

If you use yourself as the only frame of reference in trying to understand the actions of others, you are assuming that those people think the same way you do. Also, you are saying that they should value what you value and should take into account the things you take into account when deciding on a course of action. *Using only your way of thinking to understand others will lead you to be hurt or disappointed when you discover that they are not playing the game of life according to the same rules you are.* The things that matter to others may not matter to you, just as the things that matter to you may not matter to them. If you want to be realistic about others, learn to respond to what matters to them, for that's what will motivate their actions toward you far more than your wishes or expectations.

To avoid jumping to what may be erroneous conclusions, you need enough factual information to make a clear and rational decision. How do you know when you have enough relevant information? When are all the facts you've gathered sufficient to suggest a reasonable course

LEARN BY DOING #36

Discounting Others

Purpose: To help you change your negative self-image by learning to accept compliments from others as genuine statements of how they feel about you.

Some people can't accept a compliment. Not only may they not accept it; they may openly disagree. "My performance was awful; I made lots of mistakes," or "How can you think I'm good-looking when I have such big ears?" Such rejections tell the other person, in essence, "I don't think you should feel that way." Hence this exercise.

Ask people close to you to tell you something positive about yourself—something they like or respect. Then, with a straight face, respond to the compliment by saying, "I'm sorry; I can't permit you to feel that way." If you can be playful when doing this exercise, approaching it with a sense of humor, you may discover something important about how you limit or even prevent positive feedback from coming your way. How can you hope to feel good about yourself if you do not permit yourself to enjoy the kind of positive feedback that can raise your self-esteem?

of action? The answer: when you have eliminated as much ambiguity as you possibly can.

A common trap is what is known as "mind reading," where people act as if they can read the minds of others. They respond to what they presume the other person is thinking, never bothering to find out whether it is accurate! For example, you may not want to tell your parents bad news because you "know" they won't be able to handle it. When you "mind read," *you* decide how the other person will react, never giving him the chance to live up (or down) to your expectations.

You can't read other people's minds, even when you are "sure" you know what they're thinking. Is there a reason that you can't ask the person to describe his thoughts so that you can check on whether you are realistically assessing his thinking? Even if you are very sensitive and skilled in your relationships with others, even if you are correct 99 percent of the time (no one is 100 percent), how do you know this is not the 1 percent when you are way off? It is imperative for your own mental health to test your perceptions of reality by asking for feedback whenever it is available.

In another manner of jumping to conclusions, a depressed individual forms an image of the future in which something negative will happen. By anticipating that a situation will go badly, the person has all the negative and depressed feelings associated with it even though it has not yet happened! For example, an employee wants to ask his boss for a raise but is so sure he'll be denied that he doesn't even bother to ask. Then he feels as if he's been mistreated by his boss. From other things I've mentioned in this book, it should be apparent to you how powerfully your expectations influence your experience.

If you create negative expectations and are then unable to differentiate the images you've thought up from the realistic possibilities, you are heading for discomfort and depression. I highly recommend that you learn to create positive images and that you spend time sitting quietly, in a relaxed way, developing detailed images and strong feelings associated with success. (Some specific methods for doing so are in Chapter 5.) Techniques of self-hypnosis, meditation, and other such focusing methods are best for doing this. Building positive expectations of success feels infinitely better than expecting the worst. It offers the secondary benefit of serving as a "mental rehearsal" for carrying out the desired behavior later.

By avoiding conclusions based on too little information, you can avoid obvious mistakes. When you have to make a decision, or when you try to understand why something is happening as it is, it is your job to gather as much information from as many sources as possible to develop the most balanced and realistic perspective of that situation.

MAGNIFICATION (CATASTROPHIZING) OR MINIMIZATION (TRIVIALIZING)

Depression can lead people to exaggerate and focus on negative things and, likewise, minimize or discount the value of positive things. Another concept relevant to understanding your depression is "dissociation," which means breaking global experiences into their component parts. When you amplify your awareness of one part of an experience, you thereby separate it from other parts of that experience, and your awareness of them is then diminished. If I ask you to focus your attention on your right hand, you will not be paying attention to your left foot (until I direct your attention to it by mentioning it). By

LEARN BY DOING #37

Filling in the Information Gap

Purpose: To highlight how readily you can project your interpretations onto ambiguous situations, leading to the very real possibility that you will mistake your inferences for "truth."

Explain the reasons for each of the following events:

1. John drinks too much.
2. John and Mary are getting a divorce.
3. Mary was fired from her job.
4. John's car was towed away.
5. Mary did not get the raise she asked for.

Are you surprised at how easily you can create reasons for events you know nothing about? What does that have to do with your experience of depression? Write out the relevant principle.

---

focusing on the sounds of things going on around you, you will have less awareness of the feelings inside you. "Selective attention" means focusing on "this" so that we have less awareness of "that."

Your conscious mind cannot pay attention to more than a few things at once. Obviously, what you choose to pay attention to influences what you choose to ignore. For example, if you focus internally on your feelings of failure in a performance you gave, you miss the opportunity to realize that most of your audience liked what you did. Can you predict what your feelings will be if you focus on your negative thoughts instead of the positive feedback given to you by others? Focusing on what you consider your shortcoming prevents you from noticing that someone is complimenting you on that same characteristic. In the same way, focusing on the work you have not completed can prevent you from noticing how much you have finished. In a third example, focusing on the one thing about yourself that you do not like can prevent you from noticing anything about yourself that you do like.

Catastrophizing means seeing all too easily how any situation has the potential to become a disaster. It's a good idea to anticipate how things can go wrong in life and take preventive steps when possible. However, to see impending disasters everywhere is an obvious exag-

LEARN BY DOING #38

Finding Balance

Purpose: To create a balance to negativity by deliberately focusing on only the positive, emphasizing that the positive is always there. It's just a matter of whether you notice it!

Spend an entire day forcing yourself to notice and respond only to the positive. Give lots of compliments to others, be patient and understanding, and strive to be syrupy sweet. What differences in your internal state do you become aware of? What does this suggest to you about being all-positive or being all-negative? What ability does it take to become comfortable with the reality that all people's lives, including your own, have both positive and negative aspects? Can you explain how some negative things can happen without ruining everything?

geration. The anxiety so often associated with depression is a direct consequence of seeing danger even in objectively nondangerous situations. Reducing your extreme emphasis on disaster will also reduce your anxiety.

EMOTIONAL REASONING

The distortion known as "emotional reasoning" refers to relying solely on your feelings as the basis for interpreting experience. If you assume that your feelings reflect the way things really are, then you are setting yourself up for a steady flow of negative interpretations and distorted perceptions that will reinforce depressed feelings. Someone says, "I can't go out and socialize. I feel that when I walk into a room, everyone knows I'm a loser, and I just can't bear it." That person is showing evidence of emotional reasoning. In other words, he is using his subjective feelings to explain why he can't socialize rather than seeking objective evidence as to how people do, in fact, respond to him. You can end up responding to your feelings about socializing instead of recognizing how social opportunities may go well and how other people may be friendly. There can be a huge difference between what your feelings tell you and what is really going on.

Consider a woman who desperately wants romance in her life. On the basis of how much she cares for the man she is dating, she feels that he must care as much for her. She does not believe her feelings for him could be so strong unless his were as strong for her. She believes this even though he has never directly expressed any loving feelings to her. After a few months of dating, she starts planning marriage, a family, and a life with him.

In reality, however, the fellow has no intention of any serious commitment to her. He's a self-indulgent, opportunistic man who wants a regular sex partner and nothing more. He is manipulative and self-serving and will say almost anything to have his way. If she had learned more about him as a person *before* she got caught up in her marriage fantasies, she'd have known that he is not marriage material. Looking for objective evidence that things are as you think they are is the best prevention of the risky pattern of emotional reasoning.

Human emotions can be easily manipulated. It is not difficult to guide someone's feelings in a particular direction, especially when you use his wishes against him by promising him things he desperately wants that you can't or won't deliver. (How many people get conned out of their money with phony promises, or get used in relationships by someone who seemed so caring?) Based on that recognition, I say to you flatly that FEELINGS CAN LIE; FEELINGS CAN DECEIVE. What you *feel* is going on may have little or no resemblance to what is actually going on.

People who are skilled manipulators can be very good at making you feel a certain way strictly for their own personal gain. Some television evangelists, for example, can make you feel guilty enough to seek forgiveness or afraid enough of eternal damnation to seek salvation; either way, they try to get you to "send your dollars to God" at *their* address. The movie industry is perhaps the best example of how easily human emotions can be manipulated. In a couple of hours of film, moviemakers can create images and dialogue designed to move you up and down the emotional spectrum at their will. What about salespeople? Have you ever been smooth-talked into buying a lemon of a car or some useless household appliance? How did the salesperson get you to make the purchase? Obviously, at the time you bought it, you *felt* that the salesperson could be trusted and the product would be satisfying. If it turned out to be a lemon, then you probably blamed yourself for having been influenced by what you later concluded was an unscrupulous salesperson. Such examples make it apparent that people's feelings can be easily manipulated, that you need to consider more factors than just your feelings when making important decisions.

Television evangelists, moviemakers, and salespeople may seem like obvious manipulators. What catches people off guard, it seems, are the manipulations of those who "shouldn't" be manipulative, like boyfriends or girlfriends, brothers or sisters, parents or friends. To be realistic, though, you have to appreciate that they are human beings first, and whatever else they might be to you in your life follows from that fact. No one is above attempting to get what he wants from others—including you! It helps to realize, therefore, that your feelings about someone or some situation have likely been influenced by forces past or present. That's all right, *if* you come to appreciate that your feelings are not the only vehicle for making decisions.

If you believe you should rely solely on your intuition ("trust your guts") to make important decisions, you are leaving yourself vulnerable to people and situations that can influence you unconsciously. *All you have to do is think of situations in which your intuition was wrong to remind yourself how easily feelings, including "gut" feelings, can lead you to make errors in judgment.* This is *not* to say you should discount your feelings, especially since the message throughout this book has been to accept *all* parts of yourself as potentially valuable. The issue here concerns whether you rely *solely* on your feelings to make important judgments or whether you take into account additional, more objective, factors.

You can treat your feelings as one indicator of how to respond to something. I suggest, though, that you go outside yourself, beyond your feelings, in search of relevant facts whenever that is possible. In my clinical experience, the biggest mistake that depressed individuals make is in responding to their own feelings (dreams, wishes, desires, fantasies, expectations) without looking for some objective evidence that what they are feeling is realistic. It bears repeating that your feelings are one basis for deciding a course of action, but beware that they offer the most subjective and arbitrary basis. Remember, FEELINGS CAN LIE! Whenever possible, find a more objective means for deciding on your course of action.

LEARN BY DOING #39

Feelings and Facts

Purpose: To encourage you to take "gut feelings" and translate them into something more specific and objectively observable <u>before</u> acting on them.

Answer these questions in detail before you read further.

1. How do you know whether you can trust someone?
2. How do you know whether someone loves you?
3. How do you decide whether you can succeed in a challenge you want to attempt?

Do your responses reflect only your feelings about the situation? Or do they reflect objective insights about the situation itself? What do you conclude about the quality of your responses?

"SHOULD" STATEMENTS

A depressed individual often has an overdeveloped sense of responsibility. This can lead you to say, "I *should* go visit my mother"; "I *should* catch up on paperwork this weekend"; "I *should* clean the closets." If you think of all the internal "shoulds," as well as those which come at you from others, then you already know what a burden the "shoulds" are. (The psychologist Albert Ellis wryly calls the process "shoulding" on yourself!)

The standards you are "supposed to" live up to are communicated to you from the day you are born. As a child, you didn't have as much choice as you do now. It is now your responsibility as an adult to establish whether an expectation placed on you by others or by yourself is comfortable and realistic. If you live up to it and make someone else happy but make yourself miserable, it's time to re-evaluate your position. You have to know your own needs and respect them if you are to resist being pressured or bullied into a course of action that is not right for you. It's important, as a person with integrity, to be socially responsible and to honor the "shoulds," but remember that other "shoulds" may well be empty self-sacrifice.

The relationship between "shoulds" and feelings of guilt, anger, and frustration is readily apparent. Go easy on the "shoulds" in your life. You can do this by establishing your own values (instead of respond-

LEARN BY DOING #40

The "Shoulds" in Your Life

Purpose: To re-evaluate the responsibilities you've assumed in order to determine their appropriateness in your life.

List things you "should" do in your life. What "should" your profession be? How "should" you spend leisure time? How "should" you spend money? How "should" you feel about religion? To all of these questions and to the many more you think up, ask "Who says?" Who knows better than you what is good for you? Why should anyone else have the power to dictate how you "should" be? What ways are there to take that power back to use in your own best interest? When is it to your advantage or the socially responsible thing to go ahead and do what you "should"?

ing to the values of others), defining your own standards of success (instead of responding to others' ideas of what defines your worth), and becoming more realistic about what is and is not an acceptable performance by you in an area that you consider important to a positive self-image.

LABELING AND MISLABELING

From the previous discussion of overgeneralization, it may be apparent to you that people often label themselves, or others, and then respond to the label instead of the person. Why people do this is not all that difficult to understand. By labeling someone or a group of individuals, you no longer have to do the mental work of recognizing distinctions and responding to individual differences. It is certainly much easier to respond to a label than to a person.

Some research done over twenty-five years ago, and every bit as valid today, illustrates clearly the point about the problems that can result from labeling others. It involves the labels of the mental health profession.

PHONY PATIENTS

The psychologist David Rosenhan conducted an experiment in which "normal" graduate students and professional colleagues admitted themselves to a number of psychiatric hospitals. They wanted to find out just how long it would take the hospital staff to recognize they really weren't "crazy."

At the very start, each one told the admissions staff that he was hearing a voice that said, "empty," "hollow," and "thud." The assumption of the staff member, of course, was that if someone sought admission to a psychiatric hospital complaining about hearing a voice, then he must indeed be crazy. Once the phony patient was admitted, his task was to act entirely normal. How long would it take the hospital staff to discover that he was normal, not crazy? Remarkably, it took an average of nineteen days for all the individuals to be released!

Other patients, however, concluded far more quickly that these individuals were normal. In fact, many were curious as to whether the phony patients were journalists writing an exposé on the hospitals, or whether they had some other hidden purpose. The staff, on the other hand, interpreted nearly everything these individuals did as pathological. If one took a nap, he was described as "socially withdrawn." If one sat around and watched television, he was said to be "escaping into fantasy." If another sat and wrote notes about his experiences, he was "behaving compulsively." In other words, once these people had acquired the label "crazy," everything they did was interpreted according to that label.

The experiment dramatically demonstrated a profound lesson for the mental health profession. We have to learn, and keep learning, to respond to the actual behavior and patterns of an individual, rather than seeing him in terms of a convenient label.

The same point is true about labeling yourself. If you have an experience like depression, and then you label yourself according to that experience, you are "locking in" a negative self-perception. You may tell yourself or others, "I can't do that; I'm depressed." Labels can become traps. If, say, your girlfriend breaks up with you and you then label yourself a "loser," you create a negative perception about your overall ability to relate to women. That is distorted, because the breakup was with a particular woman. Even if it's a series of failed relationships you've suffered, you now know that it isn't "you"—it's

LEARN BY DOING #41

Who Are You?

Purpose: To highlight that when you label yourself or anyone else, it's all too easy to lock in a perception that makes change more difficult.

List ten words or phrases in response to the question "Who are you?" You may describe your professional, social, intellectual, or other characteristics. What emotional tone is associated with each word? Is it a label that makes you feel good about yourself, or is it hurtful to you in some way? Is the label fixed or changeable? How would you feel if it was negative and unchangeable? What labels do you attach to others of importance in your life? Do the labels work to each person's advantage or disadvantage? What would these people have to do to get you to change the label?

your way of choosing women and establishing relationships with them. You may need help with your social skills, but not because you are a "loser."

In Chapter 6, under the discussion of the stable-unstable attributional style, I emphasized that individuals who perceive their situation as unchangeable (stable) are less likely to recover from depression quickly or completely. That underscores the need to deal with each situation by itself, instead of relying on a label that represents a generalization. What does that suggest to you about the label "depression"?

PERSONALIZATION

"Personalization" refers to the tendency to take personally things that are not at all personal. For example, if your department's budget is cut and you assume it is because your work is not valued, you are personalizing an event that may have no personal basis. As you have learned, before you jump to a personalized conclusion, you'd be wise to get some objective information. Before you conclude that someone did something just to hurt you, or before you conclude that a situation happened just to victimize you, it will be to your great emotional advantage to pull yourself out of the emotional loop and attempt to find out objectively whether it has anything to do with you at all. *Ask before you react!*

Keep in mind that others may make decisions affecting you that you do not feel very good about, but they are *not* making those decisions just to hurt you. For example, your child's moving away from home and going off to college is not a slap at you as a parent. It is a stage in your child's growing up. It may not feel so good when he's leaving, but his becoming more independent is ultimately what you intended, isn't it?

People do what they want or need to. Without taking it personally, you should accept the choices others make as right *for them*. Of course, if you learn that someone consistently makes selfish decisions that hurt you, then you'll need to work at expecting much less from that person.

COMMON BELIEF SYSTEMS
UNDERLYING DEPRESSION

Earlier in this chapter I focused on patterns associated with depressed thinking. Now I present some of the most commonly held depresso-genic (depression causing) beliefs. The noncritical acceptance of these beliefs, I suggest, can put you at risk for depression. I don't mean to say that these beliefs are inherently wrong, but they are wrong enough *at times* to cause you potential emotional harm.

No "truth" operates equally well in all situations. Every situation must be judged on its own so that you can decide *whether* and *how* to respond. What is true of one situation may not be true of another. What was true yesterday may not be true today. What seemed reasonable before may be totally unreasonable now.

Unfortunately, the beliefs described in this section are casually tossed about as truisms, statements that seem beyond question. But accepting these truisms without question may lead to emotional difficulty when you find out the hard way that what you thought was true is not. In presenting each belief, I will comment briefly on its limitations to encourage some critical thinking on your part. Then you can determine for yourself when and where that particular belief system may be of use and when and where it may cause you difficulty.

LEARN BY DOING #42

Distinguish Will from Way

Purpose: To emphasize that positive motivation is not in and of itself enough for reaching a goal. Developing relevant skills is at least as important as being well-motivated.

Can you recall an instance in which someone suggested that you would have accomplished what you were unsuccessful at if you had really wanted to succeed? What was your reaction? Did you focus on your feelings of failure and incompetence, or were you able to evaluate objectively whether success was even possible? Try creating a strategy—a series of specific steps—to determine whether success is possible in an endeavor before you invest too much of your will in it. Of course, you can't always be guaranteed success, but when you do choose to take risks, you will do so knowingly. There are few guarantees in life, yet learning to invest yourself wisely is an important skill to have.

Sometime when you feel playful, experiment with trying to motivate people to do impossible things: "Fly! Flap your arms and fly!" Tell them, "If you really want to, you'll be able to!" More seriously, though, what if you were to say, "Heal yourself of AIDS"? Can you see the danger in defining accomplishments only in terms of motivation?

WHERE THERE IS A WILL THERE IS A WAY

If you reduce all problems to a simple question of motivation, where do other vital factors, such as objective possibility, emotional or physical costs, and emotional and physical limitations, enter the picture? To suggest to you that if you really want to do something, then you will, is to place on you a huge burden of personal responsibility for success. It does not give you the opportunity to question whether you are, in fact, personally responsible for, or even personally capable of, achieving the successful outcome. The net result of this belief system is an overwhelming sense of guilt if you fail. Goals must be realistic.

Your will is not enough if achieving a result is not possible or not in your control. You may have an intense desire for your child to be a brilliant physician who discovers the cure for cancer, but if he prefers to be an artist and pursues artistic interests over scientific ones, then the situation is beyond your control. Despite your will, there is no way.

200

Should he become a physician and have a strong will to discover the cure for cancer (just as countless other researchers have), that does not mean he will find a way. It is not a question of motivation; rather, it is first a question of possibility. What he wants may not be possible.

EVERYTHING HAPPENS FOR A REASON

Have you noticed how the need to find meaning in life keeps surfacing in relation to depression? Wanting to find a reason for the things that happen in your life is motivated, in part, by the need to create and maintain a sense of control. Having reasons for experiences implies that there is an order to things, an organized plan for the way things unfold in your life.

For many people, it is too threatening to think that things may happen in a random way, so whenever something happens, they look to find a reason, even if they have to make it up. If they cannot find a logical reason, they fall back on faith. Faith in a Divine Plan provides comfort for many people who still manage to be critical thinkers. For others, however, faith is a crutch that prevents their becoming more skilled in managing their lives. Belief in a Divine Plan may explain the unexplainable—it may make some people feel better—but it puts them in the shaky position of trying to guess at God's intentions or believing in incredible things, like astrology and anonymous telephone psychic advisers.

One woman I worked with, named Marta, was driving when her car was rear-ended. The accident left her in considerable pain from neck and back injuries, and when she first left the hospital, she began to look for the meaning of the event. Unfortunately, in her search for the meaning, Marta decided the accident resulted from personal flaws. She thought that because she left work early that day, she was not where she "should" have been, working away as a good employee should. Next, Marta hypothesized that her car was rear-ended because she was not doing other things she should have been doing. As she thought of these other things at which she was less than perfect, and considered them the reasons for the accident—thereby deducing "God's meaning" for her—she grew more self-blaming, anxious, and depressed.

For Marta to accept that she was the victim of a random event was not in line with her belief system that "it must have happened for a reason." The collision was certainly bad enough, but its negative effects were compounded by her interpreting it as having a reason (which

Pause and Reflect #24

Making Up Reasons

Throughout human history, people have manufactured reasons for unexplainable events. They have created sun gods and moon gods, angry gods that threaten people with displays of thunder and lightning, star alignments that predict our life, and even lines in the palm of our hand that reveal our future.

Think about life experiences that are currently beyond objective explanation, yet are "explained" by elaborate hypotheses. What about babies who die, or young people who lose their limbs to disease? What about a person whose terminal disease suddenly remits unexpectedly?

Why do these things happen? Does your belief in fanciful reasons help you or hurt you in other life situations? Does your belief have limits, or does it explain everything in a nice and tidy way? Would not believing create too much ambiguity for you to tolerate? How do you know?

My response: People make up all kinds of crazy explanations for unexplainable things, and many don't seem to recognize the absurdity of these imaginings. Desperate people, looking for reasons to believe, become easy prey to con artists, who can sound sincere while speaking utter nonsense. Unless you have the ability to think critically, as I emphasize over and over, you may easily get drawn into hurtful situations. Vulnerability comes from need. Good people will not take advantage of others' vulnerabilities, but self-serving people won't hesitate to do exactly that. Being vulnerable doesn't have to mean being foolish.

involved God's wrath, no less). There *are* events that take place in life that are random. We call them "accidents" and "coincidences."

THERE IS ONE RIGHT WAY TO LIVE

Socialization leads you to form a value system by which you judge all your experiences. If you are intolerant of others who are different from you, devaluing their beliefs, customs, or worth, you can easily evolve a belief system that, says, in essence, "My way is the right way; therefore, everyone else's way is wrong." You need look no further than your daily newspaper or the nightly news to see ample evidence that many individuals subscribe to the belief that theirs is the right way, the only way. People kill or abuse others for worshiping the "wrong" god, or for having a different political viewpoint, or for living a different lifestyle. Klan rallies, gay bashers, gang wars, skinhead violence, and other such devaluing or dehumanizing examples are evidence of these tragically distorted belief systems.

In depression, you may actually be abusive of yourself in a similar way. If you have feelings and values that make you uncomfortable, you may be your own harshest critic for not living "the right way." You may abuse yourself emotionally for feeling something you think you shouldn't, because it's "wrong." Some things *are* wrong, but some things that are labeled "bad" are not only normal but inevitable. For example, you may chastise yourself for not wanting to go to your child's school play. Or you may go, but still feel something is wrong with you for not being excited about it, when in reality it's nothing deeper than you don't like that kind of thing, especially when you're tired from work and just want some time to yourself.

What is the *right* way? It is fairly obvious, if you stop to think about it, that, despite the seemingly vast differences between cultures around the globe and individual lifestyles in a defined area, very different approaches to life are still successful. It takes flexibility to recognize that there are many ways to live successfully. The question is not so much one of "right" as of "efficient" and "useful." If what someone does works for him, leave him alone—even if it is not what *you* would do. If someone makes a career choice that you do not like, or spends money on things you do not value, or enjoys what you do not enjoy, that is the individual's decision. If the choices are acceptable or desirable to that person, and he understands their implications for himself, then it is usually (but not always) best to stay out of it.

To the extent that you are rigid and attempt to impose your beliefs on others, acting in a "controlling" manner, you are discounting their ability to make decisions for themselves. Predictably, they will eventually react negatively, and will not only reject your input but reject you as well. And you, hurt and angry, feeling rejected, naturally find that your depression deepens. If others attempt to impose on you their idea of the right way to live, you must be able to resist them by recognizing that your way, though different from theirs, is also useful and effective. There are many ways to go through life. Just make sure yours works to *your* satisfaction—and does no harm to others.

JUDGE NOT LEST YE BE JUDGED

Is it wrong to be judgmental of others? Many people are taught to be accepting of all people. Instead of being critically aware of another individual's strengths or limitations, they respond only globally to the individual. Through a lack of critical consideration, the almost "blindly accepting" person erroneously believes that others can do anything they really want to (here again is the "where there's a will, there's a way" belief). So they assume that they can motivate others to be kind, sensitive, or communicative without evaluating whether this is in the person's makeup or behavioral repertoire.

Consider, for example, the popular book by Robin Norwood called *Women Who Love Too Much.* Norwood describes women who commit themselves to a relationship with a man and then give of themselves excessively, much to their own detriment. One woman believes, "If I'm sexy enough, my husband won't cheat on me." Another believes, "If I'm supportive enough, my husband will stop drinking." Still another believes, "If I'm non-demanding enough, my husband will be more motivated to work." By engaging in distorted emotional reasoning, these women assume that if they are "this" enough, then their husbands will stop doing "that."

A big part of the problem is the apparent inability of these women to make accurate judgments about the men they are involved with. The first woman, for example, assumes that if she is sexy enough, she can prevent her husband from straying. She does not ask the most relevant question: "Is this a man who is even capable of being faithful?" She incorrectly assumes that he will make a commitment to her solely on the basis of her weight, and whether he is loyal is entirely up to her. The error in her thinking should be apparent. He may be a man who does not value commitment or loyalty, so _regardless of what she does,_ he has no intention to be faithful to her. If she believes, however, that his loyalty is based on her weight or demeanor, she will try harder and harder and get more and more frustrated and depressed when she is unable to get from him what she wants. She will blame herself instead of recognizing that the limitation is his.

So is it right to judge others? Yes—right _and_ necessary! Judging others in order to determine _whether_ they are motivated to provide the things that you want in a relationship is essential if that relationship is to be a satisfying one. It is important to _know what you want from others,_ and it is equally imperative to *know whether others can willingly provide the things you want.*

YOU ARE RESPONSIBLE FOR ALL THINGS THAT HAPPEN IN YOUR LIFE

It is virtually *impossible* for you to be responsible for *all* things that happen in your life. Others exert an influence upon you, and their influence is inescapable. It is wishful thinking to believe that if you have the right attitude or approach, you can make anything happen. The reverse is equally true. It is debilitating to believe that if you have the wrong attitude, then the worst things will happen to you. Thinking "bad" thoughts, for example, will not cause you to be rear-ended when you're sitting at a stop light. Your internal makeup plays a large role in your experience, but the external world around you also affects you to a significant extent in ways you can't do a thing about.

YOU MUST SOLVE YOUR OWN PROBLEMS

Here you are, reading a self-help book. While I hope you are finding it valuable in helping you break the patterns of depression, I know that one of the traps depressed people often set for themselves is the distorted perception that seeking help is somehow wrong, a sign

Pause and Reflect #25

The Value of Help

Of what value may another person's opinion be when you are feeling "stuck"? Can you recall a time when you felt stuck and someone said or did something that really helped? In your view, when should someone seek therapy? How much pain should someone be in before going to see a doctor or dentist? Define clearly for yourself how and when you will know it is time to seek outside help. Will it be before things reach crisis proportions?

My response: As a clinical psychologist, I have an obvious bias toward the positive value of good psychotherapy. It is a tragedy for people to suffer needlessly with misinformation or problems that could be effectively resolved. When should someone seek help? When he knows he needs to "do something different," but has no idea what that may be. And he should do it before life gets ugly.

of weakness. What an unrealistic self-imposed burden to carry! You did not learn all by yourself to view the world the way you do now. You were socialized by many people who were influential in shaping your experiences, ideas, and values. To believe that new learnings and new experiences, particularly when they are related to solving your problems, must only come from within creates an extreme disadvantage.

I have pointed out to you all along how distorted a depressed individual's thinking can be. That should make clear that if you get all caught up in your own thinking, it may be hard to find a more objective or realistic way of looking at things. Unless you have the information and tools this book provides, how will you know what you're missing? Just as you did not develop the problem-causing perceptions all by yourself, you should accept that the problem-solving perspectives may also come from outside yourself. There's a lot of great and valuable information out there. Use it!

A COMMITMENT MUST ALWAYS BE HONORED

The ability to make meaningful commitments to others is a corner-stone on which any society is built. To "be as good as your word" is a highly valued trait in *all* societies. Others base their trust in you on your ability to carry out a course of action you are committed to. As deeply as I value honoring one's commitment, however, I know there are times when circumstances demand that you renegotiate a previous arrangement.

The most obvious example of a situation in which a commitment must be re-evaluated is divorce. Most couples marry in an atmosphere of love, lust, a desire to be together always, and the wish to create a happy, healthy family. Adjusting to the reality of marriage, including the sharing of daily experiences, establishing joint goals for the future, and dealing with the stresses and strains of living, may lead to changes that create distance between the marriage partners. Situations like economic stress, different professional goals, and decisions about the quality of life can drive a wedge between the partners. Too many couples give up without trying to improve things, but it's also true that not every marriage can or should be saved.

Consider a specific example. When Rod and Patricia married, they firmly agreed that they would never have children. It is now years later, and Rod says he wants children. Patricia, however, is still clear that she does not want to be a mother. Should she sacrifice her mental health and potential for happiness by having a child she doesn't want in order to honor the commitment of "till death do us part"? Or should she recognize that circumstances have now changed to the point where it would be detrimental, even destructive, to maintain the commitment? Should Rod give up his desire to have children because years ago he didn't want them? Is there room for compromise in such a case? (As you can see, some things *are* "all or none.")

This is but one example of a difficult choice faced by millions of Americans, evidenced by a national divorce rate that slightly exceeds 50 percent. All those who divorced are not bad people who could not honor a commitment. Rather, most of them painfully and responsibly faced the harsh reality that what was worthwhile at one time had later become destructive.

I happen to be a fan of commitment, having been happily married for twenty years. But, as a realist, I recognize that circumstances can change, requiring one to "let go." Each person must decide at what point it is right to let go of a painful circumstance. In general, until you have defined that point clearly, and until you know without a doubt that you have done everything possible, including getting other views of the situation, it is premature to try to let go. My experience suggests that most people are successful in letting go of a painful commitment when they are absolutely sure, beyond the shadow of a doubt, that they have done everything they could do to remedy the problem.

There is nothing worse than having later doubts: "Did I do everything I could? Perhaps if I had . . ." Self-recrimination can cause feelings of guilt and depression by making you believe that if you had done something different, the painful circumstances might have been avoided. You can prevent doubt later by convincing yourself *before* you let go that you have done everything you possibly could.

THERE IS ONE BEST SOLUTION TO A PROBLEM

In the same way that it is unrealistic to believe there is only one right way to live, it is important to recognize that there are many ways to address the problems you face. Consider this book as an example. From the very beginning, I described different ways to conceptualize and treat depression. Each of the ways *works*, which is why I included them. It is not a question of which one works best. The better question to ask is *which one works best for a given individual in a given situation.*

Sometimes there is a clearly identifiable "best" solution. At other times, there will be a variety of solutions, each capable of producing a desirable result. In some ways, it is like being asked which is the "best" car to buy. Best for what? Speed? Looks? Reliability? Resale value? Status? Comfort? Gas mileage?

The goal in addressing this belief system is to help you evolve a stronger framework for problem-solving. Life poses continuous challenges for us. The more effective you are as a problem-solver, using different approaches according to each situation, the more likely you are to get positive results in a wider range of situations. The underlying philosophy promoted here for finding things that are effective is a practical one. If what you're doing works, then continue to do it. *If what you're doing doesn't work, do something else.* And if you're not sure what else to do, ask someone who can help you explore the possibilities.

IF YOU ARE FAIR, YOU WILL BE TREATED FAIRLY

The Golden Rule we all learn as young children teaches us that if we treat other people well, we will in turn be treated well. The problem is that not everyone subscribes to the Golden Rule. Too many individuals have a very different set of morals and ethics, and there are even some people out there who do not feel any twinge of guilt in deliberately taking advantage of or hurting another person. (Clinically, they are called "antisocial personalities.") The belief that you should not be judgmental or critical of others places you at an extreme disadvantage if you simply rely on the Golden Rule when you deal with such people.

Those people who have no intention of responding fairly in a situation will respond only to their selfish interests, regardless of whom they may hurt. I do not suggest that you develop a streak of paranoia. I do suggest, however, that you focus less on your *feelings* about someone (emotional reasoning, again) and become more aware of the true nature of the individual you are dealing with. This is especially important if you are going to form a personal or romantic relationship, where the risk of getting hurt emotionally is even greater. You need to be aware of that person's values, communication and problem-solving skills, background, expectations, ability to respect different choices you may make, and other relationship skills.

Learning as much as possible about someone you want to be involved with is necessary if you are to make a realistic determination of how much of yourself to share with this individual. As a general principle, I suggest that you exercise care in making self-disclosures until you are sure that the other person is respectful and appreciative of what you have to share.

There is a marked difference between "paranoid" and "cautious." Slowly and deliberately learning about another person is an effective way to judge realistically whether the relationship can progress in a positive way and to a satisfying degree. If the person does not have "patience" and "understanding," for example, and those are things you want in a relationship, then you may discover the person's limitations the hard way if you come to rely on him. Prevention when possible!

YOUR FEELINGS ARE THE MOST IMPORTANT PART OF YOURSELF

It is a cartoon therapist who encourages his clients to always "get in touch with your feelings." Those mental health professionals who advocate an awareness of feelings as the highest form of self-knowledge will have to come to terms with the potential limitations of that viewpoint. Since your feelings can deceive you, and since depressed feelings are often clearly distorted, why emphasize your awareness of them? This is not an all-or-none issue. Your feelings *can* be accurate and appropriate for the circumstances; I suggest, however, that no one assume feelings are always accurate or *always* the most important part of a person. They are *at times*, but at other times they can be quite irrelevant, even misleading.

EMOTIONAL INTELLIGENCE

One of the most important books I should like you to read is *Emotional Intelligence* by Daniel Goleman. Goleman does an excellent job of presenting the perspective that a great intellect can be severely constrained by the inability to respond well to life situations with emotional sophistication.

Pause and Reflect #26

Success in Spite of Your Feelings

Identify accomplishments in your life that you achieved by placing the goal ahead of your day-to-day feelings. If you have a college degree, think how you managed to stay in school for so many years. How did you make yourself go to class, write papers, study for exams, even at those times you would rather have been doing <u>anything</u> but school work? How did you maintain the continuity of your education even though there were lots of times when you felt like quitting? What personal resources did you call on? How could those same resources serve you well in other areas of your life? Think of <u>any</u> specific accomplishment of yours that took time to achieve. How did you stay with the goal despite your varying levels of interest and energy?

Goleman identifies specific skills that reflect what he calls emotional intelligence, what some are now calling EQ. Emotional intelligence embraces such abilities as knowing your emotions, managing your emotions (impulse control, for example), motivating yourself, recognizing emotions in others, and managing relationships well.

In *Emotional Intelligence,* Goleman makes the point that it's not an either-or choice of intellectual or emotional sophistication. Rather, both dimensions of human experience have value. He observes that more emphasis is placed on intellectual development than on emotional, to everyone's detriment when people engage in senseless violence or make poor life decisions. As you may now realize, this entire book is about actively building your emotional intelligence.

Clearly, focusing only on distorted negative (or positive) feelings and using them as a guideline for action can place you at a distinct disadvantage. It should be obvious that feelings are not *necessarily* the most important part of an individual in all circumstances.

In some situations, your feelings *will* be most important to you. But at other times they may be the *least* important part on which to focus, because getting wrapped up in them delays or even prevents the effective handling of a situation. The goal, as always, is to be selective. That is the core of emotional intelligence.

Take the time to consider these questions carefully: When is it important to focus on your feelings? And when is it important to shift the focus away from your feelings? Always remember, *you are more than your feelings.*

CONCLUSION

The emphasis throughout this chapter has primarily been on the cognitive dimension of your experience. While I emphasize the role of all dimensions of experience in generating depression, it seems apparent that much of your experience is determined by your belief system and patterns of thinking. For that reason, I have encouraged you (through the "Pause and Reflect" and "Learn by Doing" exercises) to challenge your subjectivity by striving to find objective evidence whenever possible. Every pattern of thought and every belief system discussed in this chapter can be useful in some place, but it can also be detrimental in some other context. Your task is to develop mastery of these principles so that you can discriminate and apply them effortlessly, situation by situation, to your best advantage.

SUMMARY OF KEY POINTS . . .
AND WHAT THEY CAN MEAN TO <u>YOU</u>

- What you think and how you think generally plays the biggest role of all the factors that create and maintain depression. After all, the choices you make in life are derived from your perceptions, whether they are right or wrong.

- There are common and easily identified cognitive distortions or errors in thinking that can fuel depression. By understanding that you can't accept whatever floats through your mind as valid, you can be more selective about what to respond to within yourself.

- All-or-none (dichotomous) thinking is the tendency to make unrealistic and extreme interpretations of your experience. An example is when someone thinks, "I must be an idiot, because I got a B on the test."

- Overgeneralization is the use of one experience to represent an entire class of experiences, as when someone thinks, "You just can't trust anyone in a position of authority."

- The "mental filter" is the distorted perception by which you focus on one aspect of experience to the exclusion of other important details. An example: "I know he canceled the date because he didn't want to see me. Sure, he said he was sick and I could hear him cough and sneeze, but still . . ."

- Disqualifying the positive is the tendency to reject or devalue positive input from others. An example: "I did a lousy job—some of the evaluations only said 'good,' not 'excellent.' "

- Jumping to conclusions involves taking a small piece of information and padding it out with your subjective thoughts, by which you reach a conclusion not justified by the facts. An example is someone thinking, "He didn't return my call because he doesn't want to face this situation."

- Magnification or minimization involves exaggerating negative things or minimizing positive things that happen in your life. An example: "My car broke down. I'll never get ahead financially," or "Sure, I got a raise and a promotion, but the lights in my office still flicker, and that bothers me."

- Emotional reasoning is the use of your feelings as the sole basis for interpreting experience (as if your feelings always accurately reflect the way things really are). An example is someone thinking, "I feel that no one ever likes me. So why is this person being nice to me if he doesn't really like me?"

- "Should" statements reflect patterns of overresponsibility, leading to guilt, shame, and self-criticism. Learning to define clearly what your responsibilities are can help you feel less burdened by others' expectations.

- Labeling and mislabeling refers to the tendency to label an experience and then respond to the label instead of to the experience. The assessment of the phony crazy patients of Dr. Rosenhan illustrate how hospital staff, misled by the "crazy" label, missed the reality of researchers' behavior.

- Labeling yourself negatively makes it difficult for you to develop positive self-regard. Labels stabilize behavior, making it more difficult to change. Be careful how you label yourself.

- Personalization means taking personally things that are not at all personal. Strive to find reasons for things that happen that *don't* put you at the center.

- Depression can distort your perceptions, and distorted perceptions can cause depression. The goal is to be as clear and objective about things as possible, actively compensating for the fact that we are not inherently rational beings. Rationality is not the ultimate goal in all situations, but it has the potential to help in many.

- Belief systems are patterned ways of thinking that may help you organize your perceptions, but when they are inaccurate representations of reality, they may lead to depression. There are few, if any, beliefs that hold true in all circumstances. The goal, then, is to respond to each situation effectively on its own merits. Learn to recognize where a principle does or does not apply, and then find a suitable one for the context at hand.

- Learning to monitor and correct your own thoughts and beliefs is essential for breaking the patterns of depression and preventing future episodes. You are not your thoughts; you are not your feelings; you are not your behavior; you are not your past; you are not *any* one part. You must recognize the limitations of human feelings and perceptions and learn to choose when to "go with them" and when to "put them on hold." This is the essence of emotional intelligence.

Chapter 8

GUILT AND RESPONSIBILITY: IS IT YOU? OR ISN'T IT?

The Case of Amanda

Amanda woke, looked at the clock, and reluctantly decided it was time to get up. She had started to get out of bed earlier, but when it took more effort than seemed worthwhile, she had let herself fall back to sleep. Now, a couple hours later, she woke again, angry with herself for sleeping so late, even though it was Sunday, her day off. It wasn't that she really had to be up earlier, but knowing that she was going to visit her mother, and how rotten her mother made her feel when she wasn't there early, she chastised herself for being self-indulgent.

Every other Sunday, Amanda drove forty miles to her mother's retirement community to spend the day with her. She hadn't minded so much when her dad was alive, but since he passed away last year, the regular visits to her mother were becoming burdensome. She had loved her dad, loved being with him. He was always happy to see her and was playful with her. Mom, on the other hand, was stern and humorless. Talking to her had always been a serious business, even when Amanda was a little girl. When her dad passed away, Amanda felt she'd lost a huge part of herself that she'd never regain. Her mother made some biting comments after the funeral to the effect that, now that Dad was gone, Amanda would probably not be coming to visit as much. She was acknowledging in sort of a mean way that she knew Amanda preferred her dad. Amanda felt horrible when her mother said that, even though she knew it was true— which made her feel even worse. She felt she had to assure her mother she'd be out to see her just as often, maybe even more often than before, since Mom was now alone.

Every once in a while, at least a couple of Sundays a month, Amanda wondered what her life would be like if her mother was no longer alive. Just as quickly as the thought would pass through her mind, Amanda would have an intense guilt attack for thinking something so awful. To atone for the thought, she'd make sure to pick up something to give her mother as a gift. Mother was a well-known fan of small gifts. She believed them the best evidence of real affection.

Amanda wondered how many gifts she'd given Mom over the years, starting with the very first she could remember—a potholder she'd made in first grade. She soon got absorbed in thinking about all the times over the years she'd been made to feel guilty and undeserving by her mother. One time, she accidentally locked herself out of the house and went to stay with a friend until someone got home. She was so wrapped up in playing that she didn't remember to call home to say where she was. By the time she did remember, her mother had been home for a half hour and was frantically looking for her. Her mother didn't talk to her at all for two weeks after that. She acted as if Amanda was invisible. No matter how many times Amanda apologized, it wasn't enough.

It seemed Amanda was always apologizing to her mother. She apologized for going off to college instead of marrying the high school sweetheart her mother thought was God's gift to the world. (So did he, unfortunately.) She apologized for getting a degree in political science instead of "something more becoming to a woman," as her mother suggested. She apologized for marrying one of her colleagues, and faced an unforgiving "I told you so" when, four years later, she apologetically announced her divorce. She apologized for never remarrying and never having children.

Amanda's whole life, it seemed, was one big apology. Not just to her mother, but also to herself, because no matter what she did, Amanda felt it was somehow not right or not good. Yes, indeed, her mother had taught her to feel guilty as a way of life, and Amanda had learned her lessons well. Now, she was so good at it she could feel guilty if she had a good meal, because there are children starving someplace. She could feel guilty if she ignored a panhandler, because "there but for the grace of God go I." She'd give a quarter to anyone who approached her asking for spare change (her two-bit guilt prevention). She could feel guilty over <u>anything</u> when she thought she wasn't being or doing what she was supposed to.

Amanda abruptly broke this train of thought, and felt guilty about feeling sorry for herself for feeling so guilty. She showered and *dressed quickly, and then drove to a greeting card store that also sold small gift items. She picked out a syrupy card she knew her mother would tolerate better than a funny one, and bought a little statuette. On the way out of the store, she stopped to call her mother to say she was leaving, and what time she'd arrive, so that Mom would know when to expect her. Her mother remarked, with obvious disappointment, "Oh, I thought you'd have left already and that you would be here by now."*

Do you feel guilty more often or more intensely than you know is reasonable? A sense of excessive or inappropriate guilt is one of the most common patterns associated with clinical depression. This chapter focuses on the issues commonly associated with guilt. Specifically, you will learn how inappropriate guilt comes about and what you can do about it.

Guilt is strongly related to your sense of responsibility. The more responsible you feel—meaning the more you feel an obligation to satisfy the wishes or expectations of others, or the more you feel an obligation to meet your own—the more guilt you are likely to experience. Amanda's case illustrates the relationship between a sense of responsibility (to please her mother) and guilt. Let's consider how we develop our sense of personal responsibility.

LEARNING THE HARD WAY

As social beings, we exist in a network of complex relationships with other people. A social network necessarily involves establishing specific roles, and each role has particular expectations, which must be met if the role is to be performed adequately. Each individual has, in fact, multiple roles to fill. You can be a father or mother, a husband or wife, an employee or employer, a son or daughter, and so forth, all at the same time. It is unrealistic to expect the different roles you play—with all their associated expectations—to mesh together smoothly at all times. You will *inevitably* face conflicts arising from the demands associated with filling multiple roles at a given moment.

A choice all of us face many times a day in our relationships is: "How much do I do for you, and how much do I do for me?" If I value my relationship with you, I don't want to disappoint you and incur your rejection and disapproval. On the other hand, doing things simply to get your approval or avoid conflict may make me feel that I'm "selling myself short," and then I wouldn't like or respect myself very

LEARN BY DOING #49

Managing Role Conflicts

Purpose: To help you define the many roles you fill and how to decide which one to respond to in a given situation when two or more roles are in conflict.

Even when everything is going well, it's hard to meet all of life's demands as parent, child, employee, citizen, and more. When your various obligations conflict, you need to make tough choices. Make a list of the different roles that you occupy in your life. What expectations are associated with each role? In other words, what behaviors <u>must</u> you engage in to fill that role adequately? What behaviors must you <u>never</u> engage in to fill that role adequately? As you review all your roles, you may see that some have conflicting expectations. How do you feel when you are caught between conflicting expectations? Identify which demands you must respond to in case of a role conflict. Doing so now can make your life easier when there is a conflict, because you won't be caught unprepared, and therefore under- or overreact. Use the outline below to get started.

Roles I Play	Behaviors Mandated by That Role	Behaviors Precluded by That Role	In Case of This Role Conflicting with Another, I Can . . . (fill in the blank)

much. It is stressful to be torn between doing something for you or doing something of importance for myself that may prevent my doing something for you. Should I lend you my car, because you asked to borrow it? Or should I use it to run personal errands that are important to me? If I give it to you, or do other such things for you at my own expense, then I may grow resentful of you and feel bad about myself as well. If I don't lend you my car, or do such things for you, I run the risk of your getting angry and withdrawing approval from me. Either way, I face the unpleasant prospect of feeling bad about myself, bad about you, or both.

EXPECTATIONS AND GUILT

Your perceptions about personal responsibility are shaped by the expectations of others, such as parents and friends. Whether and how the important people in your life have communicated their expectations to you is an important influence. It shaped your perceptions about how much freedom you have in creating a balance between meeting your own needs and your sense of duty toward others. For example, some people are reared to feel that they should never disappoint anyone, an expectation enforced through the mechanism commonly called "the guilt trip." Making others feel guilty if they don't do exactly what you want is a powerful manipulative tool. Guilt works, which is probably one of the reasons it's so "popular." It's also very destructive.

If your parents used guilt to get you to do what they wanted, you knew you'd face a heavy penalty if you disappointed them. If you have any emotional attachment to your parents, you don't want to hurt them. After all, they were (and perhaps still are) the most important people in your life, and their approval counts for a great deal. Such a background can make you sensitive, perhaps *too* sensitive, to other people's reactions. If you feel it is your job to save others from disappointment or frustration, you will be an easy target for the guilt trips they lay on you (or the guilt you place on yourself *for* them!).

Religious-based guilt is even more complex. How can you or anyone else know what God really thinks about your thoughts or feelings? Can you overcome human nature to reach the often unrealistic spiritual level that is sanctioned by religion? (Think critically!)

The best defense against inappropriate guilt is a clear sense of your standards for yourself and of the degree of responsibility you have toward others. Knowing what guilt is and where it comes from is a necessary step in protecting yourself against the manipulation of "guilt trips" imposed on you by others, often unwittingly.

Remember Amanda? Can you see how her unrelenting guilt, stemming from the need to please her mother, fueled her depression? It is exhausting to live with the constant anxiety that you will be judged harshly and will have to deal with the disappointment, anger, or rejection of those you want to please. If you allow others to determine whether you are worthy of their attention or affection, you have given away your personal power. To get over crippling guilt—the kind that makes life painful—you must assert your right to be who you are and determine how you want to live. The discussion and exercises in Chapter 4 regarding your personal values can help you do this.

GUILT AND FEAR

Beyond its association with responsibility, guilt can be associated with fear. To the extent that you fear rejection, the withdrawal of another's affection, or eternal damnation if you do not comply with his wishes, you will be afraid of letting him down. You can eventually rid yourself of this guilt and associated depression by asking, "If this person can reject me for not fulfilling his expectations, what kind of relationship do we have?" I hope you'll seek healthy relationships with people who support your decisions and respect your wish to do what you need to do. Guilt dissipates quickly when you are clear *it is not your job to manage other people's feelings for them.*

PERFECTIONISM AND GUILT

Beyond responsibility and fear, guilt also relates to perfectionism, a common theme in the lives of depressed individuals. To the rational mind, wanting to be "perfect" is an entirely unrealistic expectation. Although most depressed people recognize the impossibility of being truly perfect, they still have negative feelings about themselves when they encounter their imperfections. Here's another example of the dichotomous (all-or-none) thinking I described in the last chapter.

Pause and Reflect #28

Perfectionism Ain't All It's Cracked Up to Be

Are you a perfectionist? In what area(s) do you strive to be perfect? Is perfection possible? If you define perfection and then attempt to live up to that standard, how will you feel if other people do not also think of it as "perfect?" If others define perfection for you, how will you feel when you can't fit their definition? Do you see how this is a no-win situation?

Going through life believing that you're perfect or you're worthless is a hurtful and entirely distorted way to exist.

Understanding the motivation for wanting to be perfect is not particularly difficult. If you could be perfect, you'd risk no rejection or disapproval from others (except from those who would be critical of perfection because it makes them feel inadequate!). Perfectionism is basic to the experience of depression, and I will discuss it in more detail later in the chapter.

GUILT AND THE NEED FOR APPROVAL

Dependency on others is an inevitable part of growing up. Therefore, how can *anyone* be indifferent to the reactions of others, especially those who are our caretakers and sources of physical and emotional security? Realistically, to be immune to the reaction of others is neither normal nor healthy.

I suggest that there is a positive value in seeking approval from others. It is a way to form strong bonds that allow closeness and support. By seeking approval, you develop sensitivity and empathy, necessary for a sense of social responsibility. It is also a basis for self-esteem. Seeking and obtaining approval reinforces who we are and the things we do.

As children, seeking praise is normal and healthy. Even as adults, we continue to build our lives around the values for which we were rewarded as children, whether for education, career, family, or anything else. Like excessive guilt, though, excessive approval-seeking can be destructive. If your need for approval is so strong that it causes you to compromise your values or otherwise be untrue to yourself, then it is excessive. Furthermore, if it consistently places you in the position of being "one down"—as if others are more important than you—it is excessive.

THE STABILITY OF SELF-IMAGE

One's self-image is remarkably stable. Despite years of experience, an adult will continue to feel almost exactly the same way about himself as he did in his earliest years. There is a reason for this. A psychologist named Leon Festinger introduced the term "cognitive dissonance," nearly forty years ago, to explain how people strive to maintain the stability of their beliefs by closing out new and conflicting information. (I first described this principle in the preceding chapter.) Cognitive dissonance is a mechanism whereby a person rejects (ignores, discounts) information that conflicts with his existing beliefs. If someone contradicts the self-image you have formed, will that self-image change? Not likely. What's more likely is that you will discount the accuracy of that person's contradictory observations.

LEARN BY DOING #51

Approval-Seeking Behavior

Purpose: To emphasize that excessive approval-seeking can take place only at significant expense to your self-esteem. It works against your desire to feel better about yourself even though you obtain others' approval.

What do you do to seek approval from others? Be very descriptive of the traits by which you try to elicit approval (like generosity, hard work, or compliance). How well do these patterns work for you? When are they advantageous? When are they disadvantageous? In your judgment, do you have more or less approval-seeking behavior than is good for you? How do you know?

Spend a day exaggerating your approval-seeking behavior by saying and doing things that are specifically designed to elicit others' approval. (Give lots of unnecessary compliments, give lots of small gifts to people who are unimportant to you, make lots of syrupy sweet phone calls, and the like.) How do you feel when you do these things?

Let's put this point into a real-life context. Sam views himself as a sensitive person. When he goes out on a date, he reacts emotionally to what his date says about her views on different issues. He gets angry when she disagrees, he feels threatened when she can do something better than he can, he tries to convince her of the correctness of his views, and he feels deeply misunderstood and unappreciated when she doesn't probe and ask him lots of questions about himself. As a result, Sam sees his date as egocentric and insensitive. If she gives him direct feedback that says, "You're opinionated, unable to tolerate differences of opinion. You're so busy protecting your feelings, you don't pay any real attention to mine" and states that she no longer wants to date him, Sam concludes he's better off without such an insensitive woman.

Will Sam's image of himself change because of that dating episode? Of course not. Sam will still see himself as a sensitive person and will discount the fact that he has behaved in ways that clearly were not.

Have you ever heard a heated discussion, at the end of which one person abandons his position and says, "Okay, now I see it your way." No way! All that happens in a heated discussion is that each individual becomes more entrenched in his original position, regardless of any new information that may have been offered by the opponent.

Cognitive dissonance is a neutral mechanism, neither good nor bad. It serves to maintain the stability of your experience, whether good or bad. If you have a bad self-image, you will probably disregard positive feedback altogether or minimize its importance. If you have a positive self-image, cognitive dissonance can allow you to discount your critics as lacking insight into your true value.

Cognitive dissonance as a mechanism for maintaining stability explains how people can limit themselves unnecessarily and unwittingly. Here's another example of how it works. If you think you are not lovable (not attractive, smart, sexy, or otherwise desirable), then you are unlikely to respond positively to interest from others, because such interest contradicts your self-image. If someone shows you affection, you are likely to question his motives: "Why is he trying to be nice to me? Does he feel sorry for me? Is he trying to use me in some way?" By rejecting the affection of others, you lose the experience of being loved, which serves only to confirm your original belief that you are not lovable! How is that for a self-limiting pattern?

How about letting others decide how they feel about you instead of trying to do their thinking for them? If someone finds you desirable, even though you may not understand why, he has the right to and may genuinely feel that way. Really? Yes, really!

Consider another example. When you see yourself as helpless in life, as you often do when you're depressed, you will not expend any meaningful effort toward changing things for the better. So you will probably let circumstances control you, instead of taking control of circumstances, thereby confirming that you are a helpless victim of circumstances! This is how cognitive dissonance can sustain depression. Once again, you have to be willing to step outside your usual way of looking at things and be open to the possibility that some of the limiting aspects of what you think or believe aren't true.

This point about unwittingly creating your own "vicious cycle" is so important that I'll provide a third example. If you see the future as negative, and you feel hopeless about its ever being different, then you will not actively do anything to improve it. Thus, things going on now that you don't like will continue in an uninterrupted fashion, confirming your negative view of the future.

How do you get out of these vicious cycles? The emphasis throughout this book is on the need to *do something different.* I am stating in no uncertain terms that because of the distorted patterns of perception associated with your depression, you cannot yet trust your judgment 100 percent. Of course, as you become practiced in balancing your internal perceptions with external realities, your judgment will become much more reliable. At this point, however, I stress the need for you to work toward assessing situations more accurately. Then you can respond to each situation according to its merits, with the ability to recognize objectively what the best response would be.

The factor of cognitive dissonance is also the reason that I cannot overemphasize the need to do actively the exercises suggested throughout this book. Just reading through the exercises will not have nearly as much effect as doing them. Unless you have direct experiences that powerfully challenge your beliefs about yourself, you are likely to maintain your beliefs as they are.

SNATCHING DEFEAT FROM THE JAWS OF VICTORY

Sometimes even when people have direct contradictory feedback to what they feel, they manage to discount it. For example, the person who gives a presentation to a hundred people can do a wonderful job, according to his audience, yet still feel bad because he has an entirely subjective feeling of having done poorly. The speaker can even receive written evaluations on which ninety-nine of the hundred attendees rated the quality of his presentation as "excellent." One listener rated it as only "fair," though, so in the mind of the speaker, the presentation was depressingly unsuccessful. One "fair" evaluation outweighed the ninety-nine "excellent" ones!

The speaker demonstrates the selective perception associated with depression, namely, the uncanny ability to amplify the tiniest negative in even the most positive situations. The all-or-none pattern is also evident, leading the speaker to conclude that since his presentation was not 100 percent successful, it was a failure. Unfortunately, cognitive dissonance stabilizes such patterns of depressed thinking.

Why do I stress cognitive dissonance so heavily? Because I want to emphasize that *unless you take seriously the responsibility to challenge yourself, the momentum is in the direction of your staying depressed.* Unless you actively seek experiences to demonstrate the limitations or errors of your perceptions, you can too easily discount each new idea or technique I provide here and retain your original depressing viewpoint. You can defeat my attempts to help you—and your desire to overcome depression.

GUILT AND SELFISHNESS

In the earlier discussion about people's need to interact with others in order to enjoy the benefits of acceptance and avoid the pains of rejection, it may have become apparent to you that not everyone is equally sensitive to the way others feel about them. Why are some people so highly reactive to others, while others are not? The single most important factor seems to be self-image. People with high self-esteem are more likely to be responsible for themselves and to encourage others to be responsible for themselves. They don't feel the need to control others, rescue others, or find others to lean on.

For individuals to be guided more by their own ideas about what's right for them than by others' expectations may sound selfish to you. What are the differences between being "selfish" and being able to "take care of yourself"? Those who are the most prone to excessive guilt are usually unclear about the distinctions. They often feel that they cannot do things for their own benefit or respond to their own interests or needs because they would be doing something selfish and therefore wrong. If you have been socialized with the value that it's "right" to put other people first, then doing things for yourself may seem "wrong" and lead to feelings of guilt. If others learn this about you, you may become an easy target for their manipulations.

LEARN BY DOING #52

Revising Your Self-Image

Purpose: To encourage you to do those things which will revise your self-image in a positive direction.

Think of specific feedback you have been given in recent months that contradicts what you believe to be true about yourself. How did you reject or discount that feedback? What forms and amounts of feedback, if any, could lead you to revise your view of yourself?

On a sheet of paper, set up three columns. In the first, write a statement about the negative self-image you have held. In the second, right beside it, write a statement about yourself that contradicts your first statement. In the third column, identify the things you could say or do that would demonstrate the positive behaviors in your second column. Do you want to know how you can best revise that old negative self-image? _Do_ the things in the third column! You can use the following as an example:

My Negative Self-Image	What Actions Would Contradict It?	Behaviors to Support Column 2
I'm a lousy husband.	I can be a caring and attentive listener.	I will make time to spend at least a half hour with my wife each day, when I focus on her and nothing else.

AVOIDING RESPONSIBILITY: THE BLAME GAME

Thus far, the focus has been on people who develop such a strong sense of responsibility that they experience unnecessary and inappropriate guilt. What about the opposite sort of person? Let's consider the individuals who show no sense of responsibility for their actions, either toward themselves or others. Such people experience little or no guilt for things that they probably _should_ feel guilty about. Instead, they employ a mechanism to avoid responsibility, which nearly always involves blaming others for their mistakes. They may blame the weather, the economy, the government, their parents—anyone or anything they can fault in order to avoid being responsible for their own screw-ups.

Pause and Reflect #30

Distinguishing Selfishness from Taking Care of Yourself

Think of as many recent examples as you can of people asking you to do things for them. What was your response in each situation? Did you feel pressured to comply with their wishes? If there were any instances where you declined, were you motivated by selfishness or by the need to take care of yourself? How do you know?

My response: Doing things for others is not only acceptable; it is desirable. It's what helps make you a thoughtful and considerate person. But if you do things for others at the expense of your self-esteem, or if you do things for others who don't appreciate them, you're hurting yourself. It's usually selfish of someone to let you do things for him when he knows you're hurting yourself to do them. In other words, selfishness is self-gratification at the expense of others.

Naturally, other people want what they want. Perhaps what they want may even be realistic. The key question is whether their getting what they want must be at your expense.

Those who tend to feel guilty easily are more likely to be abused by such irresponsible people. The vulnerability comes from using *your* frame of reference, assuming that, because *you* would feel guilty and responsible, others should feel guilty and responsible. I hope you are learning to *stop using yourself as the only reference point for predicting or interpreting others' behavior.* I point out that there are many people who do not share your frame of reference. They routinely avoid responsibility and are well practiced at blaming others for their problems. You may want to read Laura Schlessinger's provocative book on this very subject, *How Could You Do That?*

It is easy to appreciate how happy a "blamer" is when he finds someone who has an overdeveloped sense of guilt and readily accepts blame without question. You need a refined ability to sort out clearly what you are and are not responsible for, situation by situation. This will allow you to avoid accepting blame noncritically and then feeling inappropriately guilty. It will also help prevent you from being a "blamer." The exercises in this chapter should help.

LEARN BY DOING #53

Amanda's Responsibilities

Purpose: To help clarify that other people's expectations can lead you to feel guilty unnecessarily when you make choices that are right for you but disappointing to them. You can learn that the attempts of others to control you may make them feel better, often at your expense.

Go back to Amanda's story at the beginning of this chapter. Identify what Amanda felt responsible for doing to please her mother. After each item of responsibility you identify, decide whether she really is responsible for that item. For example, Amanda felt guilty about marrying someone her mother didn't much care for. Was she responsible for getting her mother's approval of her fiancé? (The answer is no.) How might Amanda have responded effectively to each of her mother's guilt-inducing manipulations? Use the outline and example below to get started.

Item of Responsibility	Is Amanda Really Responsible For This Item?	An Effective Response Might Be . . .
Marrying someone Mom approves of.	No.	Mom, I know you want the best for me, but you can't arrange my marriage. I have to be with someone I choose to love, not someone you want me to love.

DEVELOPING CLARITY ABOUT RESPONSIBILITY

When you believe that whatever happens is in your control, you naturally feel responsible for the outcome. If the result you wanted is not attained, feelings of guilt and inadequacy can quickly creep in. If this happens to you more often than you'd like, it is time to develop a new decision-making process. *Before* you feel guilty or inadequate about not getting some desired result, it would be useful to pause and make an evaluation. Did you fail to get the outcome you wanted because your strategy—the sequence of steps you took—was incorrect or inefficient? Or was the lack of success a result of what is called an "illusion of control," where you believed you could control something that, you found out the hard way, you could not?

Guilt can distort your perceptions about responsibility for a given situation. You will need to evaluate whether or not something is your responsibility on a situation-by-situation basis. The distortions about responsibility take place, in varying degrees, in two forms. The first is a tendency to be underresponsible, meaning you do not assume enough responsibility for the way you relate to others or for the things that happen as a result of your choices. The second is a tendency to be overresponsible, assuming too much responsibility for other people's choices or for things that occur as a result of those choices. Let's consider both distortions in greater detail.

PATTERNS OF UNDERRESPONSIBILITY

People who demonstrate patterns of underresponsibility typically see themselves as victims of circumstance. They usually fail to anticipate how they may be affected by the choices either they or others make. When bad things happen, they are quick to blame others for their difficult circumstances.

Let's consider one couple I worked with, Len and Sally. Len would say terribly mean things to Sally when they argued. Sally would be very hurt, naturally, that Len could say such vicious things to her. Later, when the argument was over, Len would expect Sally to be warm and friendly, as if he hadn't just been nasty to her. When Sally couldn't "forget it," Len blamed her for being emotionally immature and "unable to control her anger." What do you think of Len's inability to take any responsibility for his effect on Sally? What do you think of Len seeing himself as a victim of Sally's bad temper? On a much larger scale, what does it mean when people lose, or never develop, a clear sense of their effect on other people? Hurting people either deliberately or unwittingly is one of the most destructive aspects of irresponsibility.

Let's look at the patterns frequently found in people who do not deal realistically with issues of personal responsibility.

LACK OF SELF-EXPRESSION

Many depressed people are not skilled at expressing their thoughts, feelings, and needs. In some cases, they feel it is selfish or self-centered to ask to be heard. In others, the lack of expression stems from a fear that, once they open up, they will be rejected. For others, it's because they don't know what they think or feel, so of course they are unable to express it.

Not communicating your thoughts and feelings can put you in the victim role. When you fail to disclose your needs or views, the person you are communicating with must deal with the situation from only his perspective. No matter how sensitive that person may be, he is *not* a mind reader. Inevitably, he will miss opportunities to take your feelings into account. Then you are likely to get depressed because you interpret his actions as evidence that you are not valued or appreciated!

Since there are no genuine mind readers on this planet, it is imperative that you tell other people how you feel and what you want. Not doing so usually compounds the problem, particularly when the other person makes clear what he wants, and you end up feeling overruled. Such interactions can too easily leave you feeling helpless and trapped, and catalyze all the depressed thoughts and feelings that make the situation difficult to handle. Do you see how one thing (not expressing yourself) leads to another (feeling ignored and devalued), which then leads to another (feeling depressed)? That's the "snowball effect" of depression.

I would like to add a cautionary note. Simply telling someone what you want does *not* obligate that person to fulfill your wish. It lets the other person know what you want, but he may not choose to accommodate your wishes. Of course, you stand *no* chance of getting what you want if the other person doesn't even know about it. Likewise, someone's telling you what he wants does *not* obligate you to fulfill his desire. That's the point about equality in a relationship—it means talking things out with the other person until you jointly arrive at something you *both* can live with.

To refuse to express your feelings out of the fear that others will disagree with or even discount them would be an act of underresponsibility. It suggests that you do not have to function as a full equal in the relationship. You may even be right; the other person *can* disagree with you. That's fine, because the best of relationships allows for disagreement. To discount your feelings, though, and treat them as if they are unimportant is an unhealthy sign. If that happens, then it's time to redefine the relationship and assert your feelings as being important. To place yourself, or to allow someone else to place you, in an inferior position effectively puts the other person in a superior position. A personal relationship that is lopsided cannot function in the healthiest of ways and will only lead you to suffer more depression.

So, Where Ya Wanna Eat?

I have a close friend who <u>used to be</u> very difficult to go out to eat with. Whenever I would ask her, "Where would you like to eat?" she would inevitably respond, "Anywhere is fine. It doesn't matter." Her passive response would put me in the position of always being responsible to choose the restaurant where we would eat. Almost invariably, no matter what restaurant I chose, once we were inside and ready to eat, she would make thinly veiled complaints about the restaurant.

I was aware of several choices: (1) I could let that pattern continue and get increasingly resentful about it; (2) I could confront her and directly express my anger about it; (3) I could stop going out to eat with her; or (4) I could find ways to engage her in the process of choosing. Well, rather than get too angry about it, I decided instead to do something to change her underresponsible pattern of not participating in the choosing of the restaurant.

One time when I asked her where she wanted to eat and she replied, "Anywhere is fine," I deliberately took her to the most rundown, aesthetically displeasing, gastronomically vulgar restaurant possible—but I did it with a sense of humor. After her initial shock, she took my point with a well-matched sense of humor. She was so "moved" by that experience that now when I ask her where she would like to eat, she is quick to offer an idea of where she would like to go! Likewise, I offer my preferences. If her choice is unacceptable to me, or mine is to her, at least now we can try to reach a more mutually satisfying decision.

It is important to be able to express your feelings and desires only to the extent that they matter in the relationship. There will be times when, as insensitive as this may sound, your feelings either do not matter or are irrelevant. Part of a clear sense of responsibility is knowing when it's important to assert your feelings, and when they are not applicable to the flow of events, knowing when they should be an important factor, and when other, larger issues are at stake. Sometimes it may feel good to express your feelings even though you don't particularly expect others to do anything about them. The point is for you to have choices about how to best respond in a given situation.

SELF-NEGATION OF FEELINGS

I'm often surprised at how frequently people discount their own feelings. Individuals may react to a situation and then backpedal, saying, in essence, "But I really have no right to feel this way." The effect of such self-negation is to miss the mark in managing situations well. Saying, "I have no right to feel this way," is truly at odds with the fact that you already *do* feel that way. By claiming there is no reasonable basis for feeling the way you already feel, you delay or even prevent yourself from responding effectively.

Let's put this idea about negative feelings into a real-life situation. Imagine a couple, Paul and Lorraine, arguing over an issue like family finances. Paul says, "It makes me very angry that you want to spend money on something so silly." Lorraine responds, "You have no right to feel angry! After all, it's my money, too!" If I were the therapist working with this couple, I would interrupt them at just that moment, and I would respond to Lorraine, who told Paul, that he had no right to feel angry. I would point out to her how utterly irrelevant her comment was, since Paul already *does* feel angry. To go off on the tangent of whether his anger is justified does nothing to address his feeling or show an understanding of it. "Since Paul does feel angry, Lorraine, how can you best respond to his feeling? You don't have to agree with it, but it does need to be acknowledged." Must feelings be justified before they can be acknowledged? No. Later, by acknowledging each other's feelings, Paul and Lorraine were able to devise spending guidelines they could both live with. Neither got exactly what he or she wanted, but both recognized the value of compromise.

Attempting to justify your feelings raises a question: "What justification is enough for you to feel the way you feel?" When do you have enough reason to feel angry, hurt, or happy? Each of the feelings you have is your feeling. I have not encouraged you to put your feelings first and foremost in every situation, since I have repeatedly said that sometimes your feelings will be distorted and misleading (inappropriate to the context). Nor have I encouraged you to ignore your feelings as if they are unimportant. It isn't "all-or-none." I do suggest that it is important to note your feelings and to develop enough control over them to decide *whether* to express them and, if so, *in what way* and *to what degree*. There are many times when your feelings are *very* important and should be considered carefully.

Pause and Reflect #32

There Was More Than Met Your Eye

Think about a situation you have faced recently that did not go well. What were the specific factors that you can identify now but did not take into account at the time? Was it the other person's values or feelings? The organization's politics or policies? The influence of previous traditions? Others' expectations? This kind of retrospective analysis can help you to read future situations more accurately.

You can recognize your feelings without necessarily expressing them. For example, you may be consciously angry with your boss for overloading you with unnecessary work, but you may also recognize that saying anything about your anger would not be received very well by your boss. In such a case, you may wisely choose to acknowledge your feelings but not express them. Or you may just as wisely choose to meet with your boss and express your feelings in a nonthreatening way. By being aware of your feelings, *you can choose to express them intelligently according to what the situation requires and what the other person can handle.* Simply "dumping" your feelings can feel good but may worsen an already sensitive situation.

When I advocate being in control of your feelings and recognizing that you are more than your emotions, I am *not* devaluing your feelings. Denying your feelings is the virtual opposite of everything I advocate in this book. I encourage you to recognize, accept, and utilize your feelings, but to do so in ways that are effective. I hope you will organize them according to both your internal perceptions and to the external realities of *whether* you can express them constructively in a given situation.

INTERNAL FEELINGS VS. SITUATIONAL DEMANDS

Any individual generally responds to a situation or person according to how he feels or what he wants from that person or situation. Too often, this is done without an accurate reading of the person or situation.

BLAMING OTHERS

Blaming others for things that happen (or don't happen) is the most prominent characteristic of the underresponsible individual. Putting the blame on another makes him responsible; you are then the victim of his incompetence. Many underresponsible individuals have developed the ability to get others to take responsibility so that if something goes wrong, they will not be blamed.

Accepting your fair share of responsibility also means acknowledging that sometimes you don't behave "perfectly." As you learn from the mistakes you will inevitably make for as long as you are alive, you will become a more effective problem solver and a better predictor of probable consequences. You may not eliminate mistakes from your life, but you will make far fewer of them. And you'll remember that when you do make them, it's not out of global stupidity, incompetence, or anything else that you have to beat yourself up for.

WITHDRAWAL

One of the most disturbing aspects of depression is that people may withdraw from living life. When people are caught in the grip of depression, they often suspend even the minimal effort it takes to seek out new experiences. If the depression is severe, they may not even respond to everyday things, like the telephone ringing or someone knocking at the door.

If you tend to isolate yourself and restrict your experience when you are depressed, that behavior can further hurt you. If you withdraw from people and situations for more than a day or two (which might be a useful short-term means to escape feeling overloaded), you are assuming a position of giving up. Giving up can confirm to you that you are a victim of forces too powerful to deal with. I hope that by reading this book and actively working with its exercises you will recognize that the idea is *not* just to expend energy in order to avoid giving up. Rather, the idea is to *expend energy wisely, in a goal-oriented fashion.* I'm not suggesting common-sense remedies like taking an exercise class or volunteering at the local hospital (although those *are* good ideas); I'm suggesting that instead of withdrawing, which can only complicate matters, you take active and deliberate steps, based on your recognition of which hurtful patterns you can interrupt and which helpful patterns you need to build. *Seek out, open up to, and allow new possibilities.*

PATTERNS OF OVERRESPONSIBILITY

My experience suggests that it's easier to tone down too strong a sense of responsibility than it is to create a sense of responsibility where none has previously existed. Whereas an underresponsible individual is quick to blame others, the overresponsible individual is quick to take the blame. Furthermore, the overresponsible individual may be overly considerate of others' feelings, to the point of personal detriment. You know you are overresponsible when you frequently find yourself caught up in other people's lives by getting drawn in to their problems or perhaps even butting in where you don't belong. Let other people live their lives—and be a model for how to live one's life well.

LEARN BY DOING #56

Clarifying Your Responsibilities

Purpose: To re-evaluate whether the responsibility you assume in your relationships with others is realistic.

Who are the people you feel most responsible for in your life? What are the specific things you do for these individuals as a result of your feeling responsible for them? Are these things that they could already do or perhaps could learn to do for themselves? As threatening as it may sound, if it seems reasonable to you, make a point of talking to those people about your feelings of responsibility. Be specific about what you feel your responsibilities are, and see how much agreement you get from them about your perspective. Do their responses confirm your perspective, or do they challenge your perspective in some way? Can you see how they may be motivated to keep you being responsible for them even if it's hurtful to you? Distinguish between being responsible to someone and being responsible for someone.

You can be supportive and kind, but that doesn't mean being responsible for them or their choices.

GUILT AND "HIGHER CONSCIOUSNESS"

It is easy to appreciate how, through the process of socialization, some people become overresponsible in their lives. Beyond our family dynamics, culture has played a role in encouraging overresponsibility in many of us. For example, in recent years there has emerged, in so-called higher consciousness groups, an exaggerated emphasis on personal responsibility to a level I find destructive. Many individuals have been strongly influenced by such groups but have not yet perceived the teachings as unrealistic. This includes all too many members of *my* profession. There are some groups that flatly state, "You are responsible for *everything* that occurs in your life. You are responsible for everything that happens all around you. The events of your life are a reflection of you." Proponents of such an extreme viewpoint would have you believe that if you're sitting at your computer, and it has an energy surge that causes a loss of information, you are responsible for "creating the energy" that caused that to happen!

This extreme viewpoint about responsibility has even spilled over into the world of health care. There are now many people who advocate that your health is *fully* your personal responsibility. They teach patients who have cancer and other life-threatening illnesses that the onset of the disease is *entirely* a product of personal responsibility and choice. They will say to such patients, "You have created your cancer. Your cancer is a result of your not having expressed anger appropriately to the significant people in your life. You will be able to cure your cancer when you have resolved those old emotional issues." As if it is not bad enough that the person has cancer; now he is blamed for creating the cancer. I think that's tragic.

My involvement in the field of clinical hypnosis has afforded me a great deal of insight into the relationship between mind and body, and I have much respect for the mind's ability to affect physical processes. I routinely demonstrate in my hypnosis trainings things like pain control and control of bleeding purely as a response to mental processes. Talking to me about the mind-body connection is like preaching to the choir! However, to take the extreme position that emotions directly "cause" cancer shows blatant disregard for the numerous other variables that are well known to contribute to disease processes. Emotions count, but so do other far more potent factors.

When an influential consultant identifies a clear cause-effect relationship, such as angry emotions and cancer, the patient looking for an explanation for the onset of the disease may be convinced of the claim's truth. It sounds plausible and answers the question "Why?" I find it irresponsible of some health professionals to offer patients such simplistic cause-effect statements, and I object to the ways such statements blur the lines of reality about what one is and is not responsible for. I have seen patients who have even been told they must *want* to die, because they didn't cure themselves with self-hypnosis or visualization techniques. What are they to conclude? By the time I see them, they are understandably quite depressed.

Learning to define and respect the limits of your responsibility in *any* situation is a necessary ingredient for managing your life—and depression. This is probably not as easy as it sounds. For example, consider those in my profession, the mental health profession. There are some psychotherapists who are themselves clinically depressed, substance dependent, in destructive relationships, and, in general, not doing very well. Certainly, being responsible for the complex health care of other people is a stressful position to be in. Furthermore, it is difficult to find a balance for yourself when the reason you went into the health profession in the first place is that you genuinely care about the welfare of others. However, unless you learn to establish a firm upper limit of how much you can care about others and still maintain your internal balance, you may easily become overresponsible for others.

Obviously, mental health professionals are people, too. If some of these well-educated and highly experienced professionals have a difficult time establishing the limits of their responsibilities, perhaps it's understandable that an average person without the benefit of professional training may have difficulty. I have been talking about mental health professionals here, but I could just as easily have been talking about husbands and wives, parents and children, bosses and employees.

GUILT AND RESPONSIBILITY

Guilt presupposes responsibility. You don't feel guilty about things that you don't first feel responsible for. Establishing realistic expectations for yourself, giving yourself the extra consideration and forgiveness that you probably give with ease to others, and clarifying the expectations of others are all important elements in diminishing the power of guilt in your life.

It can help you to identify clearly where your expectations for yourself came from, and also what mechanisms others use to pressure you to meet their expectations. You would then be in a position to decide whether you want to continue meeting expectations that are not of your own creation or that you may not agree with. There's no doubt that the expectations that go along with the roles you play will always be there.

The issue to consider every step of the way is how to balance others' expectations of your roles against your own expectations, based on what makes you feel best. When you resist the desire to satisfy others at your own expense, those people will learn to be more responsible for themselves. Encourage those around you to get their needs met in ways that aren't destructive to others—like you.

ANOTHER LOOK AT PERFECTIONISM

Perfectionists set exceptionally high standards for themselves and are intensely critical of themselves when they do not reach them. Perfectionism generally reflects the cognitive distortion of extreme all-or-none thinking. I remember treating an athlete several years ago who had placed second at a prestigious international competition. He convinced himself he was a *total* failure because he didn't place first. That he became famous in his sport, won money and respect, and landed lucrative product endorsement contracts seemed unimportant to him. If that is not evidence of dichotomous thinking, then I don't know what is.

For the underresponsible individual, perfectionism is a guaranteed way of attaining the approval of others. It also means never incurring the blame, negative judgments, or criticism of others. For the underresponsible individual, the perfectionist standards are usually not even his own. Instead, he usually has some "significant other" (real or imagined) who establishes the criteria that define his success. In other words, he imagines how someone important to him would be pleased or disappointed by something he does, and he then does what he thinks is most likely to gain approval.

Believe it or not, there are a lot of doctors out there who became doctors to avoid disappointing their parents, and not out of a true desire to practice medicine. Living a lifestyle to avert criticism or the disappointment of others is a hollow existence. It means living for others, not for yourself. Thus, it represents an underresponsible attitude toward yourself and an overresponsible attitude toward others.

It is important that you evolve your own definition of success. If it happens to be different from others' ideas, so be it. If you truly want long-term relief from depression, it is not only your individual right but your *obligation* to recognize and then respond to what is best for you. Hurting yourself by trying to live up to standards set by your parents, your spouse, your boss, or someone else underscores the need to evolve standards based on *your* values. The idea is not to strive for perfection in order to avoid others' judgments or attain their approval, but to establish realistic expectations for *yourself.* Setting limits on others' judgments is an infinitely more constructive way to respond than negating yourself and your personal needs in order to meet their expectations.

Pause and Reflect #33

Defining Your Standards of Success

If you are a perfectionist, ask yourself these questions: "What is my definition of success? Who established the standards for my success?" If anyone other than you established those standards, then you know now that you have been trying to suit another person, not yourself. If you genuinely accept those standards as your own, fine. But if you know that they don't match your own, then it's a problem. When you are pressured to obey someone else's wishes, how can you feel you're in control of your own life? In order to feel good, you must assert your rights to be an individual who can make his own decisions and bear the consequences.

Perfectionism can also be related to overresponsibility. It is a very responsible position to challenge yourself to never disappoint others. Be aware, though, that to take responsibility for satisfying others' wants or needs can encourage them to have overly demanding and, worst of all, never-ending expectations for you. It is not unlike the art of effective parenting. Every time a parent does something for a child, beyond the time(s) of first teaching and demonstrating it, the child is, in essence, being told, "There is no need for you to do this yourself, because I will do it for you if you are slow, uncertain, uncomfortable, or otherwise seemingly unable." Be patient and let the child learn! Let him make mistakes and practice until he is skilled. To continue to do things for others simply reinforces in them the disempowering perception that they can't do those things for themselves.

Where there is an overresponsible individual, there is also an under-responsible individual. To burden yourself unfairly by doing too many things that could be done by people who do less can make you feel overwhelmed and resentful of being taken for granted. The hardest thing for me in working with overresponsible individuals is teaching them to *let other people be responsible for themselves.* They often feel as if they are abandoning others, unfairly burdening them, or displacing their own responsibilities onto them. In fact, when you encourage others to do what they are capable of doing, and allow them to take responsibility for some of the things you were doing for them, you are improving your relationship. It will become more mature and eventually more satisfying. Initially, of course, the other person is likely to grumble a bit about having to do something he wasn't used to doing. That's predictable. You'll survive it, and so will he. Just stay with the program!

Another aspect of the responsibility issue concerns the illusion of control, your belief that you can *make* someone proud, happy, secure, or *whatever*. To think you can make anyone *anything* presupposes that you have the ability to control his reactions. As we have seen, that illusion can create unrealistic expectations. By maintaining the illusion of control and determination to satisfy another individual, you make that person the "judge" of how effective you are. It means that he can push you to try ever harder while he becomes more critical of you.

Remember Amanda from the beginning of this chapter? She illustrates the point about expectations and resentment. The stress, resentment, and, ultimately, the depression you experience when you are placed in a "dance faster" position can get deeper and deeper every day that you keep dancing. Until Amanda learns to set limits on her mother's expectations, she will be on a treadmill, doing more and more for her mother without ever getting any acknowledgment of her efforts. So much for Amanda's *ever* being the "perfect daughter."

Wanting to be perfect at something, or wanting to excel at something creates a double-edged sword. Clearly, the desire can motivate high levels of achievement and provide recognition and reward. These are positive consequences that serve to reinforce perfectionist tendencies. The downside, however, is that perfectionism can make you want to achieve ever higher levels of quality; the success itself can become a trap. This is one reason that many highly successful individuals are depressed. They are bright, forward-looking, solution-oriented, socially competent people who are so good at what they do that they continually strive for higher levels of achievement, leaving too little room to accept and enjoy the everyday aspects of life.

Since life is not continuously exciting or continuously challenging for *anyone*, getting comfortable with the everyday aspects of life is basic to feeling good. Perfectionism can rob you of that ability and, instead, foster constant worry about what to do next and how to do it better.

It's important to discover what your individual values and needs are regardless of what anyone else might expect of you. Obviously, you cannot ignore the demands of others completely, since you are a member of society and have the responsibility to conduct yourself with integrity. Nor do you want to ignore your own needs consistently as you respond to others' expectations, for that is a predictable path to depression. Live your life according to the realistic and conscientious standards you set for yourself. Remember, just as others should not be responsible for you and your feelings to their detriment, the reverse is equally true.

SUMMARY OF KEY POINTS . . .
AND WHAT THEY CAN MEAN TO <u>YOU</u>

- Excessive or inappropriate guilt is a common feature of clinical depression. Is it a feature of *your* depression? If so, to what extent?

- Guilt is strongly related to your sense of personal responsibility for others. Becoming clear that you may be responsible *to* others, not *for* them, can reduce guilt.

- Guilt can be used as a manipulative tactic by others in ways that encourage your compliance with their wishes to your own detriment. When someone lays a "guilt trip" on you, recognize its manipulative aspect; if it's inappropriate, hand it back, saying, "You can try to make me feel guilty, but the answer is still no. It's *your* responsibility, not mine."

- How reactive you are to others' expectations or judgments is determined by your degree of need for their acceptance. If you feel so "needy" of others' approbation that you will please them to your own detriment, you're in a relationship trap that can prevent you from feeling valued as an equal.

- "Cognitive dissonance" is a term which describes the need to maintain stability in your beliefs by rejecting conflicting ideas. The rationalizations you concoct about why you have to keep things the way they are even when you're unhappy with them is direct evidence of how this mechanism can maintain depression.

- There is a substantial difference between "being selfish" and "being able to take care of yourself." It's important to have good relationships that involve give-and-take, but you have to know yourself well enough to create the positive conditions that are self-nurturing and to avoid "giving until it hurts."

- Distortions of the issue of responsibility can lead you to avoid responsibility you should accept, or to accept responsibility you shouldn't. Situation by situation, you have to read where the responsibility rests—with you, with others, or shared among you.

- Developing clarity about exactly what you are responsible for is necessary if you are to manage guilt appropriately and reduce this hurtful aspect of depression. If you didn't say it or do it, you're not responsible for it. If you didn't choose it, agree to it, or commit to it, you're not responsible for it. If you didn't cause it to happen directly or indirectly, you're not responsible for it. If you did, you are!

- There are common patterns associated with underresponsibility. Among these are the lack of self-expression, negation of feelings, withdrawal, and the tendency to blame others for one's own problems. You can't pretend you don't exist or that you don't influence others. You do. Since your influence on others is inevitable, your integrity depends on your influencing them positively.

- Perfectionism can be a product of either over- or underresponsibility. You can't be perfect even if you want to be, but you could be *really* good. Define success in realistic terms, taking human factors into account. The laws of human nature *do* apply to you, believe it or not.

- Learning to accept the inevitability of mistakes and how to correct for them is necessary for a healthy self-esteem. Nobody likes to screw up, but you must be sure not to go global ("I'm so dumb") but, rather, to identify what went wrong so that you can prevent a recurrence.

Chapter 9
THE VICTIM MENTALITY

THE WORLD TODAY IS (still) filled with political hot spots. People are fighting and dying in too many places all around the world. And even where the fighting hasn't yet begun, the threat of violence simmers. On a less global, more local level there are battles of all sorts that take place on the streets of your hometown. What is this long history of human aggression all about? We see that people will often fight for, and even die for, beliefs that, from a rational standpoint, can be viewed as arbitrary and subjective. Killing people who worship the "wrong" God, or killing people for having the "wrong" skin color, shows us how irrational people can be. It also shows us how far we have yet to evolve if we are truly going to be a higher order species that survives, and not just an evolutionary "flash in the pan."

National and individual conflicts often (but not always) come about from an unwillingness to allow others to believe or act differently from one's own conception of what is "right." Aggression is an instrument used to attempt to control the beliefs others have in their minds, the spiritual connections they have in their souls, the behaviors they engage in, and how they live their lives.

Why impose religious or political beliefs on captive societies, if not for the power, wealth, prestige, and glory of controlling them? Our own nation was born from the need to escape domination and from the desire to govern itself. This struggle for independence and self-control—balanced by a need for being connected to others—continues to be the most common theme of human relations. We live in a country that blesses us with the freedom to choose how we live our lives. It's an opportunity no one should take for granted or squander.

In this chapter I consider the powerful need people have to control life situations and even other people. How you manage the issue of control can be directly related to your experience of depression. By examining more closely how you deal with what are commonly called "control issues," you will develop greater clarity about them, which is essential both to overcoming depression and preventing future episodes. I truly can't think of one depressed person I have ever treated who was entirely clear about the issue of control. Distortions in your perceptions about what you can and cannot control may lead you to make incorrect judgments about your responses to life situations. Undesirable consequences can then lead to depression when things fall apart.

In talking about control, I am really addressing the question of how much power you perceive yourself as having in a given situation. *"Power" is the capacity for influence.* It is potential, not fixed, and it will vary from situation to situation, relationship to relationship. Thus, if you tend to underestimate or overestimate your power in situations, you are at risk of misreading situations that can hurt you and trigger episodes of depression.

By clarifying your ideas about control and learning to manage power skillfully, you'll be more aware not only of your right to choose, but of your obligation to choose intelligently. _Then you can skillfully anticipate when it will be to your advantage to move into a situation and deliberately make things happen, and when it would be best to let a situation sail by because no amount of effort could make a significant difference._

SOCIETY'S RULES ARE THE START OF THE NEED FOR CONTROL

Every society has its rules, and every component of society, including the family, also has rules. The formation of a society means, in part, that all its members agree to abide by the rules. By conforming to society's rules, you contribute to its stability as well as its security. For example, it is clearly to everyone's advantage that all people who drive cars agree to follow the traffic rules. You certainly don't want someone deciding to express his individuality by driving south in a northbound lane!

Having clear and explicit rules to regulate our behavior is obviously necessary to some extent. It is also true, however, that if social or personal progress is to take place, rules may have to be bent or broken. For instance, consider the importance of the women's movement in redefining our cultural perceptions about women's roles. Thirty or thirty-five years ago, a woman who wanted to have a career had quite a bit of explaining to do to friends and relatives to justify her "unusual" position. Today, the majority of women work outside the home. _Now_ if you "only" want to stay at home and raise a family, you have quite a bit of explaining to do about why you're not out there competing in the working world.

This is a huge social change that came about in a very short time. Many people welcome such changes and have little difficulty letting go of tradition in favor of what they recognize as progress. Others, however, find such change painful, because they are losing their comfortable sense of certainty as to what is normal, familiar, and appropriate behavior.

People who violate the expectations of others frequently face disapproval and rejection. Years later, perhaps, they may recognize how their rule-breaking behavior led to substantial personal or social progress. Or they may discover that they were breaking rules blindly, fighting just to fight with others, without having anything of importance to gain.

Whether you realize it consciously or not, you are influenced by the expectations of others. The most powerful of all socialization agents is our family; family members are the ones who dress you, feed you, respond to you when you cry, talk to you, educate you, and gradually teach you to see the world as they do.

A paradox regarding the issue of control is that the more you control yourself to suppress those parts of you that others have labeled "undesirable," the more you are controlled by those people. Through their label, you are taught to see these parts of yourself in the same negative way. For example, if your depressed, humorless father hates humor and sees it as foolish, then each time you enjoy your sense of humor, he labels you "silly" (or worse) and teaches you to devalue humor and dislike it in yourself. Or perhaps you end up feeling ashamed or guilty when you have fun.

LEARN BY DOING #57

Your Family's Rules

Purpose: To identify the rules you grew up with and their relationship to the choices you make today.

One of the best ways to learn where many of your ideas about life came from is to consider the rules through which you were socialized by your family. On paper, write out in statement form the rules you grew up with, both those directly stated and those merely implied. What were you taught to believe was the "right" way to live? What were the rules regarding expressing your feelings, being ambitious, handling money, talking about sex, solving problems, getting educated, and all the countless other aspects of growing up? How did each of these rules affect your life? Is each a rule you wish to still follow, or do you need to bend or break it in order to feel better?

Use the outline and example below to get started.

Family Rule	Impact on My Life	Do I Need to Change It?
Respect other people's privacy.	A clear sense of boundaries.	No
Whoever is loudest wins the argument.	Avoid confrontations out of a fear of anger.	Yes

To be controlled by others to *some* extent is inevitable; after all, no one escapes the influence of others. There are, however, some parents who are much more sensitive to the issue of control than others. They deliberately take steps to foster a healthy sense of personal control and independence in their children at as early an age as possible. There are mothers who let their children, at an appropriate age, choose the clothes they will wear to school each day. There are other mothers who lay out the children's clothes the night before, totally excluding the children from the decision-making process. If you were raised this way, it could have reinforced the idea that even something as simple as what you wear is out of your control. The more decisions you make for another person, the more helpless you encourage that person to be.

Consider your own family. Did your parents encourage you to take risks of a safe nature, such as exploring your neighborhood or going to the grocery store? Or were you always kept within close reach because "there's danger everywhere"? Were you encouraged to make your own choices at an appropriate age about what to wear, games to play, and who your friends were? Or were these imposed upon you, requiring only your obedience? If you didn't learn how to make such choices throughout your life, how could you learn to be a good decision-maker and develop confidence that you can trust your judgment?

Your sense of personal control is a product of repeated interactions that reinforce the perception that you made things happen or that things happened to you. I hope it's becoming apparent to you how a distorted view of the issue of control can lead to misjudgments that chip away at your self-esteem, leading you to feel incompetent, self-hating, and depressed.

THE NEED FOR CONTROL

I have emphasized the notion of life as an ambiguous stimulus onto which we project our understandings and beliefs. People's need to understand is a motivating force for gathering information, sorting through it, and attempting to use those data to "make things happen." Having a need to understand is just one manifestation of our need to control our environment.

Many individuals are so fragile that only by rigidly maintaining some arbitrary belief system can they have any sense of personal control. Such people can be explosive if they feel their deeply held beliefs are being questioned or discounted. Thus, what may seem a strong reaction is sometimes only a reflection of how uncertain the person really feels and how important it is for him to hang on tight to a subjective belief. A "live and let live" attitude is a considerably more sophisticated way of going through life, but you first have to be comfortable knowing that you haven't "cornered the market" on "truth."

Considering how basic the need for control is, it is hardly "wrong" or "pathological" to want to have control over what happens in your life. In fact, I'm *encouraging* you to take charge of your life. The issue now is how to recognize and assert effectively the patterns of control. In other words, the fact that you want more control over what goes on in your life is perfectly fine. Problems arise, though, when you mismatch your needs or wants with the nature of the situations you face. When I see clients with "control issues," I'm not the least bit concerned that they want a lot of control over what goes on in their lives. *Anyone*

LEARN BY DOING #58

Assessing the Percentage of Control

Purpose: To help you to determine realistically what degree of control you have over situations in your life so that you don't ignore opportunities or try futile things.

For each of the following situations, identify (1) all the variables that influence the desired result, and (2) what percentage of control you think you have over the desired result (100% = total control, 0% = no control).

1. You apply for a job that you desire strongly.

(I'll do this one for you to get you started.) Ten variables that influence the desired result are (1) having the appropriate education; (2) having the appropriate work experience; (3) filling out a job application; (4) showing up on time for the interview; (5) dressing and grooming yourself well; (6) adopting a demeanor that is friendly, open, respectful, and cooperative; (7) answering and asking relevant questions regarding the job, work environment, and compensation; (8) sending a follow-up note expressing thanks for the opportunity to interview and restating your interest in the job; (9) the quality of the other job applicants; (10) the politics and attitudes of the interviewer (personal biases and perceptions) and how he sees you.

Here are the percentages of your control I would assign to each variable: (1) 100% (I'll assume you wouldn't apply for it if it wasn't in your area); (2) 50% (You can present your work history favorably, but it's hard to know how a new employer will view it); (3) 100%; (4) 100%; (5) 100%; (6) 100%; (7) 100%; (8) 100%; (9) 0%; (10) 25%. Do you agree with my percentages? Why or why not?

When you apply for a job, you do all you can to create possibilities. You have some control, but not total control. Without effort on your part, you won't get hired. Expending effort guarantees nothing, but it does create possibilities. Success is not a 100% phenomenon of _always_ turning to gold whatever you touch. It's about intelligent and sustained effort over time.

Okay, now you do the rest!

2. You want to ask someone you're interested in for a date.
3. You buy a present for a relative in the hope that he'll love it.
4. You buy some sharp new clothes to impress someone.
5. You negotiate with a car salesperson to buy a new car at the best possible price.
6. You want to ask your partner to be more attentive.
7. You want to ask your boss for extra time to complete a project.
8. You want to borrow money from a bank.
9. You want to go someplace different for the holidays this year.
10. You want your spouse to assume more responsibility for household chores.

Now do the same exercise with _at least_ ten important situations in your own life. To truly master this important skill, I'd recommend picking three situations a day, every day for _at least_ a month, to practice this exercise on.

who is effective in life is "controlling," but not everywhere. The wisdom is in knowing how to distinguish the situations that are controllable from those which are not. Go ahead and be controlling when it makes sense, but save yourself the grief of futile effort when you recognize that a situation is uncontrollable or that you may unfairly hurt others in the process of asserting control.

DISTORTIONS ABOUT CONTROL

The errors in judgment people make about the issue of control generally fall into two major categories: distortions that create an "illusion of helplessness," and those which create an "illusion of control." When absorbed in the illusion of helplessness, you see yourself as having no control when, in fact, you do have some. With the illusion of control, you have an inflated sense of power, incorrectly believing you can control circumstances that are objectively beyond your reach. Let's consider each category of distortion.

THE ILLUSION OF HELPLESSNESS

Too often depressed individuals passively let hurtful situations go on hurting them. They act as though they are utterly helpless to improve things when, in fact, they are not at all helpless.

Is Marie Really Stuck?

A young woman named Marie, who sought help from me for the problem of depression, felt her depression had its origin in her job situation. The feeling, though, had now grown in intensity and was interfering with all aspects of her life. She felt trapped and hopeless all the time, with no motivation to do much of anything. Marie worked for a small company in which she had an important role, and she was finding her job increasingly intolerable. But she took full responsibility for her attitude and blamed herself.

Marie described how her boss frequently made her work overtime, telling her she must work late rather than asking her, and he often did so at the last moment. Marie said she could not be promoted into any other position, simply because there were no other positions in the small business. She further told me that she was already at the top of her pay scale and was unlikely to receive any raises other than small cost-of-living increases. All in all, Marie described a dead-end job to which she had been trying to adjust. She was becoming increasingly depressed by what felt to be wasted effort. Marie had no emotional support from others at work, and she was so consumed with her job that she had no friends to lend her any emotional support.

When Marie asked for my advice about how to adjust to her job and life circumstances, I asked whether she had ever considered finding another job. Hard to believe, but it had never occurred to her that leaving her job was even a possibility! It may seem obvious to anyone else considering her circumstances, but it had never struck her as a possibility. Why not? How is it that Marie could respond in such a helpless way to a situation over which she had some control? Marie had the power to remove herself from the hurtful situation and demand of herself that she find a new job that would be more satisfying.

Any therapist who has worked with depressed clients can tell you similar stories about people failing to take obvious steps in their own behalf. How does this helplessness come about?

THE "LEARNED HELPLESSNESS" MODEL OF DEPRESSION

One of the best-known cognitive theories about depression is Martin Seligman's "learned helplessness" theory, described in Chapter 1. Seligman was perplexed by the passive acceptance of negative and painful experiences commonly found in depressed people, so he decided to do research on the problem. His experiments provide many valuable insights into depression, and I think any beliefs you may have that you are helpless will be challenged as you read on.

Seligman exposed people serving as research subjects to painful events (such as loud or obnoxious noise) beyond the range of their control. Subjects tried to escape the negative situation, but circumstances prevented them from doing so. They would continue to try, but could not succeed despite their efforts. Eventually, they would give up trying. Many developed obvious symptoms of depression, including apathy, withdrawal, sleep disturbance, and agitation. This result, in itself, had important implications for demonstrating how uncontrollable and painful circumstances can cause depression in some people.

Not all those exposed to the negative uncontrollable events became depressed, however. On the basis of what you've already learned, can you speculate why this was so? The factors of attributional style that you learned in Chapter 6 helped distinguish those who became depressed from those who did not. Understanding that hard times are unstable—that is, changeable or temporary—can help prevent helplessness. So can seeing them as external ("It's the circumstance, not me") and specific ("It's about this situation, not my whole life").

An even greater insight came when the same research subjects were placed in a new situation, where they could effectively escape the painful stimuli. Under these circumstances, many of the research subjects made no attempt to help themselves. Their previous experience had taught them that there was nothing they could do about being hurt. Thus, although the entirely new situation only superficially resembled the old one, they didn't even try to escape! They passively accepted pain. You can blame the cognition distortion of overgeneralization. Seligman termed this phenomenon "learned helplessness."

The implications of this research for understanding depression are far-reaching. Consider what happens when someone grows up in a family environment where punishment is dished out for no apparent reason. If you grew up in a home where you were punished one day for doing the same thing that you were ignored for doing the day before, you may easily have formed the conclusion that life is unpredictable, uncontrollable, and that the only thing you can do is accept whatever crummy fate comes your way. The mistake is overgeneralizing; instead of saying, "My family was unpredictable," you have become global and say, "Life is unpredictable."

An important postscript to Seligman's experiments concerns the role

Pause and Reflect #38

Your Inner Critic

How people learn to just give up and not even try to help themselves is easy to understand when they have been exposed to hurtful experiences they could not control, like sexual, physical, or emotional abuse in childhood. Such experiences are external to the individual. But what happens when the hurtful uncontrollable experiences are <u>internal?</u> For example, what if you have a critic (an inner voice) that lives in your head and criticizes and insults you for nearly everything you do? Believe it or not, everyone has such an "inner critic." How, then, can anyone ever have healthy self-esteem? By diminishing the criticism or learning to ignore it!

You cannot get rid of the critic, since it is an inevitable part of you. However, you <u>can</u> learn to limit its negative influence by ignoring or contradicting it with positive statements about yourself. You <u>don't</u> have to listen to it and accept what it says as though it speaks the truth. <u>People with good self-regard also have an inner critic; they just don't automatically listen to it or uncritically believe what it says.</u> They listen to it as one viewpoint to consider, not an inevitably correct one.

of treatment. Once research subjects formed the conclusion that they were helpless and passively "had to" accept pain, attempts were made to teach them that they were now in a situation in which they had control and *could* take action to end their discomfort. Repeated attempts to teach subjects to prevent or escape from punishment were met with indifference and a seeming lack of ability to absorb the new learning. It took many trials of demonstrating to them their ability to escape before the research subjects could overcome their helplessness and recognize opportunities to help themselves. *You* can learn quickly, though, from this research that helplessness is a frame of mind, *rarely* a reality. Don't give up!

When you automatically assume, as a general outlook on life, that you are helpless, that is a distorted view. No one's life is totally beyond the influence of the person who owns that life. Even when you can't change external circumstances, you *can* change your reaction to those circumstances. Feeling helpless about important life experiences and seeing yourself as "out of control" is a reliable trigger for depression.

When you feel out of control, your automatic response should be to make a rapid assessment as to whether circumstances are, in fact, beyond your control. Think critically, because as you now know, depressed individuals, with their distorted thinking, tend to believe they are helpless in situations in which they really are not.

THE ILLUSION OF CONTROL

The previous section focused on the distorted perception of having no control when, in fact, you have some. This section will focus on the reverse situation, where you see yourself as having control of a situation that, in fact, is not in your control. This "illusion of control" leads people to try to control things that are beyond their range of influence, and then suffer depression when things don't go the way they'd like.

There is an old wartime saying, "There are no atheists in foxholes." Pause for a moment and try to interpret what that phrase means in light of what I've been saying about control. Can you identify its meaning? In essence, the saying suggests that when a soldier is in the midst of a fierce battle, taking refuge in a foxhole while bombs explode all around and bullets whiz overhead, he does not and, realistically, *cannot* feel in control of his life. If he knows *he's* not in control of his life, he certainly hopes that someone benevolent is in charge of the situation. Who else could that benevolent someone be but God? So, many soldiers, in the heat of battle, have a "spiritual awakening" that leads them to pray to God for safe deliverance from the battlefield. They make promises of reformed behavior, charitable intentions, and even a saintly future, if only they will be allowed to survive.

The spiritual awakening and bargaining with God on the battlefield is an obvious attempt to find some control in a situation that is otherwise entirely out of one's control. In another example, a well-known religious conversion often takes place among prisoners on Death Row. Now you know one of the main reasons why that happens.

Consider the information mentioned at the start of this book, suggesting that members of the "baby boom" generation are having a significant increase in their rate of depression. I believe a main reason boomers are so depressed is that they have the "illusion of control." Boomers typically grew up believing they could do anything they wanted. They thought they could get advanced educations, high-paying jobs, could travel the world, have families, and succeed in whatever endeavor they chose. The positive side is that many boomers *did* succeed professionally and financially much more quickly than did their parents. The negative side is that their accomplishments have too often been at the expense of a good perspective on life or high-quality, enduring marital and family relationships.

When you are bright and successful, your achievements can lead you to believe you can do *anything* if you just go about it in the right way. Life would be so much simpler—and nicer—if only that were true. Believing it provides comfort to people, though, so it has widespread appeal.

The baby boomers have been socialized in an era unlike any other. Technological advances keep happening at a rate too fast for most of us to keep up with; social changes have been remarkably fast-paced; massive amounts of information are readily accessible in a variety of forms (from CD-ROM to digital recording); and great product diversity has fostered a marked increase in consumer purchases. Many people in this age group *have* been able to get what they want on demand.

What effect does such a socialization history—in which an individual essentially need only ask for something in order to receive it—have on expectations and experiences? Of course, I can't say conclusively that the high expectation of success is the primary cause for the high incidence of depression in this age group. But it certainly stands to reason that when you have been led to believe that motivation produces outcomes ("where there's a will"), you may be left wholly unprepared for the reality that life doesn't always work that way.

Trying to obtain something on the strength of merely wanting it has led many boomers to believe they can "have it all." Often, the source of depression in such individuals is their being forced to accept the reality that no one can have it all.

Every choice you make precludes other choices. For example, if you strive to build a successful career, you have less time and emotional availability for building deep and satisfying relationships. Choosing to have children means you can't go off on spontaneous trips when school is in session. Achievement as the object of intense focus can swamp a sense of comfort with just "being" and not achieving anything at all. Simply put, if you're doing "this," then you're *not* doing "that."

Life involves many difficult choices, each with profound implications for what you will eventually face. The illusion that you can control all aspects of your life, and have only desirable, happy consequences as the result of your choices, is a terribly unrealistic way to go through life. The illusion of control is manifested in many more ways, though, than just the "having it all" mentality common among younger adults. Whenever you try to make something happen that is not *directly* and *entirely* in your control, you may be laboring under an illusion of control.

The illusion of control is born of the idealistic desire we all have to make the world the way we want it to be. It's important for us to want things to happen a certain way, as I pointed out in the discussion on positive goals. Let's be clear, though: our goals must be realistic. People with the illusion of control risk depression when they attempt unrealistic goals. A vital skill for controlling depression is distinguishing clearly what is and is not within your control. The exercises in this chapter can help you do that.

I can think of many individuals I have worked with who tried to make situations or people meet their needs and wants, and then entered deep depressions when what they most wanted and valued eluded them. One case that comes to mind is that of a middle-aged, deeply depressed woman named Caroline.

Caroline, the Mom with a Vision

Caroline's college-aged son, Matt, whom she loved very much, was growing increasingly hostile toward her. In fact, their relationship was so severely strained that she feared it was in danger of breaking. In describing her relationship with Matt, she mentioned that he was attending an out-of-state college. Apparently, Matt used to come home for regular visits, but now was coming home much less frequently. When he did visit, he always seemed to have a chip on his shoulder; he was irritable, impatient, and sarcastic—quite different from his old affectionate self.

Caroline said she had always done her best for Matt. She had divorced when he was young and never remarried, and had focused all her attention on him. Caroline had attempted to raise Matt as well as possible by giving him everything she could afford to give him, even if Matt didn't particularly want it. So, Matt took piano lessons, extra courses in foreign languages, and other such pursuits that his mother considered important. When Matt first went away to college and came home for weekend visits, Caroline made a point of taking him to art galleries, museums, operas, music recitals, and almost <u>any</u> cultural events she could find. She reported that these activities, however, often gave rise to arguments. Matt didn't want to do such things anymore. She said Matt was too immature to appreciate what she was exposing him to, but she had no intention of stopping her efforts to "provide him with some polish."

Caroline was continually pressing Matt to appreciate the sophisticated things she deemed necessary if one was going to be a success in life. She had managed to get compliance from Matt all the years he was at home, until he went away to college. Now, as a maturing young adult, Matt was capable of deciding for himself which things <u>he</u> thought were of importance.

Instead of acknowledging Matt's growing maturity and ability to decide for himself what was worthy, Caroline intensified the pressure on him to see the correctness of her views. Instead of adjusting to the changing circumstances of Matt's living his own life away from home, Caroline behaved as if everything was as it had always been. She often chastised Matt by saying that if he were as grown-up as he *said he was, he would recognize the value of what she was sharing with him. Naturally, Matt got angry, they exchanged words, and their time together became difficult. Is it any wonder Matt was making fewer visits?*

Here is an example of one person, Caroline, attempting to impose on another, Matt, her idea of "right," "valuable," and "necessary." The result was that she was driving Matt away by not recognizing or accepting his ability to make choices for himself.

Caroline's attempts to tell Matt how he should think, how he should feel, and what he should value were all efforts to control him. I encouraged her to appreciate Matt's individuality and emerging adulthood by expressing an interest in things he enjoyed. And so she mustered the flexibility to listen to rock'n'roll and go to sporting events. She stopped nagging him about the holes in his jeans and his homework. She stopped bugging him to come home—and was quick to express appreciation when he did. Gradually, the relationship once again became a close, affectionate one. It took effort and flexibility to bring about the successful outcome, and, to her credit, Caroline gave up some of her illusion of control to make it possible.

You cannot control another person; you may try to manipulate him by exerting pressure on him to respond in a way you'd like, and you may even succeed. But his compliance is not voluntary. In time, he will resent the pressure you apply and eventually, no matter how long it may take, he is likely to rebel. No one likes to be oppressed by another, and the use of manipulative tactics to try to control someone almost invariably leads to the death of that relationship, either in spirit or fact.

To learn to talk to someone, and to accept and value someone, are very different goals from attempting to control someone. The fact that someone does attempt to control another person is evidence of an illusion of control. If there is someone in your life whom you want to "make" feel a certain way, respond in some way, or value a particular thing, be careful not to fool yourself into believing that, if you do everything right, you can make this person do as you wish. The illusion of control is believing you can make something happen when, in fact, the outcome is ultimately controlled by someone else.

You can care about others, you can offer them advice and perspective, and you can help support them, but *you do not control them.*

You cannot make someone else like you. You can do things that you think will make that person like you, but that's simply *you* using *your* ideas of what *you* would like about you if *you* were in that person's

LEARN BY DOING #60

If You Were Smart, You'd See It My Way

Purpose: To demonstrate the difficulties associated with trying to make people "see things your way."

Pick a safe or trivial subject to discuss, but one that you know each of your friends has a strong opinion about. If your relationship is healthy enough to tolerate this, attempt to convince them of the opposite viewpoint. Do this only with issues you don't really care much about, so that you don't get emotionally caught up in the discussion. Can you change your friends' minds? How would you feel if you really were committed to making them believe what you say?

shoes. Self-centered (egocentric) thinking is often found in depression, evidence that people use themselves as the reference point. They may think, "I wouldn't do that to someone, so they wouldn't do that to me." Then they leave themselves unguarded, and become devastated when the other person *does* do that.

I can assure you, other people do *not* value what you value, other people do *not* see things the same way you do, and other people have a different set of rules from you for playing the game of life. Sometimes those rules allow for behavior that your rules would forbid. If you want to be effective in your relationships with others and with yourself, you must *learn what other people value on their own without prodding from you.*

If another person doesn't value what you do or doesn't live by the same standards, you can maintain a relationship in such a way that you and he are not brought into conflict over the issue. And if conflict is unavoidable, you can respect that person's ability to make his own choices, and, if necessary, go your own way. Trying to control (change) his feelings or beliefs, however, is an effort that will likely fail.

The more of yourself you invest in a failing effort, the greater the chance you will feel like a failure and become depressed. You cannot make your child value a clean room or his chemistry class. You cannot make your insensitive partner sensitive or more communicative. You cannot force someone to think you are interesting and attractive. *You cannot make anyone do anything. You can only create opportunities and motivations, then leave it up to the other person to choose a course of action.* If you

265

LEARN BY DOING #61

May I Have Your Permission?

Purpose: To help make it clear why you are the only one who can set your own standards.

The fear of rejection and the fear of conflict often make someone try hard to get others' approval. The critical issue in approval-seeking behavior is how far you will go to get someone else to approve of you. If you are willing to do anything, or almost anything, to get someone to like you, then what ability to protect yourself from unreasonable or even demeaning demands do you have? In this exercise, you are to exaggerate approval-seeking behavior in order to discover firsthand how much of yourself you have to give up to do things according to what others want.

Choose harmless environments, ideally a caring relationship, to spend a few days acting out a pattern of extreme approval-seeking. Ask for permission for <u>everything</u> you want to do. "Would it be okay with you if I go to the bathroom?" "Is it all right if I get some water?"

---

use coercion or self-serving manipulative tactics to force your way, you may win in the short run, but not in the long run.

The field of social psychology offers some fascinating observations about the illusion of control. Research demonstrates the general point that when people expend effort, they expect successful results. In one experiment, individuals were allowed to buy dollar tickets for a large cash lottery. Some people were allowed to pick their own lottery numbers; others were assigned numbers. The experimenter later asked them whether they'd be willing to sell back their lottery tickets. Interestingly, those who had been allowed to pick their own numbers wanted considerably more money to sell their tickets back than did those who had had their numbers assigned. Somehow, being the one to choose the lottery number created an illusion that they stood a better chance of winning! (Statistically, of course, your odds of winning the lottery are exactly the same, no matter how you derive your numbers.)

Learn to be deliberate about choosing in what to invest your energy or emotions. You can't always know ahead of time whether you'll succeed in doing something, which is why life inevitably involves taking risks. The idea, though, is to take smart risks, not foolish ones. That

LEARN BY DOING #62

Assessing Controllability

Purpose: To solidify your ability to recognize which situations are and are not controllable. This exercise builds on the earlier one in this chapter called "Assessing the Percentage of Control." That was done retrospectively, while this one is done prospectively.

Pick <u>at least six</u> interactions or situations <u>every single day for the next month</u> and assess <u>ahead of time</u> how much control you are likely to have there. Write down (1) what the factors are that will determine what happens in that situation or interaction, (2) what overall percentage (from zero to 100) of control you think you have, (3) what actually happens, and (4) each of the factors that influenced what happened. When you are accurate most of the time in predicting 3 and 4 from 1 and 2, then you'll know your judgment about control is good. <u>This exercise is one of the most important in the book.</u> I hope you'll practice it regularly. Use the outline and example below to get started.

Upcoming Situation	Factors That Determine What Will Happen	Percent Control I Have	What Actually Happened	Factor(s) That Influenced What Happened
Asking a woman on a date.	1. Asking an appropriate person (someone not married, not otherwise involved, etc.).	1. 50% (If she's not wearing a ring, how do I know if she's involved elsewhere?)	She turned me down.	She just got out of a long-term relationship and has no interest in dating at this time (factor number 4, which was correctly anticipated as a possibility).
	2. Asking politely and in a non-threatening way.	2. 100%		
	3. Suggesting a specific activity (such as meeting for lunch or a cup of coffee).	3. 100%		
	4. Her level of interest in dating in general.	4. 0%		
	5. Her level of interest in me in particular.	5. 0% **Overall:** "It's worth a try"—50-50!		

means determining as clearly as possible just how much control you have in a given situation.

THE BALANCE OF CONTROL

From the discussion of the relationship between control and depression, you now know that depression often arises from attempting to control the uncontrollable or not controlling the controllable. No one is in control all the time, and no one is out of control all the time. The goals are to (1) develop an accurate and reliable way to recognize on a *situation-by-situation* basis where the control is, and (2) develop a balanced perspective so that *preventively* you do not expend energy in a direction that cannot pay off, and *do* expend your energy when it is likely to produce a desired result. Remember, unless you have a deliberate and detailed plan for accomplishing your goals, your efforts may be unfocused or misdirected. Once the failure dominoes begin to fall, you are at greater risk for depression. That is why I've been encouraging you to have solid plans for doing skillfully the things that matter to you. As most insurance salespeople will tell you, "It isn't that people plan to fail; it's that they fail to plan."

Attempting to control every aspect of life is certainly not evidence of actual greater mastery over life. Nor is missing obvious opportunities to take steps in your own behalf and asserting control over the direction of important things in your life. There is balance if you have a clear sense of when to walk away from a potentially hurtful situation, because you recognize it as being outside your control, and when to invest some of your energy and thought into a course of action, because a desired result is within your power.

The exercises in this chapter are meant to sharpen your ability to recognize when something is or is not in your control. If you recognize that you can meaningfully influence the outcome of a situation, and you judge that situation to be of sufficient importance to justify your effort, then it is to your advantage to strive for the result you want. If, on the other hand, you recognize that no amount of effort will be enough to succeed, then you can make a conscious choice to save your time and energy in order to prevent frustration and depression.

Control issues will surface many times every single day. That is not in your control. What *is* in your control is *whether* you attempt to influence a situation, *to what degree* you attempt to influence it, and *how specifically* you can define the point at which you are better off walking away than going down in flames.

SUMMARY OF KEY POINTS . . .
AND WHAT THEY CAN MEAN TO <u>YOU</u>

- People have a basic need to feel in control of life situations, including control of other people. This chapter is about dealing realistically with that need. As someone wise once said, "Life is what happens to you when you had other plans."

- Depression is often closely associated with errors in judgment about control issues. The errors will usually take one of two forms: not controlling things that could be controlled, or trying to control things that cannot be controlled. You may make either error at any given point unless you routinely evaluate situations clearly.

- Your perceptions about the controllability of a situation are, in part, dependent on your experience regarding whether you could make things happen, or whether things happened to you. The hazard is when you react to situations now as if they are the same as they were in the past. Time for an update!

- People can incorrectly conclude they are helpless when they have tried to do something in one situation and failed, and then overgeneralized the failure to unrelated situations. This is known as the "illusion of helplessness." Don't just "take things lying down," as if there's nothing you can do to improve your circumstances.

- An "illusion of control" exists when you believe you can control the outcome of a situation that is objectively beyond your influence. You won't always be able to change the world, but you can certainly do a lot to keep your little corner of it tidy.

- Since the relationship between your subjective perceptions of control and depression is so strong, it highlights the need for you to determine quickly and accurately what is and is not in your control. Mastering this skill will help you manage depression well. Keep practicing it!

Chapter 10

BOUNDARIES, BOUNDARIES, BOUNDARIES

Earlier in this book, I talked about socialization, the development of a personal value system that leads us to develop some patterns and abilities but not others, and the deficits in key areas that can lead to or exacerbate depression. I hope what keeps popping into your awareness is the idea that life presents us with never-ending challenges; whoever it was who said, "Life is just one damn thing after another" wasn't all that far off.

Without the ability to respond effectively to life challenges, whether internal (like coping with hurt feelings) or external (like coping with an obnoxious co-worker), it's all too easy to sink into helplessness and depression. So, thus far I have encouraged you to develop a variety of skills, such as critical thinking, clear thinking, discriminating what's in your head from what's "out there," planning, recognizing what is and is not controllable, and what you are and are not responsible for.

All of these skills require an ability to *differentiate*—an ability to recognize important differences between people, between situations, and between parts of yourself, so that you can plan your responses accordingly. When someone overgeneralizes ("You just can't trust skinny people"), for example, the lack of differentiation should be evident to you. After all, not all skinny people are alike.

Wherever there is differentiation, there are boundaries. Boundaries separate elements of experience from one another. They also separate people from one another, thus defining each person as a distinct individual. Your boundaries define who you are, what social role you are in at the moment, what you can and cannot do while you are in that

271

Pause and Reflect #42

Generalizing About Overgeneralizations

Why don't people differentiate well, reacting to situations that are only mildly similar as if they are actually the same? Do you recognize when you are making overgeneralizations about people based on gender, race, religion, age, marital status, nationality, level of education, sexual preference, and other such defining characteristics? Are there times when it is reasonable to form overgeneralizations?

My response: I think people have a difficult time escaping their own frames of reference. When they're in a situation that seems familiar, they tend to do what they did before. It is the equivalent of traveling to foreign countries and, instead of learning local customs and perspectives, judging everything by American standards. It takes effort to set aside your frame of reference and past experience and respond to what is really there. I think that's the kind of effort people don't realize they need to make, so automatic is it for them to "react from the gut."

Can overgeneralizations ever be useful? Yes. For example, an inviolable rule of conduct, like "I will never let someone abuse me," is absolute and makes no distinction of context. (And it shouldn't.) If someone overgeneralizes and says, "All people are due a fundamental respect for their basic human rights," that, too, is an overgeneralization, albeit a positive one. Our legal system also operates on an overgeneralization—that "all people are innocent until proven guilty." Can you think of other contexts where overgeneralizations are appropriate?

role, what you will and will not accept in others' treatment of you, and which part(s) of yourself you will engage with at the moment. Without clear, firm boundaries, you are at a constant risk of being victimized by others or yourself.

In this chapter, I focus on your personal boundaries. Having defined boundaries, I will discuss the vital topics of building and protecting *your* boundaries.

DEFINING YOUR BOUNDARIES

SOCIAL ROLES

How many social roles do you currently occupy in your life? Consider some of the possibilities. Parent? Child? Employer? Employee? Age? Gender? Friend? Colleague? Citizen? Group member? These terms all represent roles you assume at different times in your life. Each role has specific demands that define success when you meet them or failure when you don't.

Let's consider the role of a medical doctor. What characteristics and behaviors define a good doctor? What should a doctor almost always do, and what should a doctor *never* do? Doctors "should" provide high-quality, timely and compassionate care regarding your medical concerns. It's what defines the boundaries of good medical practice. Seducing a patient into a sexual relationship is a clear boundary violation, is it not? Yet there are some (fortunately, not very many) doctors who "cross the line" and do exactly what they should never do, violating a boundary that defines the professional doctor-patient relationship. Where are the doctor's boundaries in such a case? What should he have done to maintain the boundaries of a professional relationship and why didn't he do those things? And what are your feelings about such a doctor?

Using this scenario as an example, you can appreciate the necessity of knowing clearly the boundaries of your position. Likewise, you can recognize that it takes personal strength and integrity to maintain those boundaries, especially when your feelings (like a doctor's attraction to a patient) are pulling you in the direction of violating the boundaries. You must be able to go beyond those feelings and recognize that there is considerably more at stake than your feelings. (Here's another example of why I have stated throughout this book that your feelings are not always trustworthy and why "follow your feelings" can sometimes be terrible advice.)

Why have boundaries? They define you as a person, they define what you do and don't do, and they define your relationships with others. They define your personal, social, and professional responsibilities and your level of integrity. If you think about it, much of the deterioration that has taken place in our society has come about because people ignore or reject the positive value of boundaries. Like

LEARN BY DOING #63

Boundaries and Behavior

Purpose: To help you recognize the strong relationship between how you maintain your boundaries and your level of self-esteem.

One way to define your boundaries is in terms of the relationship between your boundaries and your behavior. Go back to the exercise you did in Chapter 8 called "Managing Role Conflicts" (Learn by Doing #48). There in column one, you listed the various social roles you currently occupy. In column two, you listed "Behaviors Mandated by That Role." In column three, you listed "Behaviors Precluded by That Role." In that exercise, I wanted you to prepare for inevitable role conflicts. Now I want you to think in terms of boundaries and self-esteem. What is the effect on your self-esteem when you live up to the mandates of column two, or when you do any of the behaviors in column three?

the unethical doctor who seduces a vulnerable patient, whenever people put their personal needs or desires ahead of their social responsibilities, the results can be harmful. *Just because someone can, doesn't mean he should.* When is ignoring boundaries a positive assertion of "personal freedom," and when is it irresponsible and self-indulgent? Finding the line and responding skillfully is not always easy.

What are *your* boundaries? They are evident in the interactions between you and others and in your interactions with yourself. Throughout your life, you have had countless opportunities to discover your boundaries by learning what you like and what you don't like, what you do and don't feel comfortable with, what is and is not acceptable to you, and what you are and are not willing to say or do to others or yourself.

DEVELOPING BOUNDARIES

How do we first learn and then develop our boundaries? Throughout our childhood, we are taught by others how to treat people, how to treat ourselves, and how to respond to the demands and expectations of others. Through all these interactions, we learn whether we are acceptable (tolerated at least, loved at most) just for being who we are, or whether our worth comes from how much of ourselves we sacrifice to gain the approval or love of others. Boundaries are easiest to build when you are encouraged to know and express yourself as an individual, and your uniqueness is valued. That is not the same, though, as "anything goes." Ideally, you are taught to honor and accept yourself, but not by acting irresponsibly at others' expense.

Consider a simple example that involves parents, children, and boundaries. When you were growing up, did you have privacy as a member of your family? Did you have your own "personal space"? I am not referring to your own bedroom, but to your space for doing routine things. Could you speak privately on the telephone to friends, or did your parents insist on listening in? Were you left alone to talk and play with your friends? If you were taking a bath or shower, did people respect your privacy, or did they intrude? Did you have a private place for your things, or did anything you have quickly become a matter of public knowledge? Did people talk openly about aspects of you that should have been private, like your body or your deeper feelings about sensitive issues?

You may think of specific instances where your boundaries were violated, as when someone revealed a secret, but such exceptional situations do not usually create poor personal boundaries. Rather, boundary problems develop from growing up under *continuing* violations, in which a sense of the importance of self is not allowed to develop. An extreme example is incest. How can you develop a sense of personal boundaries when the most fundamental boundary, which prohibits crossing the physical and sexual lines, is obliterated by an adult who makes clear that you are viewed as a sexual object, despite your feelings? In such cases, people's boundaries either never develop, or they are torn down and violated. The results can be devastating on many levels, as you can imagine. Such hurtful experiences define you as powerless to protect yourself against deeply personal intrusions. There is rarely anything empowering about such painful experiences; usually they are only destructive, requiring a great deal of effort just to cope with them.

Remember the pattern of "learned helplessness," discussed earlier? Aversive, uncontrollable events *can* lead to depression—and can prevent the building of personal boundaries that could be defended against an intruder, thereby preventing further violations. Without boundaries, there is more victimization, more helplessness, more self-loathing, and more depression. It is essential, then, as part of *any* treatment, including self-help, to learn that, though your boundaries may have been nonexistent or indefensible in the past, in your current context the boundaries can be built and protected and become a source of pride and self-value.

It is an overgeneralization—"sloppy thinking"—to believe that, because your boundaries were not very firm, they cannot be so in the future. This chapter is about building strong boundaries and protecting them—protecting *you*—consistently. The first step is to develop a better understanding of what boundaries are. You've learned something about roles; now let's consider your style of developing boundaries.

GLOBAL THINKING AND BOUNDARIES

In earlier chapters, I mentioned a global cognitive style. You may recall that I was referring to the way you gather and interpret information. As an example, consider the way you have been reading this book. Have you been merely skimming it (globally) or really reading it? Do you read in order to get the general idea (global), or do you carefully consider each new idea and exercise? Do you "have a (global) feel" for the book but can't really recall much that is specific or do you remember key points and even the examples that illustrated them?

The person who "sees the forest but not the trees" is a global thinker. That is neither a good nor bad thing until you consider the consequences in specific situations. Global thinkers are generally less critical in their thinking, responding to the entirety of something without grasping that sometimes the "little things" *can* ruin the entirety. For example, you may meet someone who is really attractive—funny, witty, great-looking, successful—but has one "tiny" flaw: he lies, blames, avoids, and never seems to take responsibility for anything he does; it's always *your* fault. Unless you can see the "trees" in the "forest" of this fellow's personality, you may easily get trapped by his attractive aspects and overlook what is surely a "fatal flaw," one that will doom your relationship with him or your self-esteem or both.

Global thinking can lead to an inability to distinguish image from substance. In our image-obsessed culture, companies spend millions of advertising dollars to create an impression. Individuals can do the same on a smaller scale. A funny example—to me, at least—occurred many years ago when *The Merv Griffin Show* was a popular talk show. One night Merv had as a guest Robert Young, and was discussing Young's current program, *Marcus Welby, M.D.* The Marcus Welby character played by Young was a kind, dedicated physician, loved by all. He didn't get sued; no one abused his generous willingness to make house calls; and he represented the ideal image of a doctor of that era. Robert Young told Merv Griffin that he received tens of thousands of fan letters every month—nearly half of them from people seeking a medical diagnosis! Let's be honest here—if you can't distinguish an actor from the role he plays, you are in serious trouble! And yet too often people do mistake someone's role for the person, and end up hurt or disappointed when they discover that the image doesn't fit. They may even feel angry and betrayed by that person. But who is

277

actually responsible—the person who didn't live up to the image or the person who mistook the image for reality?

Now, let's tie this concept into depression. Have you ever found yourself thinking, *"Everybody* else is happy, but I'm not," or *"Everyone* else is doing okay, but I'm not." To see a small part of someone and think that's *all* of him is global. It leads you to compare yourself with others in ways that will inevitably hurt you, because the comparisons are based on your projections, not on facts. You don't know that person's thoughts, feelings, or circumstances. You don't know what pains that person suffers in life. You don't know that person's history or, of course, his future. To compare yourself on the basis of some global assessment that puts that person "one up" and you "one down" is hurtful and depressing.

Good boundaries help you recognize that you don't fully know the other person or his circumstances. Healthy boundaries remind you that you are not that person, nor can you realistically compare yourself to him. Boundaries prevent you from losing your individuality by trying to be like someone else. That's a dangerous thing to want, of course, because you *can't* be someone else; you're already you! You're much better off striving to be the best *you* that you can possibly be. Boundaries remind you that anything whole comprises its parts; recognizing and understanding each of those parts is essential to defining your relationship to them.

Learning to set boundaries, to differentiate one situation from another, is an enormously valuable skill. I think it's unfortunate that people aren't routinely taught this skill early in life, because its absence can wreak havoc in their lives. Fortunately, establishing boundaries is a learnable skill at *any* point in life.

The Case of Tom, Sandy, and the Ex-Husband They Could Do Without

Sandy began the session by pointing to Tom and saying, "Tom was very nice to come here today, but the problem is really mine." When I asked her to describe it, Sandy said, "Tom is my second husband. I'm his first wife. We've been married a year. What you need to know, Dr. Yapko, is that I hate my ex-husband. I mean, I really hate my ex-husband. Make no mistake about it—I totally, completely hate my ex-husband." I said, "Okay, subtle as it was, I think I understand what you're telling me. You hate your ex-husband." Sandy said,

"Yeah, I really hate him!" I said, "Got it. Why is that relevant?" Sandy answered, "Because the longer I live with Tom, the more he reminds me of my ex-husband! I'm withdrawing from him—I don't want to sit with him; I don't want to sleep with him; I don't want to be around him at all. And Tom's a good man. I don't want to ruin this marriage because of my feelings about my ex-husband. Can you help?"

Now, pause. What would you have said to Sandy? Sandy was focused on seeing specific similarities between Tom and her ex-husband, leading to a global rejection of Tom. If I had asked, "So, Sandy, just how does Tom remind you of your ex-husband?" my question would have amplified all the similarities she was already aware of. If I had asked that, I think Sandy and Tom would be divorced today. Instead, I talked at length about superficial similarities and deeper differences. I gave trite examples of a deep point, such as how all the roses on a rosebush can look identical at first glance but, on closer examination, you discover that one rose has darker petals than another, that another hasn't fully bloomed yet, that one has spots, and so on. I described how all the trees of a forest can look the same to a casual observer. Look closer, though, and you will see that this tree has broken branches, that one has a bird's nest in it, another has moss on its trunk. I gave many more examples of seeing as similar things that are, in fact, different. Then I gave Sandy the homework assignment of writing out five hundred ways Tom is different from her ex-husband! Of course, I didn't expect her to sit down and generate such a huge list all at once, but by pushing her to focus on *differences,* I encouraged Sandy to see them, log them, and get absorbed in them to the point of never again mistaking Tom for her ex-husband. That's exactly what happened, and now Sandy and Tom live together as a happy couple.

The Case of Stan, Who Had a Bad Day

Stan's case represents another way the lack of boundaries can cause anxiety and depression. Two years ago, when Stan was about to get married, he came down with flu and was sick right up to the wedding day. But, short of death, he had no intention of canceling the wedding. After all, guests were coming from all over the country, and the ceremony and party plans were so elaborate, it would be impossible to cancel them without losing tons of money. All in all, canceling the wedding was a far worse option than just toughing it out.

LEARN BY DOING #64

Identifying Differences

**Purpose: To encourage you to look beyond superficial simi-
larities so that you develop a deeper understanding of
what makes each person or situation unique, therefore
requiring you to adapt your responses accordingly.**

Noticing the similarities between things can be helpful in developing a general understanding about them. The ability to detect
subtle differences, though, calls for a deeper analysis and leads to
a deeper understanding. Pick a category of similar experiences
(such as cocktail parties, business meetings, casual conversations,
your personal moods) to analyze for a week or two, and keep a running list of ways this one differs from that one. When your list is
long enough to suggest that you're aware of differences despite the
similarities, go on to another category and do the same. This is an
excellent exercise for developing critical thinking, a necessary step
in learning to establish clear boundaries.

During the marriage ceremony, which was held outside on a hot
day, Stan, who was wearing a black tuxedo, became so woozy that
he almost passed out. An observant usher caught Stan and got him
safely settled in a chair. Understandably, Stan was deeply embarrassed by the episode, taking place at such a sensitive time in front
of so many people. The episode grew, though, from an isolated incident at the wedding to something much bigger. Stan developed a
fear that he might pass out at any time, anyplace, but especially in
public situations. Not good, because Stan was a public speaker! So
he worked up a lot of fear and anxiety by visualizing in detail the
humiliation of passing out in almost every public situation he was in.
Stan became depressed over his inability to function as freely as he
used to, and he now avoids situations he didn't give a second
thought to in the past.

Now, pause. Define how Stan's story represents a boundary problem. Got it? Stan didn't focus on the uniqueness of his wedding day
circumstances and simply say, "I was sick and I was hot—that's why I
almost passed out." Instead, with no boundaries in place around the
episode, Stan extended the possibility of passing out into all kinds of
situations. He needed to learn that what happens in one situation,
especially a unique one, does not necessarily predict what will happen

in other situations. Remember the discussion in Chapter 6 about global thinking and specific attributions? Stan's global attributions gave rise to terrible images of public unconsciousness and private humiliation. My goal in working with Stan was clear: to help him separate with clean boundaries the memory of a negative experience at the wedding from everything else he did in his life.

From the examples of Tom, Sandy, and Stan, can you see how important boundaries—or the lack thereof—are in shaping the quality of your experience? To clearly separate an ex-husband from a current one, or to separate an uncomfortable public speaking situation that occurred due to illness from other public events, or to recognize the singularity of *any* person or circumstances can help you respond successfully in the present instead of reacting with old responses from the past. The present may resemble the past in some ways, but there are important differences, too.

While I have focused on how important it is to notice differences, I want to acknowledge that noticing similarities is valuable, too. Sometimes people get so preoccupied with superficial differences that they miss the important similarities. Perhaps the most glaring example is racism. Skin color is a superficial difference. What about all the similarities that should preclude discrimination against people because of their racial, age, gender, sexual preference differences, and so on?

It's important to recognize both similarities *and* differences. Usually, however, it's the differences between people and circumstances that force us to respond in new and creative ways. Personal growth is the positive result.

BOUNDARIES AND COMPARTMENTALIZATION SKILLS

Another potentially depressing consequence of poor (undefined) boundaries and global thinking is the inability to recognize the different parts of your "self." You can easily lead yourself to believe that "this is me, and that's all." A global representation of this sort makes it difficult to go beyond what you feel at a given moment, so that, in essence, you become your mood: "I'm depressed." You can convince yourself that your depressed feelings represent the sum total of your life experience. Your depression can become the reference point for every decision you make ("I can't think about that now; I'm depressed"), and it can become the reference point for every course of action you consider ("I can't go there; I'm depressed"). Your world can become narrower and narrower until you have claustrophobia from being walled in by depression.

How can you prevent that from happening to you? By recognizing this simple but vital fact: *You are more than your feelings. You are not your depression; you are not your depressed feelings; you are not just a mood with a body attached!*

In order to appreciate this point, you have to go from a global appraisal of your "self" to a specific or detailed acknowledgment of your many different components. No one component defines you. You are not your history. You are not your marriage. You are not your religion, nor are you your politics, and you are not your job. Each and every aspect of you that you can name—and I hope you can name many—contributes to who you are in ways big and small. But no single one of them defines you.

When you define yourself globally by one part—*any* one part—you are at greater risk of depression. Why? Because you have all your "self-esteem eggs" in one basket. To define yourself in terms of your career may seem fine when your career is going well. But what happens if you get laid off unexpectedly? Or your business fails? Or you get demoted? Depression is what happens, most typically. *You are more than your job.*

If you define yourself in terms of your relationship ("I'm a parent." "I'm a spouse"), when the relationship is going okay, no one hears any complaints. But what happens if it falters? Depression. *You are more than your relationships.*

If you define yourself in terms of your history ("I'm an incest survivor. I'm an adult child of an alcoholic"), how do you ever transcend what is unchangeable? Such a pathological self-definition may prevent you from outgrowing what is old and self-limiting. *You are more than your history.*

What I find over and over again is how frequently people's problems arise from their inability first to recognize the different aspects of themselves and then use their various parts appropriately, according to different situations. Simply put, the person is focused on the "wrong" part for the circumstance. It's like using the wrong tool for a repair job.

Let me give you what I think is a humorous example. Often in my clinical trainings, I will ask how many of my colleagues enjoy going to cocktail parties. Out of an audience of two hundred people, perhaps ten people will raise their hands. Does that surprise you? It shouldn't. Think about it. When you go to a cocktail party, what happens? You engage in pleasant, superficial conversation ("Hey, how about that local sports team?"). That is normal, appropriate, and desirable behavior in that context. In fact, if someone violates it by self-disclosing nonsuperficial things while you're standing at the punch bowl ("I'm impotent. My kids are on drugs. My checking account is overdrawn. I think my spouse is having an affair"), the normal response is to pull away from that person and carefully avoid him the rest of the night.

So why do psychotherapists often dislike and avoid cocktail parties? Because all day long they're involved in "deep" and "genuine" interactions, which they value greatly. As a result, they devalue the superficiality of cocktail party conversation. They don't like it because it seems to lack depth and sincerity. So if they don't have a positive value for "pleasant and superficial," they don't seek out experiences for developing that part of themselves.

Is superficiality "bad"? No! It is a necessary and appropriate starting place for building rapport and identifying those with whom you'd like to evolve a deeper relationship. But if the part I'll call "pleasant superficiality" is devalued, it remains underdeveloped and relatively uncomfortable. Even when a "shrink" goes to a party, he may have difficulty taking off his shrink hat and may ask probing questions inappropriately when someone casually says he saw a good movie recently.

Are you getting the point that a lot of what it takes to live well and feel good is to develop *all* your parts and recognize which parts are to be relied on in a given situation? I hope so. Only then can you evolve a sense of choice or personal control about how best to respond to different life situations. *If you are every bit as fluent in the language of your feelings as you are in the language of logic or reason, you can choose which language to speak at a particular moment based on the result you want.* To do that, you must be able to separate the emotional response from the rational response. Only a clear sense of personal boundaries can enable you to do that.

Enlarging on this crucial point, can you separate what is "best" from what is "easiest" or "most familiar" in a given context? If you choose to do what's easiest, not best, how will you like the consequences? Can you separate what's best for you from what's best for your child? For example, because of your wish not to be left alone, you may feel better keeping him home to attend a local community college. But what if he'd get a better education at an out-of-town university? What's the "good boundary" decision; what's the "bad boundary" decision?

Learning to think in terms of parts of yourself and the associated boundaries can lead to a greater recognition of which part(s) of yourself you should "tap into." You are one individual with many facets, each a valuable part of the whole. Self-awareness and appreciation of your many parts is critical to self-esteem and effective self-management.

BOUNDARIES AND SELF-ACCEPTANCE

The next exercise is useful not only for self-awareness, but also for self-acceptance. Why develop good boundaries and the ability to protect yourself if you don't consider yourself worthy? Until now, you may have not had the self-awareness or the ability to escape your one-dimensional (global) definition of yourself. But now you have the

LEARN BY DOING #66

Identifying Your Parts

Purpose: To enhance your self-esteem by realizing that every part of you is valuable at some place, some time. The skill is to know which part to "tap into" at a given point.

On a sheet of paper, make five columns. In column one, make a list of <u>at least 20 different "parts" of yourself</u>. In the second column, identify at least three contexts where that part can serve you in a positive way. In the third column, specify how it does so. In the fourth column, identify at least three contexts where that same part can serve you in a negative way. Specify how it does that in the fifth column. I hope you will discover that <u>no part of you is inherently positive or negative;</u> rather, its value comes from what it enables you to do or prevents you from doing. Use the outline and example below to get started.

My "Parts"	Contexts Where It Serves Me	How It Can Serve Me	Contexts Where It Hurts Me	How It Can Hurt Me
Desire to be with others	1. Establishing friendships	1. Allows me to show a genuine interest in others	1. When others are too busy for me	1. It can make me too urgent about getting too close to others.
	2. Establishing business connections	2. Allows me to learn from others' experiences	2. When I have to be alone	2. It can blind me to others' faults.
	3. Being connected to my family	3. Permits me to create true intimacy in my relationships	3. When others reject me	3. It can make me feel weak and dependent on others for my self-esteem.

chance to redefine yourself and come to the realization that you're more than your feelings or *any* one aspect of yourself. This can give you the motivation and rationale to develop good boundaries for your dealings with yourself and others. You are worthwhile, you are deserving, and you are the only one who can define yourself as such. It is your responsibility to do so.

Do you need to feel worthy *before* you stand up for yourself, or do you first stand up for yourself in order to feel worthy? The answer is, stand up for yourself *now*. Act as if you are important enough and valuable enough to want to take good care of, and then watch what happens. Over time, you will begin to demand better treatment from others, and you'll get it! You will demand better treatment from yourself, and you will get it! You will demand higher quality responses (actions) from yourself, you'll push yourself to deliver, and you'll do it! It is no coincidence that those people with higher expectations and demands get more of them (not all, though) fulfilled. Good boundaries means not settling for mediocrity, from yourself or anyone else.

Self-awareness and self-acceptance mean you assert your needs and wishes and you are clear about which things you are willing to compromise on and which things you have absolutely no intention of compromising on. You may compromise on where to go for dinner, but you had better not even think for a moment about compromising on whether honesty is important in your closest relationships!

It is very important that you grasp the sequence here. If you wait until you feel worthy before you start setting limits, you have it backward. You won't feel worthy until you do start setting limits—on yourself as well as others.

Recognizing that you have many different parts and accepting them is an important basis for making good life choices. For example, if you know you are a person who likes a lot of freedom to choose, then you can avoid situations that are predictably going to box you in. Remember Erica from Chapter 5? She's the woman who wanted a baby, not a child. She found it difficult to have a child because her boundaries call for control and perpetual neatness. Hers is the lack of self-awareness that so often leads people to make bad decisions that ultimately prove hurtful. For example, a woman wants to think she can adjust to her lover's fooling around on her because she wants to keep him, but monogamy is very important to her. So she sinks into depression as she tries to ignore what hurts her. Or consider a man who tries to handle a work transfer to a department he has always hated simply because he wants to stay with the company. Slowly he becomes depressed at the very thought of having to go to work in the morning.

The variety of ways that people miss opportunities to protect themselves with good self-definition is endless. Boundaries can help you know the strengths and limitations of all your parts and thereby lead you to choose wisely your investments of time, emotion, and energy.

BOUNDARIES AND ASSERTIVENESS

One of the important implications of learning to recognize and accept the different parts of your self is that you can stop asking, "Is it okay that I'm this way?" Instead, you can say, *"Since* I'm this way, how can I make this part of me work to my advantage?" *Every part of you is valuable at some time, some place.* Problems arise when you "use" the part that is inappropriate for the situation at hand.

I hear people say things like "He has a lot of control issues." What exactly does that mean? To me, someone who wants a lot of control over his life is someone who recognizes that if you want to live life well, you have to work intelligently to make it happen. Being "controlling" means wanting to control what happens. If you take control of things you actually *can* control, it's not a problem. However, if you try to control things you can't, like other people, it can be a serious problem. Good boundaries help you recognize what is and is not controllable. Being "controlling" isn't the problem; trying to control other people's right to choose by imposing your will on them is the problem. When you accept the boundary that defines treating others respectfully, allowing them their right to choose their own paths, then you can apply your controlling behavior only to those contexts where it's appropriate.

BOUNDARIES AND LIMIT-SETTING

The above point leads us to the direct relationship between having clear boundaries and acknowledging them in *all* your relationships. When must you define and protect your boundaries ("set limits")? Answer: *whenever you are dealing with anything that breathes!* Setting limits is essential with your kids, your spouse, your friends, your dates, your pet, the appliance repairman, your in-laws, your folks, the salesperson at the store, EVERYONE. *It is your job to train people how to treat you.* If you ignore their lateness, overlook their snippiness, pretend you don't notice their rudeness, or give in to their manipulations, you are silently telling them, "It's okay." But if it hurts you, *is* it okay? Ignoring what hurts is how people become and stay victims of others. The resulting lack of self-respect is fertile ground for the seeds of depression.

Why do other people put you in the position of having to define and protect your boundaries? Doesn't it make you angry that you have to be on guard and self-protecting all the time, even with your friends and family? Well, it may make you angry, but only if you are unrealistic enough to believe that friends and family shouldn't be manipulative. Why shouldn't they be? *Of course they will be manipulative!* Why? Because *all* people are manipulative. No, that's not an accidental overgeneralization. I mean it: all people want what they want. That includes you, it includes me, and it includes the nicest, most self-sacrificing people.

Manipulation can be positive or negative, depending on its methods and results. Positive manipulation is Mother Teresa using her near-saintly status to secure donations and followers to make possible her extraordinary efforts to help the poor. She is inspiring, and she is able to get much of what she strives for. Everyone wins in this context. Negative manipulation, on the other hand, involves a winner and a loser. If your boss says, "Work late on this tonight or don't bother to come to work tomorrow," that is coercive. If you comply, the boss wins and you lose (your right of personal free time and some self-esteem, too).

People will always want things from you. They may want your time, your emotional support, your money, your body, your active participation, your expertise, *whatever* it is you have that they want. The fact that they want it from you, whatever "it" happens to be, is hardly unusual. On the contrary, it's 100 percent normal. But just because someone wants it doesn't mean you have to provide it. If giving it hurts you in some way (beyond a minor irritation) or somehow sends or reinforces the wrong message ("I'll do this for you because you are too incompetent to ever do it for yourself"), then you must be able to set the limit and say no. If you send out the wrong message—"wrong" because it rewards someone's demands at a price that is hurtful to you—it will continue to make you a victim. *Being a victim and overcoming depression are mutually exclusive.*

Other people will always want what they want. The salesperson wants you to buy the product. Your mom wants you at *her* house for Thanksgiving. Your friend wants you to listen with undivided attention to his latest problem. Your boss wants you to feel lucky you even have a job. Your kid wants the "coolest" new whatever. And on and on. If you make the mistake of taking it personally (Pop quiz: What cognition distortion is that?), you're missing the fact that people turn to other people to get their needs met. They do, and it's normal. It's your job to decide how far you are willing to go to get their approval or how much you're willing to sacrifice to get them off your back. And the only way to decide those things realistically and from a position of personal power is to use your boundaries to separate what would be the "easiest" thing to do right now from what would be "best" in the long run. Giving in to a child's tantrum may make the tantrum stop for the moment, but it tells the child that throwing a tantrum will get him what he wants. Predictably, more tantrums are on the way.

The final aspect, then, of assertiveness is being able to endure the consequences of your limit-setting. When you don't buy the salesperson's product, he may make his disappointment visible or even criticize your "obvious lack of good judgment." When you have other plans for Thanksgiving, your mom may say, "How could you do this to me?" When your kid wants their gizmo and you don't buy it he may say, "You *never* understand what I want." Get the picture? People will say and do things to coerce you into complying with their wishes. If you do comply, you are rewarding some very undesirable manipulative behavior.

A vital component of maintaining good boundaries is your resistance to others' attempts to manipulate you for their personal gain at your expense. If you *choose* to comply with someone's demand because it's a situation that benefits both of you, fine. But if you are pressured or coerced into complying through someone's self-serving manipulative tactic, you are simply being victimized—always a lousy feeling, to say the least.

MANIPULATIVE TACTICS

Let's consider self-serving manipulative tactics in greater detail. The most common tactics include guilt ("Pack your bags; we're going on a guilt trip!"), intimidation, withdrawal, seduction, flattery, fast talk, and sympathy-gaining ploys. My guess is that you already know these, to some extent, from personal experience. It doesn't feel very good to be on the receiving end of such tactics, does it?

The guilt trip is an attempt by someone to make you feel guilty for not meeting his expectations or needs. Guilt is not necessarily a bad thing, of course; the truth is, you do have responsibilities and you have made commitments that you must honor if you are to maintain your integrity. But people will push you to feel responsible (and guilty) for things you are not responsible for. That's why in Chapter 8 I focused so specifically on guilt, including ways to avoid feeling it unnecessarily.

Depressed people tend to feel excessive and inappropriate guilt. Because engendering guilt often works to secure compliance, some people will use it to get what they want from you, so your task is to be clear about what you are and are not responsible for. It's *not* your responsibility to make sure he goes for his annual physical exam. It's *not* your job to make sure she gets to her job on time. If you are fooled into believing that you are responsible for another person's choices or responsibilities, you can be made to feel guilty.

Intimidation is an overtly nasty tactic. Yelling, screaming, and threatening someone's well-being (physical, emotional, financial) are all intimidation tactics. "If you don't do this, you're fired," or "I'll take the kids from you and you'll never see them again," or "If you ever say that to me again, I'll kill you," are tactics of intimidation. People get beaten up in sick relationships, the most obvious intimidation tactic of all. Violence is also a lethal tactic—if not to your very life, then certainly to your soul. It is the most brutal way someone imposes his will on another person. It may work in the short run, but it is guaranteed to breed intense anger and resentment, and an eventual rebellion and fight for independence (escape).

The tactic of withdrawal, or "freezing you out" is, no pun intended, a cold one. Whether the person sits and silently pouts, or leaves and refuses to return your calls, the manipulative message is clear: "Our relationship depends on your doing what I want." Such a tactic leaves no room for communication, negotiation, or compromise, and therefore directly undermines a healthy climate of free expression.

Being seduced softens just about anyone's feelings. You may get into an argument, mild or otherwise, and before any substantive resolution is achieved, the other person derails the discussion and changes it into a sexual encounter. And in the heat of whatever heat you may be in, the point(s) under consideration gets lost and . . . who cares? Well, you *should* care, because now he is getting his way simply because any resolve you may have had is long gone. Making love is nicer than threats of violence, but, either way, your needs or wishes can get run over.

"Flattery will get you everywhere," the old saying goes. Who is immune to the praise of others? Everyone likes to be acknowledged, and everyone likes to be appreciated and held in high regard. When others praise us, we feel good. The natural tendency is to respond to praise with positive feelings—to like the person who makes us feel good and increase our desire to please him further. There's the hook, of course. We don't want to alienate a benefactor. So we work a little harder to keep the other person happy. How far are you willing to go for his approval? And, conversely, how far are you willing to go to avoid rejection? When the praise or flattery is sincere, with "no strings attached" (there is no expectation that you must do something in return), go ahead and enjoy it. But when there *is* a string attached, beware how quickly the string can become a rope, and how easy it is to tie the rope into a noose.

If you've ever been exposed to a high-pressure salesperson, then you know what it's like to be inundated with facts and figures and superlatives (the *most*, the *best*, the *highest*). The person who can counter every point you make with some piece of information to justify why he's right and you're wrong is a tough person to deal with. There's often enough of a kernel of truth in what he's saying to make you wonder whether he might really be right. Your moment of doubt—even about something that you know—may be enough to weaken you to do things his way. That's how fast talk as a manipulative tactic works. He keeps you in the position of having to explain and having to explain some more while contradicting you with examples that don't quite seem true. He may keep it up until you doubt yourself enough to say, "Okay." To resist this, you have to work hard to keep the discussion on track, with no diversions into "conversational cul-de-sacs."

One of the most dangerous aspects of having poor boundaries is that you may put yourself in someone else's shoes so completely that he can make you want to rescue him from his problems. "Please feel sorry for me. See how sad and pathetic my circumstances are? Please help me; please take care of me." If you want the person to assume his own responsibilities and you therefore respond in an unsympathetic manner, that is used as evidence that you are "cold" and "abandoning." Being charitable or helpful isn't the same as losing yourself to someone else's needs. Helping someone out of a tough jam, especially when he didn't cause it, is a nice thing to do. Repeatedly rescuing someone from the consequences of his own foolish decisions may seem a sympathetic short-term solution, but it simply perpetuates his pattern of requiring rescue, learning nothing, and needing to be rescued once again. *The world's needs greatly exceed your personal supply.* Guard your resources carefully.

Pause and Reflect #44

They Manipulate You, You Manipulate Them

Which of the manipulative tactics described in this section are you most vulnerable to? Why do you think this is the case? Do you now have new ideas about how to resist such tactics?

Which manipulative tactics are you most likely to use to get your way? Can you see how such tactics can boomerang? How can you deal with others in a more straightforward way?

Identifying common manipulative tactics can be an empowering experience for you. It can help you smell someone's baloney coming your way from ten miles downwind. It can help you respond to all such tactics effectively by holding firmly to your position.

When you set limits and protect your boundaries, you'll learn a lot about the other person. Despite the disappointment he may feel, can he respect the lines you've drawn? If the answer is yes, then you have found a "keeper," a person who will take your wishes into account. That is the kind of person you want in your life. Such people may (and probably will) want their way, just as you want yours, but they will respect your wishes and expect you to respect theirs. (Make sure you do! That's what healthy compromise is about.) If the answer is no, then you've got a "throwaway," a person who will try to use you—taking, but not giving. Such people are *not* the ones you want in your life. As I have said, it's your responsibility to protect your boundaries and maintain healthy relationships despite the attempts by others to get you to compromise your needs in order to meet theirs.

Your boundaries will inevitably get tested countless times a day. I hope you now know a lot more about what it takes to accept yourself, like yourself, and protect yourself as you go through this complicated world we live in.

SUMMARY OF KEY POINTS . . .
AND WHAT THEY CAN MEAN TO <u>YOU</u>

- The ability to recognize differences between similar people or situations is a vital skill to master so that you can respond appropriately to present conditions without constant reference to the past. You are not the same now as you were then, and you have new resources upon which to draw. Use 'em or lose 'em!

- Boundaries separate elements of experience. They define what is appropriate behavior for your particular role. Boundaries also define what is and is not acceptable in others' behavior toward you. You have to define your roles and what you will and won't do. Self-esteem rises when you can regularly walk away from a situation and think, "I like what I did there."

- Responding globally indicates a lack of clear boundaries. So does an inability to set effective limits. The more you respond to "trees" and not "forests," the more choices you'll have about what to accept or reject in your relationships with others.

- You are made up of many different "parts," each potentially valuable in some context. Good boundaries prevent you from defining yourself solely in terms of any one part. For example, your feelings are important, but you are more than your feelings. When people get wrapped up in a "part" that is inappropriate for a given circumstance, they mishandle things and suffer the consequences. One of those consequences may be depression.

- Other people will routinely test your boundaries in their efforts to get from you what they'd like. That's normal behavior. It's your job to identify and resist their manipulative tactics (such as intimidation or guilt), and maintain the integrity of your personal boundaries.

Chapter 11

LOVE THAT HURTS, LOVE THAT HEALS: RELATIONSHIPS AND DEPRESSION

THIS CHAPTER EXPANDS ON the previous one by focusing on relationship patterns that are often troublesome for depressed individuals. Your relationship patterns are much like the other patterns described in this book: what you do may range from being very effective in achieving desirable outcomes, such as having a healthy intimate relationship, to being ineffective. My goal is to stress the need to *actively guide the direction of your relationships* so that you can make them more satisfying. Some of the patterns considered in this chapter relate to issues previously considered, especially control and responsibility. Mishandling those two issues is not only potentially hurtful at the personal level, but can be costly in terms of your relationships with others.

Having positive and healthy relationships with others is vital to your well-being. It is probably obvious to you that good relationships don't "just happen." Rather, they depend on a variety of important relationship skills. Unfortunately, though, the skills for building and maintaining such satisfying relationships seem to be on the decline in America. The high rate of divorce is an indication of the relationship problems Americans have. Other indications are the growing rates of such interpersonal problems as child abuse, domestic violence, custody battles, and discrimination. These problems and others all suggest that people are having a harder time than ever getting along with one another.

I believe a primary reason interpersonal skills are on the decline is that we interact with each other less and less as we do more and more independently. The need to interact is gradually being minimized in our lives. For most of us, there isn't a corner grocer who knows us from years of our shopping at his store; now there are huge supermarkets where we could probably die in an aisle and nobody would notice for a couple of days. There isn't a mechanic at the corner gas station who knows us from years of our buying gas there; now we walk up to a mirrored window and ask to have "ten dollars on number four," as if we're placing a bet at the racetrack. We don't have to interact with bank tellers, travel agents, or anybody else. We can replace all of them with a computer and modem.

These examples show how our interactions with others are too often brief and anonymous. The sad result is that there are a lot of people not connected to any, or very many, others. Statistically, more people in this country live alone than ever before. Many of them are happy to be alone, but many more are not.

TECHNOLOGY AND THE DECLINE IN SOCIAL SKILLS

What leads to the decline in relationship skills evident in these social problems? One pertinent observation by experts is that as the emphasis on technology increases, so does the emphasis on solitary pursuits. Consider the fact that surveys indicate the average American watches more than seven hours of television a day. Seven hours! Cable television, satellite dishes, videocassette recorders, and video disk technology can make watching television a full-time occupation. Interpersonal ("people") skills suffer.

Watching television is *not* an interactive process. Perhaps other people are in the room while you watch television, but your attention is diverted away from them. Television does not contribute to your ability to express your own ideas or feelings, nor does it encourage an understanding of your family and friends that's more profound than what's on sitcoms or the network movie of the week. Add to the amount of television watching time the hours an individual spends in front of a computer screen at work and alone in a car driving to and from wherever, and you'll see how the need and opportunity to interact with other people is decreasing.

The more time you spend alone with television, video games, or computers, the less opportunity you have to meet people and interact with them in casual ways. As casual interaction declines, it can create in you an even greater sense of urgency to have interactions of a deeper meaningful nature. Realistically, of course, you cannot create instant intimate relationships or immediate close friends, and the greater the urgency you feel to do so, the more likely it is that you will make mistakes by trying to have too much happen too quickly.

The divorce rate in America is high, exceeding 50 percent; the average dating relationship, statistically, lasts only a matter of weeks. The "quick fix" mentality—wanting to feel good and solve problems quickly or avoid them altogether (remember the "all-or-none" cognitive distortion?)—leads to a low frustration tolerance, that is, an inability to stay with a task until its completion. This desire for immediate results, or immediate gratification, keeps you from establishing long-term goals or attempting things that seem too time-consuming. And low frustration tolerance increases the likelihood that when a relationship problem does arise, as it frequently does, the relationship will get abused or even thrown away, instead of both partners taking the time to achieve a reasonable resolution.

The fact that we live in a "throw away" society which, unfortunately, includes marriages and families as well as disposable lighters and cameras, often makes it hard to develop a sense of personal security. How can you feel secure in a relationship when the threat of losing it hangs over your head? Each partner must be especially careful, if the relationship is to last, to *protect the other person's sense of security*. For example, when your impulse is to storm out of the house during an argument, the best and healthiest message you can give your partner is to stay and try to address the issues rationally. Your impulse may be to hurt the other person by making him feel afraid or jealous, but if, instead, you put your arms around him, the enduring message of caring is a powerful one. The last chapter's focus on boundaries, particularly the discussion about learning to distinguish between the fast or easy response and the best one, is relevant here. Healthy relationships require that both partners have clear boundaries about the importance of what can and cannot be said and what can and cannot be done when they are angry.

Each individual has needs that can be met only in the context of a relationship with another person. Your needs for emotional support, intimacy, and the expression of your sexuality are best met in a relationship with someone about whom you feel good. When your needs are *not* met, you become frustrated, with an amplified sense of urgency to try to get them satisfied. As the urgency increases, so does the likelihood of your making mistakes in judgment about how to meet your needs. So, Mr. Right gets sacrificed for Mr. Right *Now*. The most common mistake is one you can avoid: attempting to get your needs met in relationships with individuals who are not able or willing to meet those needs.

GENDER ROLES AND RELATIONSHIPS

In the earliest stages of socialization, our roles are based solely on gender: "Here's what a girl does; here is what a boy does." Those gender roles are called sex-role stereotyping, and they are created by society— the same society that shapes you to fit those roles. The result is that you establish expectations for your own gender-based behavior as well as that of others.

Sex-role stereotyped behavior has been the subject of a great deal of

Pause and Reflect #47

Do You Fit the Cultural Gender Model?

Do you fit your gender's sex role stereotype? If so, to what extent? How were you reared to fit this stereotype? If you don't fit the sex role stereotype, then how did you learn to do what you do, regardless of your gender and socialization?

study by social psychologists and relationship experts. If we consider the stereotypical woman, for example, we can observe that she is likely to be "other-oriented." She is taught to be highly sensitive to others' needs and wishes, and to place herself in a secondary role in relation to them. She is told, "Be a good daughter. Be a good wife. Be a good mother. Be there for everyone else, and if you make everyone else happy, then you'll be a success." Is it any wonder that women frequently feel unfulfilled? It is no coincidence that nearly twice as many women are diagnosed as depressed as are men. I repeat what I said before: building your life around things you cannot control seems fine when things go your way, but when they don't, look out!

Traditional male socialization leads the stereotypical man to be competitive and achievement-oriented. Is it any wonder, then, that men have historically had a far greater number of stress-related illnesses? It may interest you to know that as sex roles continue to undergo change, leading to a blurring of the lines separating the genders, an increase in women's stress-related illnesses is being documented. Given the cultural emphasis on men being high achievers and good providers, it may be more understandable, though not necessarily excusable, that men have more trouble than women in developing intimate relationship skills. Their focus has been on accomplishment, not relationships.

ROLES AND EXPECTATIONS

The important point about roles being assigned by our culture or our family is that wherever there is a role, there is also a set of expectations. Your competence in a role is judged on the basis of how well others' expectations are met. For example, consider what happens when a dating relationship first turns sexual. It may never be verbalized, but there is often a new expectation that this relationship is now a more deeply committed one. What happens, then, when he leaves the morning after and doesn't call for several days—or ever again, for that matter? Your expectations for the seriousness of the relationship have been unfulfilled. Predictably, you will feel negatively (hurt, betrayed, misled) about the person, and that will likely trigger some depressed feelings. If, on the other hand, he becomes more loving and attentive, your expectations and hopes will be fulfilled. Only then can you feel positively about him.

In relationships, expecting someone to meet your needs is, to a certain extent, necessary. After all, the chief benefit of being in a relationship is that your partner can provide dimensions of experience that you can't provide for yourself.

EXPECTATIONS OF OTHERS

Are the expectations you have for others realistic and appropriate? Perhaps your expectations are too high, too low, or too irrelevant for a specific person you have a relationship with. If your expectations are inappropriate or unrealistic, primarily because they are based on what you want rather than on what the other person can offer, then you have set yourself up to be disappointed. If you do not recognize that your expectations are unrealistic or inappropriate, you will be aware only of disappointment or anger, because your expectations will be unfulfilled.

When you form an explanation as to why your expectations went unfulfilled, your reasoning may end up hurting even more than the original disappointment. You may blame the world as a hostile place that is unpredictable and unmanageable, and thereby assume a victim's position of helplessness. Or you may heap blame on yourself by concluding that you are unworthy of having your needs met. Naturally, this reinforces a poor self-image and builds more expectations of failure and rejection. Can you see how important your interpretation of events is in influencing how you feel and what you do? That's why I have heavily emphasized learning skills in making accurate interpretations.

Some people attempt to protect themselves from disappointment by trying not to have any expectations at all. Can you recognize this strategy as an example of the cognitive distortion of overgeneralization? To dismiss in one broad sweep the potential value of expectations is a far less realistic way to manage yourself than is learning to be realistic about your expectations. You need to have *some* expectations in your relationships with others, and you need to be able to make realistic and appropriate demands on others (did you notice my deliberate use of the word "demands"?) if you are to maintain the give-and-take of a balanced and healthy relationship. Realistic expectations must represent a good fit between your needs and the other person's abilities to meet them, as well as the other person's needs and your ability to meet them.

Can one individual meet all of your needs, and can you meet all of his? It is probably unrealistic to burden yourself or your partner with "having to do it all." It is more realistic to recognize that a variety of needs can be met in a variety of ways. It is up to you and your partner to decide jointly which needs are best met within the relationship, and which needs are best met elsewhere. Keep in mind that for true intimacy to evolve, the security and well-being of each partner must be protected sensitively. In order for a relationship to endure, the ideal attitude of both partners is that their mutual well-being is generally more important than any specific issue or problem. Such an attitude surfaces as "us against the problem" instead of "you against me."

SELF-AWARENESS OF PERSONAL NEEDS

It is difficult to have your needs met if you don't know what they are. Clearly, in order to have a satisfying relationship, you need to *recognize* your own needs, *accept* them as basic and valid parts of who you are, and *assert* them to others as important. Think about the things that you may need in a relationship: honesty, security, love, passion, adventure, monogamy, fun . . . *Whatever* you value in a relationship, your values are legitimate *for you*. You can have and are entitled to have your desire met.

The things that you value as important are correct for you. Of course, the fact that you want those and value those things carries no assurance that your partner will also want and value them. Relationships take the most negative turn when something you value is openly devalued or even just ignored by your partner. The recognition of your needs as valid is vital to self-acceptance. It permits you to take the healthy position that you expect your needs to be acknowledged and responded to by your partner. It is your job to educate the other person about you and your needs, and about what kind of environment you thrive in. In essence, it's your job to provide your partner with a "user's manual" that will teach him about you, your inner world, and your way of looking at and doing things. By doing so, you will make it possible for your partner to relate to you in positive, effective, and loving ways. The value of the "dating" process is the time it gives you to learn as much as you can about another person *before* you become too emotionally attached.

To discount or minimize your own needs by focusing instead on the other person's needs is a strategy for failure. For any relationship to be vital and healthy, there must be a high level of shared responsibility and sensitivity between the partners. That is not to say that you two must be exactly alike, although, typically, people *are* attracted to each other on the basis of perceived similarities. Rather, I point out that there is a good balance when each person is sensitive and responsive to the other's needs. The strategy is that of *both* partners giving in order to get. At any one moment, if you were to "freeze-frame" the interaction, one might be giving and the other getting. Overall, though, the relationship needs balance.

If you place yourself in the role of a "rescuer" or a "martyr," regularly sacrificing your well-being for someone else, then you are actively

LEARN BY DOING #68

Write Your User's Manual

Purpose: To organize your perceptions about who you are and what you require, and set them down so that you can easily transmit the information to others.

It may sound strange, but pretend you are a product that someone has just purchased. He opens the box, finds you inside, and sees a user's manual attached to you. What will the manual say? Write a user's manual (a guide) to the "proper use and best care" of you. Provide guidelines for how much communication you need, how much fun and entertainment, exercise, intellectual stimulation, sex, social contact, and as many other things as you can think of. When you do this, it will become apparent to you that no one can know you or what you need until you actively teach him about you.

guiding your experience in the direction of being underresponsible for yourself. Sacrificing yourself makes the indirect statement that the other person has greater worth than you do. It's hard to feel valuable in a relationship that has been built to accommodate only the greater worth of the other person.

Now, take care not to think in all-or-none terms. I'm not suggesting that you ought not make sacrifices for others. I do suggest that it not be a one-sided relationship on an ongoing basis that uses you up and puts little or nothing back.

One aspect of the "martyr" role that is frequently associated with depression is the tendency to protect others from your depression. Realistically, this pattern is not entirely lacking in sensibility, since most depressed individuals learn, often the hard way, that other people don't really want to hear much about their personal problems. However, in the context of an intimate relationship, with a lover, close friend, or family member, protecting your partner from your true thoughts or feelings prevents closeness. Worse, perhaps, is that keeping silent prevents you from getting other perspectives on your situation, views that might be more helpful than just your own. I believe that one of the reasons people in relationships are less depressed is that they get others' viewpoints, which keep them from being stuck in their own depressive attributions.

Pause and Reflect #48

If You Keep It to Yourself, You'll Always Have It!

Can you see how someone who keeps his thoughts to himself may not recognize they are distorted and then be at higher risk for things staying depressingly the same? What does that suggest to you about the importance of learning other perspectives in order to break the patterns of depression? Do you talk to people about what's going on with you?

My response: The goal isn't to just talk, of course, but to get useful feedback from someone who is both perceptive and supportive enough to challenge your thinking in helpful ways. As you've learned, you are blind to your own blind spots. Others can help you learn and understand useful things that you would probably not have come to realize on your own.

Assuming a "victim" role is another mechanism for denying your own needs. When you take a helpless posture, you show an inability to assert your needs. Thus, you end up unintentionally building a relationship in which your needs can be ignored. Denying yourself encourages others to take you for granted or otherwise mistreat you. If you place too few or no demands on the other person to be aware of and sensitive to your needs, it is like saying to him, "My feelings aren't really important." Trust me, you don't want to train your partner to disregard you!

Your awareness and acceptance of your needs is your recognition and affirmation of your own individuality. It isn't a question of "Is it all right to want or need these things?" Rather, it is a statement: "*Since* I want and need these things, this is how I would like to be treated." Simply put, it is your responsibility to be aware of and to assert your preferences, feelings, and needs. Bear in mind that just because you communicate what you want doesn't mean you'll get it. If your partner is unable or unwilling to respond to your needs, the needs will not be met. This is why it is so important to know whether your partner has the desire and ability to meet your needs. Read on to find out how you can determine that.

303

ASSESSING OTHERS

How do you know whether you can trust someone? What are the *specific* criteria you use to evaluate another person to determine whether he can be relied upon? If your answer is some variation of "I trust my gut feelings," you are showing evidence of the cognitive distortion of "emotional reasoning." To rely solely on gut feelings is evidence that you are responding to you, *not* to the other person.

If you are internally focused on your gut feelings or other internal states, you are more likely to miss external information that might suggest a different reaction or perhaps a different choice. The fact that people can get so absorbed in their own viewpoints is precisely what limits their ability to read and handle situations more objectively. They may make errors in judgment, which lead them to become depressed when things go badly.

A superficial but clear example of internal focus is the behavior of many individuals when they are first introduced to someone. If you are so absorbed in wondering things like, "Am I okay? Do I look okay? What should I say?," your preoccupation will limit your ability to pay attention to the other person. That is one reason why, only a few seconds later, you're trying to remember the other person's name, which you were just told!

You cannot be effective in dealing with other people if you are too internally focused. Instead, as a general strategy, it is important for you to focus externally when meeting or first getting to know someone. Specifically, observe the person's attributes, values, and patterns so that you can quickly develop a strong sense of who he is and how he does things. Even though you may not actually feel this way right now, the best position for you to take in meeting someone new is to *assume that you're okay and it's your job to find out whether he is.*

Assessing others may sound cold and clinical to you. However, the need to recognize what matters to another person and what he is capable of is of utmost importance in determining the sort of relationship you will be able to have with him. An idea of the specific things you'd like to consider learning about someone else will give you a structure for better understanding who this other person is, and you'll be in a stronger position to determine what type of relationship, if any, you can expect to have with him. People's deep disappointment in others is a very common theme among my depressed clients. It shows me

LEARN BY DOING #69

Learning to Assess Others

Purpose: To help you "read" people so that you can better determine what realistically to expect of them. This is a preventive tool that can save you lots of hurt and disappointment.

When you meet someone for the first time and begin to form an impression of him, on what specific traits do you judge him? Divide a sheet of paper into four columns. In the first column, write down the names of people you have met recently. In the second column make a general (global) statement about your impression of each person. Then, in the third column, describe specifically what this person said or did to warrant your judgment. When that column is clear and detailed, you'll know your assessment skills are improving. Now, in the fourth column, specify what you still don't know about the person that may eventually prove significant. Use the outline and example below to get started.

Individuals I Recently Met	My Global Impression of Him/Her	Specific Observations That Led to My Assessment	Things I Don't Know About Him/Her That May Prove Significant
John Smith	Nice guy	Helped me change my flat tire; stuck around to make sure I was okay; expressed concern for my safety; recommended where to get my tire repaired.	I don't know anything about him— what he does, what he values, nothing! "Nice" in one context says next to nothing about what he's like anywhere else!

how frequently they misread (or fail to read) the people they get involved with, usually because they see others as they'd like them to be instead of the way they really are.

Here are some of the traits and behaviors that I think would be useful to assess in others. I don't exactly want you to put people under bright lights and interrogate them using implements of torture, but I do want you to be observant and think about the implications of what you're observing and hearing.

CONTROL

Does this person attempt to impose on you his standards and values, or does he respect you as you are? If you feel some subtle, or not so subtle, pressure telling you that you should somehow "be different," then beware. He may be attempting to control you and make you see or do things his way, and the message coming to you is "You're not okay." The extent to which he lets you know "You're not okay unless you do it my way," is the extent to which you will be getting negative and hurtful messages from him. If it's helpful feedback about something you realize does need changing, great. But, if it's something you're okay with and he's not, be careful.

If you feel the need to have that fellow around, regardless of his telling you that you're not okay, you're choosing to stay in an environment that will prove harmful to your self-esteem. The healthiest environment in which to co-exist with another person is one in which you both recognize the differences between you, but can accept those differences rather than use them as ammunition against each other. The whole idea is for the two of you to be stronger together than either one is alone.

RESPONSIBILITY ISSUES

Does this person accept responsibility for himself? Or does he consistently blame others for whatever happens to him? Consider the following scenario. You are a single woman who meets a man socially for a lunch date. Eventually, you naturally ask, "Have you ever been married before?" He says, "Yes. As a matter of fact, I have been married three times." You (casually) ask what happened to his marriages, and he responds, "Well, my first wife trapped me into marriage to escape her parents' house. My second wife ran around with every guy in town, and my third wife was a gold digger; she was only after my money."

If you meet a guy like this and feel sorry for him because he's been so "unlucky in love," then you need to reread the last few chapters. If you meet a guy like this, my advice is to RUN! Don't finish your meal.

RUN! A man's explaining his three divorces in terms of "blame, blame, blame" is strong evidence that he's a highly irresponsible individual. Nowhere in his explanation does he accept any responsibility for whom he married, nor does he demonstrate any awareness of his part in the breakup of the marriages. If you meet such an irresponsible person, get away! But if you have to be around someone like that (at work, for instance), keep things safe and superficial between you. Don't expect him to become a responsible person if that isn't already a part of his makeup. It happens, but only rarely. Teaching irresponsible people to behave responsibly is one of the toughest challenges of psychotherapy. The reason it fails so often is that the irresponsible person doesn't want to assume the extra pressures that come with responsibility. No surprise.

In much of the relationship counseling I do, the imbalance that first leads the couple into conflict, and subsequently into therapy, revolves around the issue of responsibility. One partner wants to address their issues; the other does not. One wants to blame the other for problems, and often his partner is foolish enough to accept the blame. Responsibility in *any* relationship is a shared phenomenon. No matter how bright or strong you may be, you are only half of the relationship with any other person.

PROBLEM-SOLVING CAPABILITIES

Does this person face problems directly and demonstrate an ability to work through them, or does he deny or attempt to run away from them? Just as life inevitably lobs problems at each of us, so will every relationship. The fact that there are problems in a relationship is hardly unusual. But because they are there, it is especially important to have two effective problem-solvers facing them jointly and realistically. If one partner wants to solve problems but the other partner only wants to have fun, the imbalance may well prove fatal to the relationship. Does the person even have relevant problem-solving skills, like the ability to address unpleasant situations in a timely and direct way?

The reverse situation is equally true. Depressed individuals, in particular, often focus so narrowly on problems that they seem to forget how to relax and have fun. It is important to be a good problem solver, but it's also important to compartmentalize problems so they are not always looming. Before you quickly label the other person as less than competent in dealing with problems effectively, you should try to evaluate realistically whether you're creating gloom and doom in the relationship that the other person is trying to avoid. Fun is *fun*damental!

COMMUNICATION SKILLS

Is the individual able to express his feelings, needs, and views? Or is he closed-mouthed to the point of creating uncertainty and insecurity about the best way for you two to relate? Many people do not express their feelings. For some, it's because communication skills were never encouraged in the family. For others, they just don't have much to say. Expressing your thoughts and feelings in a clear and direct way presupposes enough depth and awareness for you to communicate them. Some individuals do not have depth and awareness, and they're *not going to* have depth and awareness. Not everyone has a deeper self.

A common scenario in therapy has the woman in the relationship continually putting pressure on the man to express himself. She *assumes* he is holding back the great things he really feels and thinks. She is hurt because he holds back, and agonizes over how to get him to open up to her. In fact, he is exactly as he appears to be and isn't holding back *anything*. What she sees is all there is! Someone once said, quite sarcastically, "If you take a walk through the ocean of most people's souls, you will barely get your feet wet." To assume that everyone has deep feelings or deep thoughts is a false assumption. Many people are remarkably superficial and have no deeper perceptions or insights. Nor do they have some great organization for the way they live their lives.

Before you push for depth and openness, it's to your advantage to *look for evidence* that there is anything deeper awaiting your discovery. Don't assume that if you do everything right, this person will open up with all kinds of "good stuff." There may not be any hidden gems in there to go mining for, and to assume they are there is potentially hazardous. Here's another example of what I meant when I cautioned you against using yourself as the frame of reference for assessing others. Other people are not necessarily like you, and can, in fact, be very different from you. Keep your eyes and ears open!

CONSISTENCY

Do the actions of the individual match the things that he says? Or is there a mismatch, an incongruity, between what he says and does?

Remember the concept of cognitive dissonance? Cognitive dissonance, as a way to keep perceptions basically the same, permits distortions in one's self-image. This can, you'll recall, include your distorted view of yourself. Earlier, I discussed cognitive dissonance primarily in the context of someone's forming a negative perception about himself and, on that basis, closing out contradictory positive feedback.

Clearly, an individual's self-image can be distorted. In fact, it is fair to say that *most* people's self-image is distorted to some degree. If you meet someone who tells you, "I am a sensitive individual," he is only telling you how he sees himself. That self-disclosure says *nothing* about whether he really is sensitive. The person who says he is can, in fact, turn out to be abusive. *No one* is likely to say, "Hi. I'm mean, I'm insensitive, and I treat people very badly." To respond only to what someone says is to miss the more important dimension of what the person actually *does*. Talk *is* cheap, and action *does* speak louder than words.

If you feel an urgent need to get emotionally involved with someone quickly, you are far more likely to respond to his words alone. After all, you would not yet have experienced enough of his actions to know anything more about him than what you've been told. Remember the discussion on low frustration tolerance? That is why I place a HUGE emphasis on patiently taking your time in getting to know someone. Then you will be in a stronger position to understand what degree of consistency there is between what he says and what he does.

There is a phenomenon psychologists call "honeymooning," which refers to the tendency at a first meeting to share with someone only your "best face." You do this, of course, to create a positive image of yourself. The other person may do the same. Thus, when you begin to establish a relationship with him, especially—but not only—if it's in a dating context, you're seeing that person's "best stuff." On a first date, he will probably not be argumentative, sarcastic, critical, or inconsiderate, unless those characteristics are so strong in his personality that he cannot help expressing them. Most people, however, have enough finesse to hold those parts in check until they feel it safe to let them out.

There is simply no substitute for taking time to get to know someone by being with him in a variety of situations (socially with your friends, socially with his friends, alone in unstructured situations, alone in structured situations). Only by experiencing him in different situations over a reasonable length of time can you develop some insight as to how consistent he is in the way he treats you and how skillfully he responds to the demands of his life.

BUILDING A HEALTHY RELATIONSHIP

You may have noticed my use of the word "building" in this section's heading. I use it deliberately to stress that a healthy relationship does not just spontaneously "happen." The magical images created for us in romantic movies and television series do not portray real life. People don't happily and effortlessly ride off into the sunset to share a trouble-free life together.

It takes purpose to guide a relationship in a progressive and positive direction. At the outset, the first direction involves establishing healthy patterns of relating. To be actively guiding a relationship presupposes that you are not a victim (passive, helpless). Being in the role of a depressive victim places you at great risk for missing opportunities to steer the relationship. It is then that the relationship will go off course, perhaps so much so that it will eventually self-destruct.

DOES LIKE ATTRACT LIKE?

As a rule, optimists don't enjoy hanging around pessimists. People who are not depressed often find it a drain to be around depressed individuals. Whom do you want to attract into your life and why?

The kind of relationship you would like to have with another person is something to think about beforehand so that you can determine which parts of yourself to share and in what order. Should you build a relationship with another depressive based on shared negativity? Should you build a relationship with a "do-gooder" based on your need for sympathy? What about your need to have someone there to listen to you complain? Starting a relationship on the basis of negativity, sympathy, or complaints is often a bad first step. Establishing a relationship on a negative basis, even if it feels good at first to share your negativity, means there are two negative people reinforcing some of the worst patterns in each other. In essence, you have the "blind leading the blind" when two depressed people swap stories of pain and anguish. I don't discount the value of having someone there to listen and support you during difficult times. I do suggest, however, that a relationship based solely on shared negativity and complaints is one that contains its own seeds of destruction.

It is best to build a relationship with a positive future in mind. After all, depression won't always be there. Having your eye on a mutual goal of sharing good times together—*and expending effort to do so*—encourages the relationship to develop in a more balanced and positive way. I have encountered many couples whose relationships started in the midst of personal crises (failing jobs, failing marriages). These people did very well commiserating with each other, but they have no idea of how to have fun together. *Never underestimate the value of fun in a relationship.*

PRESCRIPTION: FUN

I value the ability to solve problems well, but a sense of balance in a relationship comes about only when having fun is also a priority. Many depressed couples reinforce each other's depression. By paying no attention to the need for fun, leisure, and recreation, their emphasis is on "deep exploration of important issues." Such nonstop seriousness creates an aura of intensity around the relationship that is draining. Balance comes from having serious time together but also time spent on superficial endeavors and activities that have no deeper meaning beyond being enjoyable. My advice is: Dare to be superficial! Dare to be silly sometimes, instead of forever hashing out the deep intricacies of life. Life isn't meant to be a burden.

Depressed people are often intolerant of what they perceive to be superficial. Many place a negative value on such experiences, thinking

LEARN BY DOING #71

Learning the Value of Leisure

Purpose: To highlight the <u>fundamental</u> truth that if you do things to feel good, you can feel good.

What things do you do to play? Do you do them regularly, or only once in a great while? Make a list of <u>at least</u> twenty things you do to relax and have fun. Identify the ones on your list that you like to do alone and those you enjoy doing with others. Identify which ones require planning and which you can do spontaneously. Identify the activities that require money and those which cost nothing. Last, note the last time you participated in that activity. If it's been a long while, you may wonder how you're supposed to feel good if you don't do the things you enjoy.

Keep this list handy for the next time you feel down and are trying to find something to make you feel better. Build lots of play into your life to counterbalance your depressive emphasis on problems.

Use the outline and examples below to get started.

Fun Things I Enjoy Doing	Activities I Prefer to Do Alone	Activities I Prefer to Do with Others	Activities That Require Planning	Activities I Can Do Spontaneously	Free Activities	Activities Requiring Money	When Was the Last Time I Did This?
Hiking	No	Yes	Yes	Yes	Yes	No	2 weekends ago
Listening to music	Yes	No	No	Yes	Yes	No	This morning
Horseback riding	No	Yes	Yes	No	No	Yes	3 months ago

them useless. Such a value system can lead you to want to get right to the deeper feelings of others you meet. This is usually a bad strategy. Why? In order to answer this question, we'll need to understand more clearly the process of self-disclosure.

SELF-DISCLOSURE IS AN ART

How do you know how much to reveal about yourself to someone else? When to reveal it? Is it better to be an "open book" in relating to others? Is it better to be secretive and withholding? The answer: "It depends on what outcome you want." If you want to find a sympathetic ear or a sounding board, then walking through life telling any-body and everybody all your problems is likely to bring you into contact with a steady supply of "rescuers." There *are* rescuers out there. They love to help. A relationship established on that basis, though, will automatically be a "victim-rescuer" relationship, reinforcing negative roles for each.

You can learn to self-disclose selectively at a pace determined by two key factors: (1) according to a rate that is reasonable for the context; and (2) the rate at which the other person self-discloses. How do you tell what's reasonable? If it's a business relationship, you keep your personal life out of it. If it's a professional relationship, you keep your personal life out of it. If it's a casual friendship, you leave intimate top-ics out of it. Go back and review in the previous chapter the boundaries that define relationships. Many people are much too quick to share deep, personal information before the relationship is strong enough to support the weight of such disclosures. The relationship then collapses before either person knows whether the other can accept such intimate or deep information. When it collapses, one individual or the other may feel abused, misunderstood, trivialized, and depressed. Hopes and expectations fall apart. The reason that things fall apart, though, is that too much was introduced too soon into the relationship!

Your urgency to make a relationship "happen" increases the likeli-hood of your making mistakes in the weight and quality of self-disclosures. The solution: Go easy! Slow down and take the time to learn about the other person's ability to relate, self-disclose appropri-ately, and accept you for who you are. The idea is to *disclose at a rate that gradually adds depth to the relationship.* The key word in that phrase is "gradually." You can't make someone your best friend instanta-neously; it will take time—*if* he even has the potential to be a great friend. The process requires the patience (frustration tolerance) it takes to let the relationship grow over many months.

The ideal I encourage you to strive for is a close relationship with someone who can appreciate and accept you for who you are. Each time that you self-disclose, you run the risk of being rejected. That is precisely the reason for sharing only selected parts of yourself at a gradual pace. Learn whether this person is accepting of you or whether, as you self-disclose things, you experience negative judg-ments and messages suggesting that this person feels you're not okay and should be different. Be careful not to let another's threats of rejec-tion control you. Likewise, be careful not to invest yourself in someone who lets you control him. "Give and take" in relatively equal proportions is the essence of a healthy relationship.

LIMIT-SETTING IS VITAL

As we saw in the previous chapter, building a relationship means establishing a set of rules for conducting the transactions within the relationship. What good are rules if they are not clearly stated and enforced? Enforcing clearly defined rules is known as "setting limits." The inability to set limits effectively on others is the mark of a "victim" mentality, which can make you an easy target for the manipulations of others.

It is human nature to want what you want when you want it. That's hardly a new observation. The question is, how far will someone go in order to get what he wants? There is a range of tactics an individual may use to get whatever he wants. These are the tactics of manipulation described in the previous chapter.

The chief problem with manipulative tactics is that while they may, in the short run, enable you to get what you want from another person, they allow you to devalue that person. In essence, you're saying, "Getting what I want is more important than how you feel." Such tactics work against the longer-term health of the relationship by hurting the self-esteem of the other person. You've learned this from your own experience, I'm sure. If you have ever had someone lay a guilt trip on you, you know that you felt not only guilty, but also angry that the person would manipulate you. It didn't help your self-esteem to feel you were being used.

NO ONE COMES TO YOU HOUSEBROKEN

Consider the following everyday scenario. A man asks a woman for a date, and she agrees. He says he will pick her up on Friday at 8 P.M. On Friday night, he does not show up until 8:45. He offers no explanation or apology for his lateness. The woman is faced with a critical decision. Does she ignore his being late because she does not wish to seem confrontational lest that create tension between them or cause him to never ask her out again? Or does she make an issue of his being late, letting him know of her irritation at his lack of consideration?

If she says nothing to him, she is, in effect, saying that she passively accepts his lateness. If she says something about his lateness, perhaps

Pause and Reflect #49

Are You Easy to Manipulate?

Think of the last three times you felt manipulated by someone. What was the tactic used? How did you feel about yourself for having been manipulated? Why did the manipulation work? Does this sort of manipulation work with you consistently? If so, you can now recognize how you unwittingly helped the other person to be a manipulator by not setting and enforcing limits.

politely requesting a phone call under similar circumstances in the future, she is letting him know that her time is just as valuable to her as his time is to him. Pause for a moment and think of three or four different ways (from humorous to serious) in which she might communicate her displeasure.

The question here is not one of *whether* she should let him know about her need to have her time respected. She must do so. The question is one of *how* she communicates that need. "Attacking" him is a strategy that is effective only if she never wants the guy to ask her out again. Saying politely, "In the future, I'd appreciate it if you'd call and let me know when you're running late" is an appropriate assertion on her part.

What if he gets angry at her polite assertion? If he does, he's making a statement that says, "Anything I do should be okay." At a deeper level, that reaction says, "My needs come before yours." Establishing a relationship with someone who is that self-centered and insensitive is a poor risk. She's better off knowing about him on a first date than investing time and energy, not recognizing until later what he's like.

To help yourself set limits, perhaps the best thing to do is ask yourself, "What am I communicating to this person if I do not establish a limit?" If you intend to let others know they can disregard your feelings, then by all means, be passive and say nothing when people make you feel guilty (afraid, isolated . . .). If, on the other hand, you want to be respected and acknowledged as important, it is your responsibility to let people know what is not acceptable to you.

When someone violates your limits, you will feel abused and devalued. If you are manipulated because you did not enforce your limits, or never established them in the first place, you will most likely become angry with yourself. And you will also be angry with those who manipulated you for their personal gain. Much of the anger found in depressed people arises from their perception of being victimized. Anger can dissipate quickly, though, once you establish and enforce the limits that interrupt the pattern of your being abused in this way. This is a decidedly better and more direct approach to managing your anger than pounding pillows (although that can help, too).

Do not expect other people to protect you. It is your job to protect yourself. Other people will always want to get from you whatever they want—your money, your time, your body, your emotional support, your expertise. It is your job to *define your limits and enforce those limits in your own behalf*. To expect others to be protective of you is unrealistic. It is up to you to determine *whether* to give of yourself and, if so, *how much*.

Predictably, any time you say no to others, they will be inconvenienced at least, hurt at most, because they aren't getting what they want. *That doesn't mean you are wrong.* But when they're standing there, expressing disappointment or anger to you, and you become focused on how it feels to say no and become the target of someone's anger, you will feel guilty at having upset him. But if you then back down and give in, you are violating your own limits, and later you won't feel very good about yourself.

The whole point of this section on setting limits is that *the path to self-respect involves setting clear limits and enforcing those limits* in a manner consistent with your needs. Whenever the limits you set prevent others from getting what they want, you can expect negative feedback. Learning to tolerate negative feedback is necessary if you are to effectively set and enforce limits. This is why others should not be given the power to determine your self-image. Whether they approve or disapprove of you should be incidental to your doing what is sensible and reasonable *for you.*

If you are able to recognize other people's motives for using manipulative tactics, you will more easily resist their self-serving demands. *Ask yourself why this person is trying to manipulate you.* What does he want from you? Perhaps more important, why is he willing to make you feel bad for his personal gain? What does this say about him? What does it say about his perception of you? When you are able to identify people's manipulative tactics, you will see why you need at all times to *be firm.*

If you build good relationships on the basis of acceptance and respect, does that eliminate manipulation? No. Even if others love and respect you, they still want what they want, just as you do. Ideally, when you set limits, the other person can respectfully accept them or choose to end what would otherwise be a pretty unhealthy relationship. *Not having a relationship is better than having a bad one.*

Manipulation can go two ways, of course, and so it is important that you do your best to deal with others fairly. Respect for and acceptance of another person (and the position he takes on some issue) precludes your using negative manipulations at his expense. Respecting another individual means accepting his right to choose for himself. That means that you cannot impose your desires on him, to his detriment.

CONCLUSION

Becoming aware of and practiced in the skills presented in this chapter will undoubtedly lead you to develop better, more satisfying relationships. Having good relationships with others is a wonderful source of satisfaction and comfort, but they are just one part of your life. If your entire self-esteem or sense of well-being rests on a relationship, then too much rests on factors that are not entirely in your control.

Global thinking may have erroneously led you to believe that good relationships come about from "chemistry" or other such vague factors. In fact, good relationships require very specific skills; they don't "just happen." Like nearly everything else I've talked about in this book, success in relationships comes from your taking specific steps to establish healthy patterns that make good things possible.

SUMMARY OF KEY POINTS . . .
AND WHAT THEY CAN MEAN TO <u>YOU</u>

- Healthy relationships don't just happen. Good relationships require such specific skills as setting clear boundaries, having realistic expectations, self-awareness, assertiveness, skills in assessing others realistically, sharing control, being realistic about responsibility, good problem-solving capabilities, and consistency. Build up your skills!

- Unless relationship skills are practiced, they will decline in effectiveness. Take deliberate steps to put yourself in social situations where you can develop and hone your skills.

- Technology can discourage meaningful contact with others. For example, spending a great deal of time watching television limits meaningful contact with others. If you want to have decent relationships with members of our species, you'll have to leave the comfort and safety of your home.

- Caring about another person means being willing to protect that person's sense of personal security. Trust and depth can evolve only in an atmosphere of safety. You can't say or do anything you feel like saying or doing when you have influence with someone else. If you draw someone into a relationship with you, you have an obligation to treat him respectfully.

- While it is important to have expectations of the way others will relate to you, it is also important to determine whether they have the abilities to live up to your expectations. The reverse is true as well. Never ask someone for something he doesn't have!

- It is your responsibility to educate others about the best way to relate to you. Other people are not mind readers. If you communicate clearly about what you want, it guarantees nothing, but it certainly gives the other person knowledge he can choose to make good use of.

- Do not assess others solely in terms of how they make you feel. Instead, learn how this person deals with such issues as control, responsibility, problem-solving, communication, and consistency. As you now know, a "nice" person isn't necessarily suited to be a good partner.

- It takes time to get to know someone well. Reduce your sense of urgency to get attached to others and try to be more objective about the people with whom you get involved. It may help you to remind yourself of all you don't know about the person before things go too far too fast.

- In general, like attracts like. Therefore, attaching yourself to another depressed person and building a relationship on negativity may initially feel comfortable, but eventually may prove to be a problem. Misery may love company, but it's the equivalent of deciding to stay in a rut and just redecorating it.

- Self-disclosure is an art. Your rate of practicing it is determined by the rate at which the other person self-discloses, and a rate that is reasonable for the context. In general, do not share sensitive information until you have a pretty good idea of how the other person will respond to it.

- Establishing and enforcing clearly defined rules is known as "setting limits," one of the most important mechanisms for building strong and healthy relationships. If it breathes, you must set limits on it!

- All people, to one degree or another, use tactics of manipulation (such as guilt and intimidation) to get the things they want. Your job is to keep your self-protection in mind as you deal with those tactics.

- The anger commonly found in depressed people often arises from the perception of being victimized. Anger can dissipate when you effectively enforce the limits that you set on others, thereby preventing further victimization. You can't let go of anger if you're still being hurt!

- Learning to tolerate others' feedback is necessary in order to set limits that are effective. People may tell you things you don't want to hear, but when you can put the good of the relationship ahead of your feelings, you can learn to appreciate the other's honesty.

- Relationships are just one part of your life. Do not make your entire self-image dependent on your relationships with others. You can't control other people or how they choose to relate to you.

Chapter 12

NAVIGATING
THE THERAPY WORLD

This book is intended to be a self-help book, and while I expect it will help everyone to one degree or another, it would be unrealistic to believe that it can be effective in helping *everyone* who reads it. As I said at the outset, depression can vary so much from person to person that it may be more accurate to talk about *depressions*, in the plural, rather than as a single disorder. If you have read this book carefully and have actively experimented with its ideas and exercises, and you find that your depression continues, it is *not* a sign that you are hopeless. It *is* a sign, however, that your experience of depression is unique or complex enough to require further consideration.

If that is the case, it would be wise to seek the help of a professional, someone who can help you continue the recovery process you have now begun. A skilled psychotherapist can identify what may help you and get you started on a personalized approach to recovery. After all, depression is not necessary or inevitable. It does need to be approached from an angle that *works.*

It is not easy for most people to step outside their usual way of looking at things in order to see themselves or their situations differently. We all tend to live inside our heads and individual frames of reference, often making objectivity about ourselves a most complex task. Yet such objectivity is desirable if you are to experiment with your perceptions and develop new and better ways of responding to old feelings or situations.

I include this chapter on finding professional help not only to encourage you to continue your recovery, but for three very important additional reasons. First, as statistics indicate, only about a quarter of depressed individuals seek professional treatment. Sometimes it's because of misdiagnosis, but often it's because of the seeming hopelessness of the disorder. The attitude of "Why bother? Nothing is going to help me" has been challenged numerous times in this book, and is challenged here again. Professional treatment can work and work well. But you'll never know how much better you can feel if you give up before you even try, by dismissing the possibility of help with "Why bother?"

Second, it is true that there are some psychological problems that the mental health profession does not know how to deal with very well. Fortunately, depression is *not* one of them. The mental health profession knows a great deal about depression and its effective treatment. You may want to go back and reread Chapter 2, where I described the body of literature that has been amassed about successful treatments. The success rate for people receiving treatment is high. You really can reasonably expect positive results when you let well-trained professionals do what they have been trained to do.

Third, many depressed people have considered seeking professional help but were so overwhelmed by the task of finding a qualified psychotherapist that they gave up before they even started. (Do you recognize the global thinking?) On the basis of the points discussed in this chapter, you will have enough basic knowledge about the therapy process to be competent in obtaining professional help for yourself or for the depressed person you care about.

If you have seen a psychotherapist in the past and found the experience less than satisfying, you are not alone. However, be careful not to overgeneralize; there are many excellent therapists and there are some mediocre ones, as in any profession. Remember all you have learned throughout this book about therapy, depression, relationships, and your particular needs. Use this knowledge to find a competent professional who can help you get the job done. And do not let low frustration tolerance lead you to give it only one chance. At the end of this chapter, I will give you specific ideas about how to "shop" for a competent therapist.

In Chapter 2 I described to you the cumulative wisdom in the mental health profession regarding the best treatments for depression. The results of what are known as "therapeutic efficacy" studies led to the formation of the treatment guidelines discussed in that chapter. Efficacy studies are carefully controlled studies of specific methods of treatment under carefully controlled conditions. They are considered the most objective and scientific way to determine that a therapy approach really works.

An interesting thing happened in November 1995, though. *Consumer Reports* (*CR*) published an article about how their readers, responding to a *CR* survey, evaluated the effectiveness of their experiences with therapy. Unlike standard efficacy studies which involve random assignments to treatment, rigorous controls, standardized treatments, preassigned lengths and frequencies of treatment, and rigid eligibility criteria for who will receive treatment, *CR*'s effectiveness study went right to the consumer who actually experienced the treatments "in the field." The *CR* survey was the largest such therapeutic effectiveness survey ever conducted.

Unlike what happens in efficacy studies, in "real life" therapists can do things like "throw away the manual" and adjust to ongoing feedback from the client, thereby better tailoring their treatment to a specific client's individual needs. They can provide treatment as required on an individually determined need for length and frequency. They can aim for "better quality of life," and not "just" specific symptom remission. In short, going directly to the consumers as *CR* did in their survey may offer, in some ways, a more realistic picture of how therapy fares than do controlled efficacy studies.

So, under "real life" conditions, how well did therapy fare? Extremely well, as the following results indicate:

1. Eighty-seven percent of respondents said they felt better following treatment.
2. Perhaps surprisingly, given our field's heavy emphasis on brief therapy (and mine as well), long-term therapy produced greater improvement than short-term therapy. I interpret this as evidence for the positive value of an ongoing relationship between therapist and client, but reaffirm the value of teaching short-term problem-solving strategies even in a longer-term therapy.
3. There was no statistically significant difference between psychotherapy alone and psychotherapy in combination with medication for *any* disorder, including depression.
4. Not surprisingly, people whose choice of therapist or whose length of treatment was dictated by their insurance coverage did worse than those who could actively shop for and choose both their therapist and style of treatment.

5. Psychologists, social workers, and psychiatrists had roughly the same rates of success in treatment.

The *CR* study, which was able to meet strict survey criteria surprisingly well, gives us considerable evidence that when it counts, therapists do very well in helping their clients.

WHEN TO GET HELP

How do you know when to get professional help? As a general answer, *you should seek help long before things get really bad.* To be more specific, there are at least five factors to consider when you are deciding whether you should seek professional treatment.

SUICIDAL THOUGHTS OR FEELINGS

If you often find yourself thinking about death, killing yourself, or fantasizing about the relief of being dead and not having to deal with your emotional distress anymore, then you are experiencing suicidal thoughts. They should not preoccupy you, so if you have them often, they are a legitimate basis for concern. If they are vivid thoughts, detailed to the point where you have even thought of specific ways to kill yourself and the consequences of your death, then such suicidal thoughts are an even greater reason for immediate concern. It would be wise for you to give them immediate attention in therapy.

Suicide has appropriately been called "the permanent solution to a temporary problem." To believe hopelessly that your future holds only more pain is distorted, depressed thinking. Suicide is a global, irreversible, and terrible solution to specific problems. If you are at all suicidal, I urge you to get into therapy *immediately*, where your self-destructive thoughts and feelings can be addressed and resolved as quickly as possible. *Think preventively.*

ACUTE DEPRESSION TURNING CHRONIC

If your depression had a rapid onset following a traumatic event (such as the death of a loved one, the breakup of an important relationship, the loss of a job, an illness or accident, or *any* other such personally distressing event), then your depression, though painful in the short run, could be considered a normal response to painful circumstances. However, if you interpret your feelings incorrectly, and the depression continues beyond a reasonable length of time—from a few weeks to a few months—then there is concern that an acute (short-term) situation may be becoming a chronic (long-term) one.

Most people who suffer a depressive episode experience a full return to their normal level of functioning in a few weeks or months at most. Some individuals, however, never seem to "bounce back" completely. If you feel that your experience of depression is lasting longer than it should, or if you worry that it will, it may be wise to get a professional opinion. Or if you recognize you are making lifelong negative decisions or pronouncements during a depression ("I'll never be happy again"), then it's important to get help from someone who can challenge you to think more clearly.

LIFESTYLE DISRUPTION

If your experience of depression is severe enough to impair your ability to function well in various areas of your life, it would be best to *seek help well before life situations deteriorate further.* Losing your marriage, losing your job, or abusing your body and physical health with drugs or apathy because of depression will only add to your problems. Take steps *now* to prevent the downward spiral, which could cause you more hurt and pain than the depression already has.

REALITY TESTING

If you are in a position of relative isolation and there isn't anyone close enough for you to talk with about your thoughts and feelings, then you have no one with whom you can "reality test." Reality testing means checking out your perceptions with others who have a more objective viewpoint. Considering all the patterns of distorted thinking I've described in this book, it should be apparent to you that speaking to someone with an objective view can be extremely valuable in getting you back on track. A good therapist can be a valuable partner for reality testing, particularly if he is experienced in recognizing the common distortions in depressed people's thinking.

Because it may be beyond the range of your capabilities at this time to step outside your own (depressing) frame of reference, seek someone to help you effectively. A person outside your frame of reference can provide feedback that is refreshingly beyond anything you are able to generate on your own. A fresh pair of eyes on your problems can allow for fresh solutions. Furthermore, a caring relationship, like the collaborative partnership of good therapy, has healing qualities that go far beyond what you can experience on your own. (And if relationship problems are a primary source of distress in your life, how do you solve relationship problems *by yourself?*)

EXTREME SYMPTOMS

As you have learned, many of the symptoms associated with depression can exist on a physiological level. If you are severely depressed—unable to sleep well, without appetite, with no energy, unable to concentrate, or feeling just plain lousy—then you may benefit from more immediate interventions of a biological type, such as antidepressant medications. In Chapter 2, I presented current information on the effectiveness of antidepressant medications. They may help you achieve a more receptive state to the additional benefits of psychotherapy, which I would encourage you to pursue simultaneously.

Once you make the decision to seek professional treatment, you will need a strategy to help you find competent help. The information in the next section will be helpful.

APPROACHES TO TREATMENT

It is little wonder that people are confused by the intricacies of the mental health field. After all, there are many categories of mental health professionals, each with a different title and educational background, and each with different ways of looking at problems like depression. There are psychiatrists, psychologists, marriage and family therapists, pastoral counselors, lay counselors, and social workers. All are called "psychotherapists," defined as those who provide therapeutic intervention for emotional disorders or psychological problems.

How can you know which is the best psychotherapist for you? In a broad generalization, we can divide the mental health field into two major areas, biological and psychological. The areas have a great deal of overlap, but I exaggerate their differences here in order to clarify some points. Bear in mind that they are not mutually exclusive approaches, nor should they be. You will recall that biological, psychological, and sociological factors all contribute to depression.

BIOLOGICAL APPROACHES TO TREATMENT

The primary psychotherapeutic practitioner in the biological realm is the psychiatrist, a person with an M.D. A physician who specializes in the diagnosis and treatment of psychological disturbances, according to a medical model, the psychiatrist has had advanced training in the use of psychoactive medications (drugs that affect the mind) and physically based treatments for psychological disturbances. Psychiatrists also learn psychotherapy techniques to complement their use of medications.

In the case of depression, the psychiatrist's primary tool is antidepressant medication. In cases of severe and unrelenting depression (where the person is unable to function), the treatment may also be severe, calling for hospitalization and even, in extreme cases, the use of electroconvulsive treatment (ECT), commonly known as "shock treatment." While ECT has historically been the subject of fear and horror stories, many clinicians and researchers have come to believe that ECT is the "treatment of choice" in very severe depressions. It remains a controversial treatment, though, and is usually advised only in the most extreme cases. *Only* a psychiatrist can administer ECT.

For the great majority of severely depressed individuals, the condition is managed by psychiatrists with the use of antidepressant medications, which have repeatedly been shown, in the best of clinical studies, to be effective in providing relief from the symptoms of depression. While it is not yet fully understood how such medications work, most depressed individuals can experience relatively rapid relief (in two to six weeks) with their use. Thus, if your depression is highly disruptive to your life and you are experiencing uncomfortable symptoms, particularly on a physiological level, you may consider consulting a psychiatrist for an evaluation as to the appropriate use of antidepressant medication. Using the guidelines I described in Chapter 2, you can participate in the process, so that you do not blindly take whatever is prescribed. The individual who participates in the treatment process is more likely to recover.

There are a number of concerns to be aware of in using medications. While antidepressant medications may provide marked symptom relief in a relatively short period of time, they do not significantly change your attributional style, cognitive style, relationship style, and other key patterns described throughout this book. Despite the media hype for drugs like Prozac, which can be effective for many people, the potential for a recurrence of depression is higher if you receive only antidepressant medications and no additional psychotherapy.

Another concern is that the medications have side effects that, until you adjust to them, may be a source of discomfort. The newer antidepressants, such as the selective serotonin reuptake inhibitors (SSRIs, like Prozac and Zoloft), have fewer side effects than the older tricyclic antidepressants (TCAs). Fewer side effects means a higher likelihood of your being able to continue on the drug, which increases its chances of working. For most people, the issue of side effects is a minor consideration.

A final point about medications: I am concerned that the medication may discourage the client from actively striving to change his depression-causing patterns. The use of medications alone may encourage you to assume a passive role in treatment at a time when it is critical that you actively learn new and healthy life-management skills. I emphasize *action!*

There are other forms of physical intervention beyond drugs and ECT, such as physical exercise, diet, and changes in sleep schedules. I acknowledge these as potentially useful in a general way, so I encourage you to be active in pursuing exercise, rest, and a good diet regimen.

PSYCHOLOGICAL APPROACHES TO TREATMENT

Psychological approaches to treatment assume that your emotional disturbance is a product of your experience, including the things you learned as well as the things you did not learn from life. These approaches primarily involve "talk therapy," usually an exchange between therapist and client of ideas, perspectives, and philosophies. The ideas and techniques of this book fall into the psychological realm. They encourage you actively to consider and experiment with the ways that you think about and relate to the different aspects of your life.

There are dozens of types of psychological therapies, each with its own assumptions and approaches. Since the typical depressed individual does not know the differences between approaches, he may be confused about what the "best" therapy is. From having read this book, you are now quite well informed, so you already know there isn't one "best" therapy. You also know especially from the first two chapters, that not all therapies are equally effective, and some *are* better than others for depression.

If what you still imagine therapy to be, after all I've said, is a matter of your confessing all your problems and going on endlessly about what your parents did to you when you were growing up, then your idea about therapy is common but inaccurate. Of the many different approaches to treatment, the ones that work best for depression do not rely on such past-oriented methods. They involve building a future that is compelling and positive.

In pointing out that there are many different types of therapy, I want to suggest that the type of therapy you seek for depression is important to your eventual recovery. More important than the type itself, though, is the nature and level of skill of the therapist with whom you work. I have emphasized the cognitive, behavioral, and interpersonal models of psychotherapy because these have *consistently* been shown to be the most effective in treating depression. There are many qualified professionals trained in these approaches, including all levels and backgrounds of psychotherapists (psychologists, psychiatrists, family therapists, and social workers). The academic degree of the person you consult (Ph.D., M.D., M.A., L.C.S.W.) may be of importance to you *if* you equate level of education with level of expertise. It is *not* a reliable indicator, however. There are some highly educated but unskilled clinicians, and there are some lesser educated but highly skilled clinicians. It is more important that the therapist be able to apply efficiently the principles and methods of these therapies; a more advanced or specialized degree does *not* offer assurance that this will be the case. I directly suggest to you that it is less the academic degree and more the professional skills of the individual that will determine how effectively he conducts the therapy.

SHOPPING FOR A THERAPIST

It is unfortunate that at a time when you are probably least motivated and energized, you most need to expend energy in "shopping" for a therapist. Finding a good therapist is not always an easy task. There are many questions to ask, many factors to take into account, and many possibilities to consider. Certainly on the basis of what you now know about depression, you can see that therapy can and should be done actively *and* briefly in most cases. You also know that spending time going over endless details about your unhappy past is unnecessary, unless you need to explore it or vent your feelings about it. You know that focusing on hurt, anger, or any other negative feeling can amplify it and still not teach you any new skills or correct any distortions. Therefore, it is reasonable to ask for specific information from potential therapists about how they would approach the treatment of your depression.

A good place to start your search is a referral. Your family physician may have psychotherapists to whom he refers patients. Physicians, who often have an exclusively medical or biological viewpoint, are more likely to recommend a psychiatrist and the use of antidepressant medication. That's fine, but you'll still need a therapist to talk to if the psychiatrist you see doesn't also employ psychotherapy. You may raise the subject with friends or relatives you trust who themselves have had experience with therapy. Perhaps you're new to your area and don't know anyone you can ask for a referral. In that case, I recommend that you call some of the professional organizations and groups listed in Appendix D and seek a referral from one of them.

If you use the phonebook as a reference source, you can look up "Psychologists," "Counselors," "Mental Health," and related headings, and then call specific psychotherapists, especially if they advertise themselves as interpersonal, cognitive, or behavioral therapists. When you call, you can ask for certain basic information, such as the therapist's academic degree, (even though *which* advanced degree one has doesn't matter so much, an advanced degree *is* important), whether he has been licensed by the state to do psychotherapy, and what his treatment of depressed clients usually involves. (See *only* a state-licensed, reputable clinician.) It is unrealistic to expect that a therapist will spend an inordinate amount of time with you on the telephone, but it is not at all unreasonable to ask for just a few minutes of the therapist's time to get some basic information and a sample of his professional demeanor.

You can ask the average length of treatment, the fee per session, whether any health insurance you have will cover the costs (and, if so, what your cost share might be), how your progress in therapy will be evaluated, the frequency of sessions, and the general availability of the therapist for regular appointments.

Once you have this sort of information, you can tell whether to schedule a first appointment. During that appointment, you can expect to describe your experience of depression, including your symptoms, your ideas of what your depression is about, the things you have already done to try to get over it, and so forth. During this first session, you should also get an idea, from the way the therapist responds, whether he will be able to provide you with support, feedback, direction, structured learning activities, and other key ingredients of successful therapy.

It may not be easy, but keep in mind that while you are intelligently evaluating whether you can work effectively with a therapist, many of the cognitive distortions and negative relationship patterns that may be a part of your depression can creep into the therapeutic relationship. It is important, therefore, that you maintain an awareness of your need to set limits, avoid emotional reasoning, keep from jumping to conclusions, and do no personalizing on the basis of feedback you get from your therapist.

If you find that your response to this person, based on his treatment of you, is negative, or if you feel that his level of expertise is not enough to meet your needs, then it is not only desirable but *necessary* for you to interview more therapists. Do not allow yourself to be manipulated by a therapist speaking "psychobabble" who attempts to convince you that it is your depression that prevents you from forming a meaningful therapy relationship with him. It is very important to your therapy's success that you feel valued, supported, and positively challenged to grow by your therapist. You must definitely have the feeling your therapist is on your side, especially when you're dealing with tough issues.

A therapeutic relationship is a special type of relationship, but it follows many of the principles of other positive and healthy relationships. A good therapist is, in most ways, an educator, *not* a substitute parent. It is important to have within the therapy relationship the same expectations of acceptance and respect that you want in any relationship. That's why it's imperative that you be clear about setting limits. You are half of the therapy relationship, so even though the therapist has greater expertise in an area of vital interest to you—namely, depression—that is *not* a legitimate basis for him to discount or ignore your needs or views. After all, you know your experience, background, and thoughts better than anyone else ever will. You are the expert on you. It is your job to educate the therapist about who you are and how you do things so that he can get a good sense of where and how to intervene. If the therapist repeatedly goes off on things you find irrelevant or unnecessarily hurtful, you can say so. Be an *active* participant in your therapy.

The therapy relationship is a confidential one; whatever you say about yourself *must*, both by law and professional code, be kept in the strictest confidence. There are only two exceptions in which confidence may be broken: if you threaten harm either to yourself or to someone else; and if you are abusing a child or an elderly person. Thus, for all intents and purposes, nothing that you talk about will ever go beyond the therapist. When he provides you with a secure environment in which to explore distorted perceptions, depressing beliefs, and self-limiting patterns, and when he teaches effective life-management skills, remember that the likelihood of your recovery is great.

It is worth remembering, too, that the therapy relationship is based on your problems and needs. You can take an active role in shaping the direction of the treatment, even though you may not know what things you need to learn or how to best learn them. Therapy is not something that is done *to* you. It is a process in which you participate. Your input, your willingness to self-disclose, and your eagerness to carry out well-intentioned therapeutic assignments are all vital to the process. It is one of the great paradoxes in the world of therapy that even the best of therapists can help only to the extent the client permits.

It bears repeating that therapies are as subjective as the therapists who practice them. No psychiatrist can predict exactly how you will respond to a particular medication, and no psychologist can predict exactly how long it will take you to learn a new skill. As with all things discussed throughout this book, if you try something and it does not work, do something else. If you go for therapy, give it a reasonable chance to succeed. You should expect to see some positive results in six to twelve weeks of treatment. If the experience does not prove to be beneficial, do not overgeneralize, in a distorted way, that it is a negative statement about the value of *all* therapy. Nor should you personalize, in a distorted way, that therapy works for everyone else but that somehow you cannot benefit from it.

You now have many explicit criteria to help you be a smart consumer of therapy services. There are lots of very skilled, very talented therapists out there. With a little bit of persistence and some self-awareness of your needs and, therefore, the kinds of approaches you might best respond to, you will, I have no doubt, find the quality help that you want.

Chapter 13

GETTING ON WITH YOUR LIFE

In "getting on with your life," you can use all you now know about the nature of depression and its treatment to see that there will be significantly fewer, and less painful, depressive episodes in your life. In this short final chapter, I want to pull everything together and leave you with a strong sense of what it takes to break the patterns of depression.

Life continually presents challenges to all of us. That makes each of us vulnerable to the pains of depression when important things do not go our way or, worse, when catastrophe befalls us. Though it may sound trite, it is nonetheless true: *When things fall apart, there is an opportunity to rebuild.* Do you want to just survive life, or transform it into something wonderful?

The first step to managing your life well is to recognize early warning signs that something important is happening that requires your attention. Bad things do not have to grow into terrible things if you react quickly and effectively to curtail them. The chapter on future orientation should come in handy for just this reason. *Always remember, prevention whenever possible is the first and best choice.*

RISK FACTORS FOR DEPRESSION

A "risk factor" exists when anything increases the likelihood of the occurrence or recurrence of a particular problem or challenge. For example, just as we all know that cigarette smoking puts people at risk for developing lung cancer, we also know that there are risk factors for developing depression.

The emphasis throughout this book has been on identifying common patterns for interpreting and responding to life experience. The implications for recognizing these patterns as risk factors for depression may already be clear to you. *Any* pattern that reflects an imbalance in an important area of your life puts you at risk for depression. Depression comes about when you are unable to find within yourself the necessary resources to cope with the demands you face, whether those demands are internal or external in origin. In a broad sense, it can be said that *any* pattern that leads to a "one size fits all" approach to life will put a person at risk. I hope by now you know the value of adapting skillfully to the ever-changing landscape of your life.

Each cognitive distortion represents a characteristic thinking style that, because of its automatic (unconscious) nature, can surface at any moment and cause you the pain of its consequences. Learning to recognize quickly and correct actively the cognitive distortions associated with depression is an ongoing challenge. You have an opportunity to do so nearly every moment you are alive, so please do!

Attributional style as a second set of risk factors is also of great significance. To the extent that you erroneously form attributions that are internal ("It's me"), stable ("It will always be this way"), and global ("It ruins my whole life") for negative events, you are at risk for personalizing things that are *not* personal, assuming things will stay hurtful forever, and that they will negatively affect everything that you attempt to do. Depression is a predictable consequence of patterned errors in explaining the things that happen in your life.

A third risk factor concerns your degree of personal adaptability. The ability to shape your experience and create new experiences for yourself, rather than being passively shaped by whatever happens to you, is the core of mental health. You must be able to recognize *quickly* and *flexibly* when it is time to "do something else." If you automatically dismiss ideas or experiences that conflict with what you believe, or if you bar others from having access to your thoughts and feelings, then you'll never have your ideas opened up to helpful questioning by concerned others. And by so doing, you will be trapped inside your own frame of reference, unwittingly keeping things uncomfortably the same.

Life presents all of us with opportunities to seek and experience new things; each new experience gives us a chance to develop new resources within ourselves. It is these internal resources (such as the ability to take risks, learn new skills, anticipate the consequences of our actions, address and solve problems, and so forth) that each of us must effectively draw upon in response to life's demands. You have so many fine characteristics and resources already, and each day you're in the position of being able to develop even more. When you watch yourself moving through life handling things skillfully, you'll discover how great it feels to be living the way you want to.

THINGS **NOT** TO DO

Throughout this book I have emphasized things you can actively do to help yourself, and very deliberately so. In this section, though, I want to offer a brief list of things *not* to do if you are attempting to overcome depression. As you read each point, you can recall the associated discussion from earlier in the book. If not, go back and re-read it!

DO NOT DWELL ON THE PAST

The past is over, and history can't be changed. Depression is not about bad events in the past; it's about how you interpreted those events and the skills you didn't have at the time for dealing with them. What matters now is what happens tomorrow and throughout all your tomorrows. Make changes *now* and learn skills *now* so that things will be better from now on. Learn *how* to overcome the teachings of your past that were hurtful, wrong, or ineffective. Focusing on the past does *not* teach you new skills; it simply rehashes old stuff. Look forward, because tomorrow hasn't happened yet, and the possibilities are wondrous.

DO NOT COMPARE YOURSELF TO OTHERS

You are unique as an individual, trite as that may sound. By making comparisons to others, you distract yourself from the more immediate task at hand, which is identifying the specific experiences *you* need to have and the skills *you* need to learn in order to move forward with *your* life. There will *always* be people who are a little better and a little worse than you; your most important task is developing yourself to the fullest extent possible. You are you, and there isn't another you anywhere—so be the best you that you can possibly be.

DO NOT CREATE AND DWELL ON
NEGATIVE POSSIBILITIES

While it can be good to anticipate potential snags in your plans, the larger picture should be one of what you can do that is useful, not the negatives to be avoided. Whoever said, "Obstacles are what you see when you take your eyes off the goal" definitely had the right idea. Your goals help define your character, the purpose of your life, and they fuel the optimism of what the "good life" can be for you. Aim for the target.

DO NOT LEAVE IMPORTANT THINGS UNSAID
OR UNDEFINED

You have learned that it is necessary to make the abstract more concrete, and the global more clearly defined, in the course of day-to-day life. Save the abstract philosophies about "the meaning of life" for things that are not essential to your well-being. For all the things that directly affect your feelings about yourself—your relationships, your health, your job—these are the things that should be well defined and skillfully managed. Keep yourself focused on how to do things skillfully. If you don't know *how* to do something, learn it. *Don't* give up!

DO NOT REJECT BASIC PARTS OF YOURSELF

Each part of you is valuable to some degree somewhere, sometime. Rather than trying to "get rid of" parts of yourself that you have labeled "bad," it is far more advantageous to acknowledge and accept the presence of those parts. Then you can discover in what specific circumstances they can actually work to your advantage. For example, "anger" is not "bad." It is a basic and necessary emotion. Throwing tantrums, however, is not an effective way to deal with anger. Learning when and how to express anger (as well as your other feelings) appropriately is a valuable skill for staying healthy. Learn about your different parts and enjoy discovering how each is a facet of you. And always remember that you are *more* than your parts, either collectively or singly. When you master that concept, you'll have little choice but to realize how much greatness there is in you.

DO NOT IGNORE YOUR OWN NEEDS

As you have learned, depression often comes about from letting your inner world become imbalanced, because you invest more and more heavily in others or in external situations (such as getting a promotion at work). The necessity of balancing your needs against the needs of others is vital to maintaining good mental health. Other people matter, but you're in no position to help if you don't take good care of yourself first.

DO NOT IGNORE REALITY IN ORDER TO BLINDLY FOLLOW YOUR OWN WISHES AND DESIRES

To focus on your own goals and wishes to the exclusion of understanding the realities of the environment in which you live means that you will respond ineffectively to the world around you. Remember, you can't always trust your feelings. Your feelings can deceive you, so make "reality testing" a habit. Watch for evidence, listen carefully to things people say (and don't say), and set your feelings and reactions aside until you're clear about what's going on. A little "impulse control" can go a long way.

DO NOT GIVE UP

To expend effort and fail, in whatever way failure might be defined, is undoubtedly painful. The things you want to do are most likely possible. Success or failure comes as a result of the strategy (series of steps) you follow to produce an outcome. If you try to do something and fail, don't give up and don't just do the same thing harder. *Do something else!* If you see other people who can do it, that means it can be done. If you do not know what to do, find someone who can show you how. *If you fail, it is not a reflection of your capability as much as it is a statement of how you went about doing it.* It is vitally important that you continue to expend effort and do so intelligently, in a focused way. When you do not know what to do, get help; that is a far more effective response than giving up and assuming you can't succeed. No one succeeds in all things they attempt to do. As Thomas Edison once said, "Genius is about 5 percent inspiration, and 95 percent perspiration."

DO NOT LEAVE TIME UNSTRUCTURED

Time can be your greatest ally, depending on how you use it. Actively structure your daily experience to bring out your best. If you feel good when you are out in nature, for example, then get out there as much as you can. Build your schedule to include a balance of work with play, time with others with time alone, physical rest with physical exertion, and so forth. Activity is a natural and highly effective antidepressant. Schedule yourself for good times.

DO NOT STOP WORKING TO IMPROVE YOURSELF WHEN YOUR DEPRESSION LIFTS

You now know that you can be at risk for depression even when you are not depressed. Continually monitor your attributions, thoughts, relationships, perceptions of control and responsibility as your best means to prevent recurrences. If you are in therapy and it's working, stay until you are certain you are clear about all the relevant issues. If you have too much difficulty identifying in yourself the patterns that get you down, then make use of professional help. Always remember, the quest for self-improvement is never-ending. You may not ever be perfect, but you can be *really good*.

THINGS TO DO

All of the ideas and techniques presented in this book have given you many different paths on which to walk in the direction of self-discovery. This is not meant to be a book that you read once, as if it were a novel. Instead, I hope you will continually use the exercises and ideas to keep developing new understandings and competencies, and new ways to enhance all the good things you already are.

Since so much of what to do has already been discussed throughout this book, my final pieces of advice are quite brief and to the point:

1. Appreciate that stressful things happen in *every* life, not just yours. Stressful experiences can easily lead to depression. *Managing stress effectively, thinking ahead, being able to relax, and stepping outside the immediacy of the situation* are all important skills for maintaining your balance and for

quickly recovering your balance when it is temporarily tipped.

2. Developing *effective problem-solving* skills is vital to managing your life effectively. Dealing with what *is* instead of fantasizing about how things should or can be is the necessary starting place. Having dreams and goals is great, but reality is the starting place to build the bridge between "here" and "there."

3. A heavy emphasis has been placed on *self-awareness*, particularly in the areas of your personal needs and values. The importance of personal integrity—your behaving in a way that is consistent with your needs and values, and respectful of others as well—cannot be overstated. I want you to watch yourself liking what you see as you move through life. Living a life with integrity is the foundation of good self-esteem.

4. The need to *build your life around factors within your control whenever possible* is particularly critical if you are prone to depression. Be especially careful about whom or what you get attached to or dependent on. The tendency to get victimized easily or assume too much control means any situation you invest yourself in emotionally is potentially hazardous.

You can't control other people, of course, but you can choose carefully whom you bring into your life. Bring in people who enhance you, who evoke the parts of you that you really like, such as your sensitivity, sense of humor, playfulness, and affection. Treat yourself as if you deserve good people in your life who can appreciate you. Why? Because you deserve good people in your life who can appreciate you!

CONCLUSION

Depression is not the mystery it once was. We now have a good idea about who gets depressed and why. More important, we know a great deal about how to deal with depression. As you continue to learn more about your internal world and the way that you function in dealing with the external world, you can develop more and better choices about ways to respond to the life situations you face. Although it may not seem this way to you at times, it is nonetheless true that *the power to choose is yours.* Your life is *so* important, and you're the only one who can live it well. I wish you a future of happy times and satisfying personal growth.

Appendix A

A Complete List of the "Pause and Reflect" Exercises

Appendix B

A Complete List of the "Learn by Doing" Exercises

Appendix C
Audiotape Support

I have created a series of self-help audiotapes for depression involving hypnotic methods of relaxing and focusing. They teach you to create feelings of comfort while you build a positive frame of mind in order to deal effectively with common problems associated with depression. (You may wish to review the discussion in Chapter 4 about the benefits of such methods.) These tapes can help you to think more clearly and take appropriate action, and thereby better accomplish specific goals and resolve bothersome issues.

The tapes are listed below; each is titled according to the specific issue it addresses.

FOCUSING ON FEELING GOOD

- Depression as the Problem; Hypnosis as a Solution
  (A discussion about how to overcome depression)
- The Power of Vision
  (Build positive expectations)
- Try Again . . . But Do Something Different
  (Manage life circumstances flexibly)
- Is It In Your Control?
  (Learning to control the controllable)
- You're the Border Patrol
  (Build self-defining boundaries)
- Presumed Innocent But Feeling Guilty
  (Resolve issues of guilt)
- Good Night . . . And Sleep Well
  (Curtail rumination and facilitate sleep)
- Prevention Whenever Possible
  (Integrate preventive learnings)

Price: All 8 sides on 4 audiotapes: $39.95 (plus shipping $ handling)

For further information about these and Dr. Yapko's other audiotape programs, or to place an order, you can call, write, or fax:

Michael D. Yapko, Ph.D.
P.O. Box 234268
Leucadia, Ca. 92023-4268
(619) 259-7300; (619) 259-6271 FAX

Appendix D
Organizational Support

The following professional organizations can provide general information or specific referrals to assist you in your efforts to find a skilled psychotherapist.

American Association for Marriage and Family Therapy
1100 Seventeeth Street, N.W., 10th Floor
Washington, DC 20036-4601
(800) 374-2638

American Psychiatric Association
1400 K Street, N.W.
Washington, DC 20005
(202) 682-6220

American Psychological Association
750 First Street, N.E.
Washington, DC 20002
(202) 336-5800

American Society of Clinical Hypnosis
2200 East Devon Avenue, Suite 291
Des Plaines, IL 60018
(847) 297-3317

Depression Awareness, Recognition and Treatment (D/ART)
National Institute of Mental Health
5600 Fishers Lane, Room 10–85, Dept. GL
Rockville, MD 20857
(800) 421-4211

National Association of Social Workers
750 First St., NE
Washington, DC 20002
(800) 638-8799

National Foundation for Depressive Illness
P.O. Box 2257
New York, NY 10116
(800) 248-4344

National Mental Health Association
1021 Prince Street
Alexandria, VA 22314
(800) 969-6642

Bibliography

Alloy, L., and Abramson, L. (1988). Depressive realism: Four theoretical perspectives. In L. Alloy (ed.), *Cognitive processes in depression* (pp. 223–265). New York: Guilford.

Alloy, L. (April 1995). Depressive realism: Sadder but wiser? *The Harvard Mental Health Letter,* 4–5.

American Psychiatric Association (April 1993). Practice guidelines for major depressive disorder in adults. *American Journal of Psychiatry,* 150:4, 1–26.

Antonuccio, D., Danton, W., and DeNelsky, G. (1994). Psychotherapy for depression: No stronger medicine. *Scientist Practitioner, 4* (1), 2–18.

Antonuccio, D. (1995). Psychotherapy for depression: No stronger medicine. *American Psychologist, 50, 6,* 450–452.

Antonuccio, D., Danton, W., and DeNelsky, G. (1995). Psychotherapy versus medication for depression: Challenging the conventional wisdom with data. *Professional Psychology: Research and Practice, 26, 6,* 574–585.

Arieti, S., and Bemporad, J. (1994). *Psychotherapy for severe and mild depression.* Northvale, NJ: Jason Aronson.

Beach, S., Nelson, G., and O'Leary, K. (1988). Cognitive and marital factors in depression. *Journal of Psychopathology and Behavioral Assessment, 10,* 93–105.

Beach, S., and Nelson, G. (1990). Pursuing research on major psychopathology from a contextual perspective: The example of depression and marital discord. In G. Brody & I. Sigel (eds.), *Family Research, Vol. II: Clinical populations.* Hillsdale, NJ: Erlbaum.

Beach, S., Sandeen, E., and O'Leary, K. (1990). *Depression in marriage.* New York: Guilford.

Beck, A. (1967). *Depression: Causes and treatment.* Philadelphia: University of Pennsylvania Press.

Beck, A. (1973). *The diagnosis and management of depression.* Philadelphia: University of Pennsylvania Press.

Beck, A. (1976). *Cognitive therapy and the emotional disorders.* New York: International Universities Press.

Beck, A. (1987). Cognitive therapy. In J. Zeig (ed.), *The evolution of psychotherapy* (pp. 149–163). New York: Brunner-Mazel.

Beck, A. (1991). An interview with Aaron T. Beck, M.D., by Michael Yapko. *The Milton H. Erickson Foundation Newsletter, II* (2).

Beck, A., Rush, J., Shaw, B., and Emery, G. (1979). *Cognitive therapy of depression.* New York: Guilford Press.

Beck, A., Steer, R., Kovacs, M., and Garrison, B. (1985). Hopelessness and eventual suicide: A 10-year prospective study of patients hospitalized with suicidal ideation. *American Journal of Psychiatry, 142,* 559–563.

Beck, A., Brown, G., Berchick, R., Stewart, B., and Steer, R. (1990). Relationship between hopelessness and ultimate suicide: A replication with psychiatric outpatients. *American Journal of Psychiatry, 147,* 190–195.

Bernstein, N. (1982). Affective disorders and the family system. In E. Val, F. Gaviria, and J. Flaherty (eds.), *Affective disorders: Psychopathology and treatment* (pp. 441–453). Chicago: Year Book Medical Publishers.

Birtchnell, J. (1991). Negative modes of relating, marital quality, and depression. *British Journal of Psychiatry, 158,* 648–657.

Blackburn, I., and Davidson, K. (1990). *Cognitive therapy for depression and anxiety.* Oxford: Blackwell Scientific Publications.

Braiker, H. (1988). *Getting up when you're feeling down: A woman's guide to overcoming and preventing depression.* New York: G. P. Putnam's Sons.

Breggin, P. (1991). *Toxic psychiatry.* New York: St. Martin's Press.

Breggin, P., and Breggin, G. (1994). *Talking back to Prozac.* New York: St. Martin's Paperbacks.

Brown, G., and Harris. T. (1989). *Life events and illness.* New York: Guilford Press.

Burns, D. (1980). *Feeling good: The new mood therapy.* New York: William Morrow.

Burns, D. (1989). *The feeling good handbook.* New York: Plume.

Burns, D., and Nolen-Hoeksema, S. (1991). Coping styles, homework compliance, and the effectiveness of cognitive-behavioral therapy. *Journal of consulting and clinical psychology, 59,* 305–311.

Charney, E., and Weissman, M. (1988). Epidemiology of depressive illness. In J. Mann (ed.), *Phenomenology of depressive illnesses* (pp. 45–74). New York: Human Sciences Press.

Cleve, J. (1985). *Out of the blues.* Minneapolis: CompCare Publishers.

Cohen, D. (1994). *Out of the blue: Depression and human nature.* New York: W. W. Norton & Co.

Coyne, J. (ed.) (1985). *Essential papers on depression.* New York: New York University Press.

Cronkite, K. (1994). *On the edge of darkness: Conversations about conquering depression.* New York: Doubleday.

DePaulo, J., and Ablow, K. (1989). *How to cope with depression.* New York: Ballantine.

Depression Guideline Panel (1993a). *Depression in primary care: Vol 1, Diagnosis and detection* (Clinical Practice Guideline No. 5, AHCPR Publication No. 93–0550). Rockville, MD: Department of Health and Human Services, Public Health Service, Agency for Health Care Policy and Research.

Depression Guideline Panel (1993b). *Depression in primary care: Vol 2, Treatment of major depression* (Clinical Practice Guideline No. 5, AHCPR Publication No. 93-0551). Rockville, MD: Department of Health and Human Services, Public Health Service, Agency for Health Care Policy and Research.

BIBLIOGRAPHY

Depression Guideline Panel (1993c). *Depression in primary care: Detection, diagnosis, and treatment: Quick reference guide for clinicians* (Clinical Practice Guideline No. 5, AHCPR Publication No. 93-0552). Rockville, MD: Department of Health and Human Services, Public Health Service, Agency for Health Care Policy and Research.

Depression Guideline Panel (1993d). *Depression is a treatable illness: A patient's guide* (Clinical Practice Guideline No. 5, AHCPR Publication No. 93-0553). Rockville, MD: Department of Health and Human Services, Public Health Service, Agency for Health Care Policy and Research.

DeShazer, S. (1985). *Keys to solution in brief therapy.* New York: W. W. Norton.

DeShazer, S. (1991). *Putting difference to work.* New York: W. W. Norton.

Dowling, C. (1991). *You mean I don't have to feel this way?* New York: Scribner's.

Egeland, J., and Hostetter, A. (1983). Amish study. I: Affective disorders among the Amish, 1976–1980. *American Journal of Psychiatry, 140,* 1, 56–61.

Elkin, I., Shea, M., Watkins, J., Imber, S., Sotsky, S., Collins, J., Glass, D., Pilkonis, P., Leber, W., Docherty, J., Fiester, S., and Parloff, M. (1989). National Institute for Mental Health Treatment of Depression Collaborative Research Program: General effectiveness of treatments. *Archives of General Psychiatry, 46,* 971–982.

Ellis, A. (1987). The evolution of rational-emotive therapy (RET) and cognitive behavior therapy (CBT). In J. Zeig (ed.), *The evolution of psychotherapy* (pp. 107–125). New York: Brunner-Mazel.

Emery, G. (1988). *Getting undepressed: How a woman can change her life through cognitive therapy.* New York: Simon & Schuster.

Fieve, R. (1989). *Moodswing.* New York: Bantam Books.

Fieve, R. (1994). *Prozac: Questions and answers for patients, family, and physicians.* New York: Avon Books.

Fisher, S., and Greenberg, R. (1993). How sound is the double-blind design for evaluating psychotropic drugs? *The Journal of Nervous and Mental Disease, 181,* 345–350.

Flach, F. (ed.) (1988). *Affective disorders.* New York: W. W. Norton.

Garber, J., and Seligman, M. (eds.) (1980). *Human helplessness: Theory and applications.* Orlando, FL: Academic Press.

Glick, E. (ed.) (1995). *Treating depression.* San Francisco: Jossey-Bass.

Gold, M. (1986). *The good news about depression.* New York: Bantam Books.

Goldberg, I. (1993). *Questions and answers about depression and its treatment.* Philadelphia: The Charles Press.

Goleman, D. (1995). *Emotional intelligence.* New York: Bantam Books.

Gotlib, I., and Hammen, C. (1992). *Psychological aspects of depression: Toward a cognitive-interpersonal integration.* New York. Wiley.

Greenberg, R., Bornstein, R., Greenberg, M., and Fisher, S. (1992). A meta-analysis of antidepressant medication under "blinder" conditions. *Journal of Consulting and Clinical Psychology, 60,* 644–669.

Greenberger, D., and Padesky, C. (1995). *Mind over mood: A cognitive therapy treatment manual for clients.* New York: Guilford Publications.

Greist, J., and Jefferson, J. (1984). *Depression and its treatment.* New York: Warner Books.

Haley, J. (1987). Therapy—a new phenomenon. In J. Zeig (ed.), *The evolution of psychotherapy* (pp. 17–28). New York: Brunner-Mazel.

Hazleton, L. (1984). *The right to feel bad.* New York: Ballantine Books.

Hillman, J., and Ventura, M. (1992). *We've had a hundred years of psychotherapy—and the world's getting worse.* San Francisco: Harper Collins.

Hollon, S., Shelton, R., and Loosen, P. (1991). Cognitive therapy and pharmacotherapy for depression. *Journal of Consulting and Clinical Psychology, 59,* 88–99.

Hollon, S., DeRubeis, R., Evans, M., Wiemer, M., Garvey, M., Grove, W., and Tuason, V. (1992). Cognitive therapy and pharmacotherapy for depression: Singly and in combination. *Archives of General Psychiatry, 49,* 774–781.

Johnson, L. (1995). *Psychotherapy in the age of accountability.* New York: W. W. Norton.

Johnson, L., and Miller, S. (1994). Modification of depression risk factors: A solution-focused approach. *Psychotherapy 31,* 2, 244–253.

Kantor, M. (1992). *The human dimension of depression.* New York: Praeger.

Klein, D., and Wender, P. (1993). *Understanding depression: A complete guide to its diagnosis and treatment.* New York: Oxford University Press.

Kleinman, A., and Good, B. (eds.) (1985). *Culture and depression: Studies in the anthropology and cross-cultural psychiatry of affective disorder.* Berkeley: University of California Press.

Klerman, G. (1988). The current age of youthful melancholia. *British Journal of Psychiatry, 152,* 4–14.

Klerman, G., Weissman, M., Rounsaville, B., and Chevron, E. (1984). *Interpersonal psychotherapy of depression.* New York: Basic Books.

Kocsis, J., and Frances, A. (1988). Chronic depression. In J. Mann (ed.), *Phenomenology of depressive illness* (pp. 126–140). New York: Human Sciences Press.

Kramer, P. (1993). *Listening to Prozac: A psychiatrist explores antidepressant drugs and the remaking of the self.* New York: Viking.

Kuhs, H. (1991). Anxiety in depressive disorders. *Comprehensive psychiatry, 32–33,* 217–228.

Lankton, S., and Lankton, C. (1986). *Enchantment and intervention in family therapy.* New York: Brunner-Mazel.

Lewinsohn, P., Munos, R. Youngren, M., and Zeiss, A. (1986). *Control your depression.* New York: Prentice Hall.

McGrath, E., Keita, G., Strickland, B., and Russo, N. (eds.) (1990). *Women and depression: Risk factors and treatment issues.* Washington, DC: American Psychological Association.

McGrath, E. (1992). *When feeling bad is good.* New York: Henry Holt and Company.

McMullin, R. (1986). *Handbook of cognitive therapy techniques.* New York: W. W. Norton.

Miracle drugs or media drugs? (March 1992). *Consumer Reports,* pp. 142–146.

Monroe, S., Kupfer, D., and Frank, E. (1992). Life stress and treatment course of recurrent depression: 1, Response during index episode. *Journal of Consulting and Clinical Psychology, 60,* 718–724.

Munoz, R., and Yu-wen, Y. (1993). *The prevention of depression.* Baltimore: The Johns Hopkins University Press.

Munoz, R., Hollon, S., McGrath, E., Rehm, L., and VandenBos, G. (1994). On the AHCPR Depression in primary care guidelines: Further considerations for practitioners. *American Psychologist, 49,* 42–61.

Murphy, G., and Wetzel, R. (1990). The lifetime risk of suicide in alcoholism. *Archives of General Psychiatry, 47,* 383–392.

Nezu, A., Nezu, C., and Perri, M. (1989). *Problem-solving therapy for depression.* New York: John Wiley & Sons.

Nolen-Hoeksema, S. (1987). Sex differences in unipolar depression: Evidence and theory. *Psychology Bulletin, 101,* 259–282.

Nolen-Hoeksema, S. (1991). Responses to depression and their effects on the duration of depressive episodes. *Journal of Abnormal Psychology, 100,* 569–582.

Nolen-Hoeksema, S., Girgus, J., and Seligman, M. (1986). Learned helplessness in children: A longitudinal study of depression, achievement, and explanatory style. *Journal of Personality and Social Psychology, 51,* 435–442.

Ornstein, R., and Ehrlich, P. (1989). *New world, new mind.* New York: Touchstone.

Papolos, D., and Papolos, J. (1987). *Overcoming depression.* New York: Harper & Row.

Preston, J. (1989). *You can beat depression.* San Luis Obispo, CA: Impact Publishers.

Pushing drugs to doctors. (February 1992). *Consumer Reports,* pp. 87–94.

Rehm, L., and VandenBos, G. (1994). On the AHCPR depression in primary care guidelines: Further considerations for practitioners. *American Psychologist, 49,* 42–61.

Reich, T., VanEerdewegh, P., Rich, J., Mullaney, J., Endicott, J., and Klerman, G. (1987). The familial transmission of primary major depressive disorder. *Journal of Psychiatric Research, 21,* 613–624.

Robins, L., Helzer, J., Weissman, M., Orvaschel, H., Gruenberg, E., Burke, J., and Regier, D. (1984). Lifetime prevalence of specific psychiatric disorders in three communities. *Archives of general psychiatry, 41,* 949–958.

Rosellini, G., and Worden, M. (1987). *Here comes the sun: Finding your way out of depression.* New York: Harper & Row.

Rounsaville, B., Weissman, M., Prusoff, B., and Herceg-Baron, R. (1979). Marital disputes and treatment outcome in depressed women. *Comprehensive psychiatry, 20,* 483–490.

Rude, S., and Rehm, L. (1991). Response to treatments for depression: The role of initial status on targeted cognitive and behavioral skills. *Clinical Psychology Review, 11,* 493–514.

Rush, A. (ed.) (1982). *Short-term psychotherapies for depression.* New York: Guilford Press.

Safran, J., and Segal, Z. (1990). *Interpersonal process in cognitive therapy.* New York: Basic Books.

Salmans, S. (1995). *Depression: Questions you have, answers you need.* Allentown, PA: People's Medical Society.

Schad-Somers, S. (1990). *On mood swings: The psychobiology of elation and depression.* New York: Plenum Press.

Schulberg, H., and Rush, J. (January 1994). Clinical practice guidelines for managing major depression in primary care practice: Implications for psychologists. *American Psychologist, 49, 1,* 34–41.

Schwartz, A., and Schwartz, R. (1993). *Depression: Theories and treatments.* New York: Columbia University Press.

Segal, Z., Shaw, B., Vella, D., and Katz, D. (1992). Cognitive and life stress predictors of relapse in remitted unipolar depressed patients: Tests of the congruency hypothesis. *Journal of Abnormal Psychology, 101,* 26–36.

Seligman, M. (1988). Boomer blues. *Psychology today, 22,* 50–55.

Seligman, M. (1989). Explanatory style: Predicting depression, achievement, and health. In M. Yapko (ed.), *Brief therapy approaches to treating anxiety and depression* (pp. 5–32). New York: Brunner-Mazel.

Seligman, M. (1990). *Learned optimism.* New York: Alfred A. Knopf.

Seligman, M. (1993). *What you can change and what you can't.* New York: Alfred A. Knopf.

Seligman, M. (1995a). *The optimistic child: How learned optimism protects children from depression.* New York: Houghton Mifflin Co.

Seligman, M. (1995b). The effectiveness of psychotherapy. *American Psychologist, 50,* 12, 965–974.

Shea, M., Imber, S., Sotsky, S., Watkins, J., Collins, J., Pilkonis, P., Beckham, E., Glass, D., Dolan, R., and Perloff, M. (1992). Course of depressive symptoms over follow-up: Findings from the NIMH treatment of depression collaborative research program. *Archives of General Psychiatry, 49,* 782–787.

Shimberg, E. (1991). *Depression: What families should know.* New York: Ballantine Books.

Simons, A. (1992). Cognitive therapy for cognitive theories of depression: Restructuring basic assumptions. *Psychological Inquiry, 3*, 264–265.

Simons, A., Angell, K., Monroe, S., and Thase, M. (1993). Cognition and life stress in depression: Cognitive factors and the definition, rating, and generation of negative life events. *Journal of Abnormal Psychology, 102*, 584–591.

Simons, A., Gordon, J., Monroe, S., and Thase, M. (1995). Toward an integration of psychologic, social, and biologic factors in depression: Effects on outcome and course of cognitive therapy. *Journal of Consulting and Clinical Psychology, 63, 3*, 369–377.

Sotsky, S., Glass, D., Shea, T., Pilkonis, P., Collins, J., Elkin, I., Watkins, J., Imber, S., Leber, W., Moyer, J., and Oliveri, M. (1991). Patient predictors of response to psychotherapy and pharmacotherapy: Findings in the NIMH Treatment of Depression Collaborative Research Program. *American Journal of Psychiatry, 148*, 997–1008.

Steinbrueck, S., Maxwell, S., and Howard, G. (1983). A meta-analysis of psychotherapy and drug therapy in the treatment of unipolar depression with adults. *Journal of Consulting and Clinical Psychology, 51*, 856–863.

Styron, W. (1990). *Darkness visible: A memoir of madness.* New York: Random House.

Tavris, C. (1989). *Anger: The misunderstood emotion.* New York: Touchstone.

Terman, S. (1980). Hypnosis and depression. In H. Wain (ed.), *Clinical hypnosis in medicine* (pp. 201–208). Chicago: Year Book Medical Publishers.

Thase, M., Simons, A., and Reynolds, C. (1993). Psychobiological correlates of poor response to cognitive behavior therapy: Potential indications for antidepressant pharmacotherapy. *Psychopharmacology Bulletin, 29*, 293–301.

Thompson, T. (1995). *The beast: A reckoning with depression.* New York: Putnam's.

Weiner-Davis, M. (1995). *Change your life and everyone in it.* New York: Fireside.

Weissman, M. (1983). Psychotherapy in comparison and in combination with pharmacotherapy for the depressed outpatient. In J. Davis and J. Maas (eds.), *The affective disorders* (pp. 409–418). Washington, DC: American Psychiatric Press.

Weissman, M. (1987). Advances in psychiatric epidemiology: Rates and risks for major depression. *American Journal of Public Health, 77*, 445–451.

Wells, K., Hays, R., Burnam, A., Roger, W., Greenfield, S., and Ware, J. (1989). Detection of depressive disorder for patients receiving prepaid or fee-for-service care. *Journal of the American Medical Association, 262, 23*, 3298–3302.

Wetzel, J. (1984). *Clinical handbook of depression.* New York: Gardner Press.

Wexler, B., and Cicchetti, D. (1992). The outpatient treatment of depression: Implications of outcome research for clinical practice. *The Journal of Nervous and Mental Disease, 180,* 277–286.

Willner, P. (1985). *Depression: A psychobiological synthesis.* New York: John Wiley & Sons.

Yapko, M. (1985). Therapeutic strategies for the treatment of depression. *Ericksonian Monographs, 1,* 89–110. New York: Brunner-Mazel.

Yapko, M. (1988). *When Living Hurts: Directives for treating depression.* New York: Brunner-Mazel.

Yapko, M. (1989). Disturbances of temporal orientation as a feature of depression. In M. Yapko (ed.), *Brief therapy approaches to treating anxiety and depression* (pp. 106–118). New York: Brunner-Mazel.

Yapko, M. (1990a). *Trancework: An introduction to the practice of clinical hypnosis* (2nd ed.). New York: Brunner-Mazel.

Yapko, M. (1990b). Directive psychotherapy. In J. Zeig and W. Munion (eds.), *What is psychotherapy? Contemporary Perspectives* (pp. 378–382). San Francisco: Jossey-Bass.

Yapko, M. (May–June 1991). A therapy of hope. *Family therapy networker,* 34–39.

Yapko, M. (1992a). Therapy with direction. In S. Budman, M. Hoyt and S. Friedman (eds.), *The first session in brief therapy* (pp. 156–180). New York: Guilford Press.

Yapko, M. (1992b). *Hypnosis and the treatment of depressions: Strategies for change.* New York: Brunner-Mazel.

Yapko, M. (1992c). *Using hypnosis in treating depression* (audiotape series). New York: Brunner-Mazel.

Yapko, M. (1993). Hypnosis and depression. In Rhue, J., Lynn, S., and Kirsch, I. (eds.), *Handbook of clinical hypnosis* (pp. 339–355). Washington, DC: American Psychological Association.

Yapko, M. (1995). *Essentials of hypnosis.* New York: Brunner-Mazel.

Zeig, J. (ed.) (1980). *A teaching seminar with Milton H. Erickson, M.D.* New York: Brunner-Mazel.

INDEX